DECOLONIZING CHRISTIANITIES IN

CONTEMPORARY NIGERIAN LITERATURE

WORLD CHRISTIANITY

Dale T. Irvin and Devaka Premawardhana, Series Editors

ADVISORY BOARD:
Akintunde E. Akinade
Adrian Hermann
Leo D. Lefebure
Elaine Padilla
Peter C. Phan
Yolanda Pierce

Moving beyond descriptions of European-derived norms that have existed for hundreds of years, books in the World Christianity series reflect an understanding of global Christianity that embodies the wide diversity of its identity and expression. The series seeks to expand the scholarly field of world Christianity by interrogating boundary lines in church history, mission studies, ecumenical dialogue, and interreligious dialogue among Christians and non-Christians across geographic, geopolitical, and confessional divides. Beyond a mere history of missions to the world, books in the series examine local Christianity, how Christianity has been acculturated, and how its expression interacts with the world at large. Issues under investigation include how Christianity has been received and transformed in various countries; how migration has changed the nature and practice of Christianity and the new forms of the faith that result; and how seminary and theological education responds to the challenges of world Christianity.

OTHER BOOKS IN THE SERIES:

Krista E. Hughes, Dhawn Martin, and Elaine Padilla, eds., *Ecological Solidarities: Mobilizing Faith and Justice for an Entangled World*

Aminta Arrington, *Songs of the Lisu Hills: Practicing Christianity in Southwest China*

Arun W. Jones, ed., *Christian Interculture: Texts and Voices from Colonial and Postcolonial Worlds*

Edward Jarvis, *The Anglican Church in Burma: From Colonial Past to Global Future*

Jifeng Liu, *Negotiating the Christian Past in China: Memory and Missions in Contemporary Xiamen*

Gideon Elazar, *Christian Missionaries, Ethnicity, and State Control in Globalized Yunnan*

Briana L. Wong, *Cambodian Evangelicalism: Cosmological Hope and Diasporic Resilience*

Elochukwu E. Uzukwu, *Memorializing the Unsung: Slaves of the Church and the Making of Kongo Catholicism*

Yun Zhou, *The Woman's Messenger: Evangelical Literature and the Missionary Movement in Republican China*

DECOLONIZING CHRISTIANITIES IN CONTEMPORARY NIGERIAN LITERATURE

Adriaan van Klinken

The Pennsylvania State University Press
University Park, Pennsylvania

Library of Congress
Cataloging-in-Publication Data

Names: Van Klinken, A. S., author.
Title: Decolonizing Christianities in contemporary Nigerian literature / Adriaan van Klinken.
Description: University Park, Pennsylvania : The Pennsylvania State University Press, [2025] | Includes bibliographical references and index.
Summary: "Explores how twenty-first century Nigerian novels engage with Christianity as a locally rooted aspect of postcolonial society. Examines how authors use Christian traditions, beliefs, and symbols to address themes of gender, sexuality, ecology, and interreligious relations in the pursuit of social transformation"— Provided by publisher.
Identifiers: LCCN 2025039227 | ISBN 9780271100395 (hardback) | ISBN 9780271100401 (paperback)
Subjects: LCSH: Nigerian literature (English)—21st century—History and criticism. | Nigerian fiction (English)—21st century—History and criticism. | Christianity and literature—Nigeria—History—21st century. | Christianity in literature. | Postcolonialism in literature. | Nigeria—In literature.
Classification: LCC PR9387 | DDC 820.99669—dc23/eng/20240701
LC record available at https://lccn.loc.gov/2025039227

An open access digital edition of this book is available with the generous support of The Pennsylvania State University Libraries under the Creative Commons Attribution-NonCommercial-NoDerivatives 4.0 International License. To view a copy of the license, visit https://creativecommons.org/licenses/by-nc-nd/4.0/.

Except for the uses authorized by this license as well as brief quotations for reviews and critical articles, no part of this book may be reproduced, in whole or in part, in any form, without written permission from the publisher.

Copyright © 2025 Adriaan van Klinken
All rights reserved
Printed in the United States of America
Published by The Pennsylvania State University Press,
University Park, PA 16802–1003

The Pennsylvania State University Press is a member of the Association of University Presses.

It is the policy of The Pennsylvania State University Press to use acid-free paper. Publications on uncoated stock satisfy the minimum requirements of American National Standard for Information Sciences—Permanence of Paper for Printed Library Material, ANSI Z39.48–1992.

To my parents,
Adrie van Klinken and Annie van Klinken-van de Vreede,
for guiding me to read the world
with faith, hope, and love.

Can religion peacefully cohabit with humanism in the twenty-first century? Can religion cohabit with humanity itself?

—WOLE SOYINKA, *OF AFRICA* (2012)

Contents

Preface xi

Acknowledgments xiii

Introduction: Reading Christianity and Social Thought in Nigerian Literature 1

chapter 1 Forgiveness: Christianity, Civil War Trauma, and Religious Memory 29

chapter 2 Deliverance: Christianity, Sexuality, and Queer Embodiment 52

chapter 3 Apparition: Catholicism, Marian Devotion, and Gender 78

chapter 4 Prophecy: Christianity, Environmental Degradation, and Ecology 102

chapter 5 Spiritual Warfare: Christianity, Islam, and Interreligious Recognition 125

chapter 6 Prosperity: Pentecostalism, Charismatic Leadership, and the Prosperity Gospel 153

Conclusion: Nigerian Literature as African Religion and World Christianity 174

Notes 183

Bibliography 196

Index 217

Preface

During my childhood and teenage years, I grew up with some family habits and rituals that may have laid the early foundations for this book. First, the habit of reading and, related to that, the ritual of weekly visits to the library. I have childhood memories of my dad reading for my siblings and me, when we were at an age too young to read ourselves; I remember how he would play with the intonation and volume of his voice, bringing the story to life and transporting us into its fantasy world. Other memories are of my mum taking us every Friday evening to the public library in our town, where my siblings and I would browse for an hour or so, carefully selecting the maximum number of books (was it five?) that we were allowed to borrow and that we would devour in the following week, only to return them the next Friday in exchange for another stack of books. Second, the habit of family devotion (which also included reading, from the Bible in this case, after every meal we would share) and of churchgoing every Sunday, and several other rituals that put faith central in our lives. Growing up in a family without a television, in the conservative environment of a town in the Dutch Protestant Bible belt, reading children's and youth literature became for me an alternative window to the world, an avenue to explore worlds out there that were different from the one with which I was familiar. During my late teenage and early adult years, reading religious, and later theological, texts also fed into a process through which the Calvinist Reformed faith I was raised in was gradually internalized but also critically reinterpreted, broadened, and transformed in a more ecumenical and progressive direction.

At some moment in my youth—I cannot remember when, exactly—I learned that I could have been born in Nigeria. Early in their marriage, my parents were destined to move there because my dad (having studied tropical agriculture) had been offered a job as an agricultural specialist with a mission agency in this West African country. Yet these plans were thwarted at the last minute due to health-related reasons. Thus, I ended up being born and growing up in the coastal southwestern region of the Netherlands, where my dad was a secondary school teacher and my mum, in addition to running the household, was actively involved in church and community work. I still sometimes wonder what my childhood would have looked like if things had taken a different turn, and how this would have shaped me—but I will never know. Perhaps this book is an attempt for me to explore the country I did not get to grow up in (and until recently did not get to visit) and to learn about its diverse and dynamic religious culture and social environment, not from firsthand experience but through reading its literary representations. If reading was an avenue to explore different social, cultural, and religious worlds during my childhood, it continues to be so, even if it has also developed into a professional skill and an academic method, as illustrated in this book.

This is to say that, as much as this book was conceived of as a scholarly project, its focus, methods, and interests link to and are embedded in my autobiography in various ways. Whether the significance of this is merely anecdotal or adds personal, intellectual, or political meaning is a question for further reflection. In any case, given the above, I dedicate this book to my parents, with deep gratitude for the joy of reading, the virtue of faith, and a heart for compassion and social justice, which they embody and have instilled in me.

Acknowledgments

Having played with the idea of a possible book project on Christianity and African literature for several years, I started working seriously on conceptualizing and writing this book in 2020. That year, I was supposed to enjoy research leave granted by the University of Leeds, but many of the plans I had for fieldwork- and research-related travel abroad became impossible due to the restrictions imposed by the COVID-19 pandemic. Locked down in my study at home, I decided to try make the best of the circumstances by prioritizing the literature project that, until then, had just been a latent research idea. Luckily enough, postal and delivery services were not affected by COVID-19 restrictions, so I was able to order and receive a steady flow of books that helped me do an initial review of the representation of, and engagement with, Christianity in contemporary African literature. I soon realized that I would need to narrow the scope of the project, and for various reasons (outlined in the introduction), the focus turned to twenty-first-century Nigerian literature specifically.

Although the book was conceived in the context of social isolation during a global pandemic, I am indebted to a remarkable number of people for their input and ideas, and for their willingness to brainstorm and serve as sparring partners about the shape and direction of the project. I remember early-stage conversations via email and Zoom with several colleagues—most notably, Grace Musila, Brendon Nicholls, and Ranka Primorac—while we grappled with the difficult circumstances of the pandemic and its effect on our personal and professional lives. These conversations continued, in one way or another, after we gradually moved out of the pandemic. I am grateful to many valued colleagues and friends who, at some point in the process of researching and writing this book, have been sparring partners in one way or another, and have offered advice, insights, and feedback. This includes Afe Adogame, Abiodun Alao, Sindile Bongela, Nadine Bowers Du Toit, Nella van den Brandt, Ezra Chitando, Sicco Claus, Carli Coetzee, Chris Dunton, Louisa Egbunike, Anthony-Mario Egbunonu, Jörg Haustein, Nina Hoel, Nathanael Homewood, Johnathan Jodamus, Benjamin Kirby, Anne-Marie Korte, Karen Lauterbach, Belinda Makinana, Sarojini Nadar, Gibson Ncube, Abraham Waigi Ng'ang'a, David Ngong, Insa Nolte, Ebenezer

Obadare, Aiwan Obinyan, Olukoya Ogen, Kwame Edwin Otu, Damaris Parsitau, Devaka Premawardhana, Janet Remmington, Alison Searle, Jonathan Smith, Johanna Stiebert, Nathan Suhr-Sytsma, Ashwin Thyssen, Abel Ugba, Asonzeh Ukah, Auli and Mika Vähäkangas, Tamanda Walker, Kevin Ward, Emma Wild-Wood, Corey Williams, and Martin Zebracki. Several of these conversations were, directly or indirectly, facilitated via the academic associations I am involved with, most notably the African Association for the Study of Religions and the African Studies Association in the United Kingdom, and I am grateful for these networks and all the good things they make possible.

In the aftermath of the pandemic, I was able to publicly present and talk about parts of this book as a work in progress and to rediscover the stimulating experience of in-person (rather than virtual) interaction, such as at research seminars and symposiums hosted at the University of Birmingham (Department of African Studies and Anthropology, with thanks to Insa Nolte), the University of Cambridge (Centre for Christianity Worldwide, with thanks to Muthuraj Swamy and Jörg Haustein), the University of Cape Town (Department for the Study of Religions, with thanks to Nina Hoel and Sa'diyya Shaikh), the University of Copenhagen (Centre for African Studies, with thanks to Karen Lauterbach), the University of Edinburgh (Centre for the Study of World Christianity, with thanks to Emma Wild-Wood), the University of Lancaster (Religious Studies seminar, with thanks to Emmanuel Ossai and Chris Macleod), the University of Oxford (School of Anthropology, with thanks to Antonio Montañés Jiménez and Matthew Porges), the University of Southampton (Centre of Imperial and Postcolonial Studies, with thanks to Ranka Primorac and Chris Prior), and the University of the Western Cape (Desmond Tutu Centre for Religion and Social Justice, with thanks to Sarojini Nadar). I also presented papers related to this project at the conferences of the African Studies Association of the United Kingdom, held in Liverpool (2022) and Oxford (2024), and of the European Research Network on Global Pentecostalism, held in Cambridge (2022), and I have benefited from the discussion and feedback on those occasions.

In 2024, I had the honor and privilege of delivering keynote lectures at two conferences, which I used as an opportunity to frame my work on this project in relation to the conference themes. Thus, at the conference of the British Association for the Study of Religions, held in Leeds in September 2024, I spoke about "Rewriting Colonial Legacies: Indigenous Religion, Christianity and Embattled Gods in Nigerian Literature" (with thanks to

Melanie Prideaux and Aled Thomas for the invitation). Earlier in the same year, I spoke about "Engaging African Realities Through Contemporary Nigerian Literature" at the joint conference of the African Association for the Study of Religions and the Nagel Institute for World Christianity, held in Abuja, Nigeria (with thanks to Benson Igboin and Damaris Parsitau for the invitation). The latter conference was a particular highlight, as it was an opportunity to present my work on Nigerian soil and to a mostly Nigerian academic audience, which made for a stimulating discussion.

Having worked gradually on the project for several years, significant progress in the writing of this book was made in the first half of 2024, when I enjoyed a semester of research leave from my home institution and during which I spent a three-month residential fellowship at the Stellenbosch Institute for Advanced Study (STIAS) in South Africa. I am grateful to the STIAS director, Edward K. Kirumira, the program manager, Christoff Pauw, and the program coordinator, Nel-Mari Loock, as well as all the support staff at the institute, for offering me space for concentrated thinking, reading, and writing in such a wonderfully conducive environment. I am also grateful for the other fellows in my cohort, for the stimulating interactions and conversations over our shared daily lunches and in the weekly research seminars. Specific mention should be made here of Ayodeji Olukoju, for enhancing my understanding of the Nigerian context; Faith Kandie, for amazing weekend hikes in the scenic mountains surrounding Stellenbosch; and Makhosazana Xaba, for sharing her passion for literature, specifically poetry, and for becoming a treasured neighbor and friend during the time we shared together.

The University of Leeds, specifically the School of Philosophy, Religion and History of Science where I am based, and the Leeds University Centre for African Studies, as well as the Centre for Religion and Public Life, with which I am associated, have offered me a very supportive and stimulating working environment ever since I joined the institution in 2013. I am particularly grateful to my colleagues in Theology and Religious Studies, who on two separate occasions discussed and offered feedback on draft material in our regular work-in-progress seminars, and from whose comments, questions, and suggestions I greatly benefited. The Centre for African Studies also offered a space to test and discuss ideas reflected in this book, and I specifically thank Brendon Nicholls, Abel Ugba, and Megan Fourqurean for the fruitful conversations about anything related to African literature and African religions. Through the experience of supervising the PhD projects of Gloria Adichie, Bonaventure Chia, Emmanuel Erhijodo, and Grace Nwamah, I have learned a great deal about Nigeria's rich and complex religious, social, and political environments. The same applies to the experience of mentoring Zaynab Ango, Adaobi Muo, Ibukunolu Isaac Olodude, and Nduka Udeagha as visiting fellows at Leeds. A particular source of inspiration in recent years has been the presence of Megan Robertson as a Marie Curie Postdoctoral Fellow and Tendai Mangena as a British Academy Global Professor at Leeds, and I am grateful for the stimulating conversations (including about this book as work in progress) and ongoing collaborations we share.

Emmanuel Erhijodo, Alistair McFadyen, and David T. Ngong each read draft versions of particular chapters and provided insightful feedback, for which I am very grateful. My thanks also goes to Mikel Burley, Tendai Mangena, Devaka Premawardhana, and Tasia Scrutton, who made helpful suggestions and comments on the draft introduction. Nathanael Homewood went the extra mile by volunteering to read the full draft manuscript and offering valuable thoughts, criticisms, and suggestions—a gesture of collegiality and friendship that I do not take for granted. The anonymous readers arranged by the press, whose names were revealed to me afterward, provided reports that were a real encouragement to bring this project to completion: Thank you, Chielozona Eze and Emma Wild-Wood, for being such constructive and supportive readers. Having had an incredibly positive experience with the Penn State University Press previously, with the publication of my book *Kenyan, Christian, Queer*, I was keen to work with them again—a publisher that truly cares about the project one is working on makes the endeavor so much more rewarding. I am grateful to acquisition editor for religious studies Kathryn Yahner, whom I first approached, and to Tristan Bates, who soon after took over this role, for their warm support of this project, and to all the PSUP staff who have played their part in the journey of bringing this book into the world. A note of thanks also goes to Dale Irvin, Peter Phan, and Devaka Premawardhana as the editors of the World Christianity series, who from the beginning expressed a strong commitment to the project.

Lastly, I am grateful to the many friends and family members I am lucky to have in my life. At times they may show some interest in my academic work, which I appreciate, but more importantly, they show a constant and genuine interest in, and care about, me as a human being. These relationships remind me of the constant need to put academic matters into perspective, and they help me keep a healthy balance between my professional and personal lives, even if the boundaries between these two are often blurred. On this note, I particularly express my thanks to Casper, for offering me a solid base and warm place to call home, and for being an unwavering source of support and love.

All the chapters were specifically written for the purpose of this book. However, two of the chapters have some overlap with other publications in which I discuss the same literary texts, with the analysis and argument following somewhat similar lines. Thus, chapter 2 ("Deliverance") may share some similarity with:

> Adriaan van Klinken and Belinda Qaqamba Makinana, "'Deliver us from Evil': Pentecostal Christianity, Queer Sexualities and the Language of Deliverance in Nigerian Literature," in Transafrica: The Languages of Postqueerness, edited by Chantal Zabus and Chris Dunton, 95–111. London: Bloomsbury, 2025.
> Adriaan van Klinken and Ezra Chitando, "Infinite Possibilities in a Nigerian Lesbian Love Story: *Under the Udala Trees*," in *Reimagining Christianity and Sexual Diversity in Africa*, 165–80. London: Zed Books; New York: Oxford University Press, 2021.

Similarly, chapter 3 ("Apparition") may have some overlap with:

> Adriaan van Klinken, "The Problem of 'Redemptive Masculinity' in Chimamanda Ngozi Adichie's *Purple Hibiscus*," in *The Palgrave Handbook of African Men and Masculinities*, edited by Ezra Chitando, Obert B. Mlambo, Sakhumzi Mfecane, and Kopano Ratele, 373–84. New York: Palgrave Macmillan, 2024.

INTRODUCTION

Reading Christianity and Social Thought in Nigerian Literature

The all-time classic of Nigerian literature, Chinua Achebe's *Things Fall Apart*, originally published in 1958, tells about the first Christian missionaries arriving and settling in Umuofia, a fictional village in southeastern Nigeria. Although the missionaries soon win a handful of converts, the clan leaders are initially not too bothered because they consider the converts insignificant people, and they believe "that the strange faith and the white man's god would not last."[1] Obviously, these leaders got it wrong. The novel narrates how the new religion gradually gains traction and how the church, helped by newly introduced colonial structures of government and law, becomes a powerful force in society. As one of the characters, Obierika, famously puts it in a conversation with the novel's protagonist, Okonkwo: "The white man is very clever. He came quietly and peacefully with his religion. We were amused at his foolishness and allowed him to stay. Now he has won our brothers, and our clan no longer acts like one. He has put a knife on the things that held us together and we have fallen apart."[2]

With its narrative depiction of the disruptive and divisive impact of missionary Christianity on local communities, their belief system, and their traditional way of life, *Things Fall Apart* is the major Nigerian example of what the literary scholar Simon Gikandi has described as the "canonical African texts," in which Christianity is represented "as the cultural arm of imperial expansion and as the major agent in the alienation of Africans from their traditional cultures, the source of self-hate and mimicry, and one of the sources of the violence that separates families, communities, and nationalities." He continues by adding that "when Christianity is not represented as an agent of colonial domination and violence, it appears as the ambiguous force of civilization and Europeanization." Together with other classics, such as the Kenyan writer Ngũgĩ wa Thiong'o's *The River Between*, Achebe's novel exemplifies how missionary Christianity tends to be depicted in twentieth-century African literature as "nothing less than the source of the crisis of modernity and modernization."[3] Admittedly, these twentieth-century writers had a complex relationship to Christianity. As much as they offer a postcolonial critique of this religion for its links to European colonialism and imperialism, they also draw on Christian symbols and biblical imagery in their creative writing, and, in several cases, such as Achebe, they did not radically break with their Christian upbringing.[4] As the literary scholar Femi Ojo-Ade observes, some African creative writers are primarily critics, and others children, of Christianity; however, in his assessment, both "perceive a certain rigour and rigidity in the religion imposed upon the African" as they problematize the "complementarity between christianity [sic] and colonialism."[5] Hence, the critique of Christianity has become a dominant theme, both in African literature and in the scholarship thereon.[6]

As much as the clan leaders of Umuofia believed that the white man's God and faith would not last, Christianity has firmly settled itself. It has become the majority religion in southeast Nigeria, where *Things Fall Apart* is set, as well as elsewhere in the country and in many other parts of Africa. Numerically, according to the *World Christian Encyclopedia*, the Christian population of Nigeria grew from 176,000 in the year 1900 (1.1 percent of the total population) to over 95 million in 2020 (46.3 percent) and is projected to grow to 197 million by 2060 (48 percent).[7] These figures are part of a broader picture of demographic growth, yet they are nevertheless astonishing. By 2060, Nigeria is projected to become the country with the third largest Christian population in the world, and the largest in Africa.[8] This growth is part of a broader trend on the continent, with sub-Saharan Africa projected to be home to more than 40 percent of Christians worldwide by 2060.[9] Both in Nigeria and across the continent, Christianity is competing with Islam over which religion has a larger following and influence (see chapter 5). In the process, African indigenous religions—in spite of their resilience and, in some cases, revitalization—have become increasingly marginalized, with only a small percentage of the population primarily identifying with these (although, arguably, many Christians continue to respect and practice indigenous beliefs and rituals in one way or another alongside their Christian faith).¹⁰

These quantitative figures are only part of the story of Christianity establishing itself in the region. More interesting are the qualitative developments, described by scholars with terms such as religious adaptation, appropriation, contextualization, indigenization, inculturation, hybridity, and innovation, through which Christian traditions introduced by European missionaries have become an "African religion," and through which the Christian God is said to have become African, and specifically Nigerian.¹¹ Thus, in a sense, one could indeed say that the white man's faith did not last, because Christianity in the postcolonial period belongs to local converts and subsequent generations of Christians who have reshaped, and are reshaping, it by demonstrating considerable religious agency and creativity, in Nigeria and elsewhere in Africa.¹² As the historian Ogbu Kalu puts it, Christianity in Africa is being written as an "African story."¹³

Now, what does this rooting of Christianity mean for the way it is engaged with in African literary texts? As Gikandi has argued, after independence, which for most African countries came in the 1960s, "the Church could no longer be represented as a direct agent of colonialism or neocolonialism," and "Christianity could no longer be represented as a force extraneous to the African experience but a crucial part of the social and cultural fabric of postcolonial society."¹⁴ Ojo-Ade appears to be more reserved, writing that in twentieth-century African literary accounts "Christianity is a burden, the Black man's burden. As with other aspects of our life, the weight is being carried confusedly. Colonialism became cooperation—some call it neo-colonialism—and the Church became africanized [*sic*]. We are still strangers on our land."¹⁵ Clearly, he is skeptical about the nature of postcolonial transformations in African Christianity, suggesting that nothing changed substantially. Yet his review focuses on twentieth-century literary texts, written by first-generation African creative writers for whom Christianity continued to be linked to the experience of European colonialism and "civilization." What about the work of the current generation of writers, who were born and grew up after independence?

The literary scholar John Hawley has pointed out that, compared to the classic texts by Achebe, Ngũgĩ, and the like, "a new generation of novelists now incorporates Christianity into its writing with less of an edge." Referring specifically to contemporary Nigerian writers such as Chimamanda Ngozi Adichie, Chris Abani, and Uwem Akpan—each of whom is featured in the present book—Hawley observes that their writings display "appreciative treatments of Christianity," which "suggests the maturing of the Christian church in Africa."[16] Further elaborating on this, he points out that the work of these writers displays "a higher degree of comfort with the increasingly Africanized version of Christianity in which they themselves were raised, and in which they locate the characters in their novels."[17] Indeed, Adichie's 2003 novel *Purple Hibiscus* is often seen as representing this shift in the African literary engagement with Christianity, as it acknowledges but also moves beyond the status of Catholicism as a European missionary religion and actively explores the question of its potential to be rooted in late twentieth-century Nigerian society.[18] Although one of the staunch Christian characters is referred to as "too much of a colonial product," through some of its other characters the novel narratively explores the possibility for Christianity to be decolonized—that is, for it to be dissociated from its colonial heritage and to become part of a liberatory future.[19]

Referring to another major trend in African Christianity in the postcolonial period, the emergence of Pentecostal-Charismatic movements, the cultural sociologist Michael Okyerefo has pointed out that "one would expect that African writers today, just as Achebe or Ngũgĩ engaged with the religious question as it pertained to their time, would dwell heavily on this 'new' development."[20] Okyerefo's implicit criticism appears to be that contemporary African writers do not adequately engage with current trends and developments in African Christianity, although he discusses the 2005 novel *Sun by Night*, by the Ghanaian author Benjamin Kwakye, as an exception. He notes that Kwakye treats Pentecostalism as a phenomenon "that has gained acceptance in Ghanaian society today," thus suggesting that this writer has moved on from the notion of Christianity as a foreign influence, a concept that dominates the work of earlier writers.[21]

If *Sun by Night* was among the first novels engaging with the rapidly growing Pentecostal-Charismatic forms of Christianity on the continent, it is fair to say that other writers have followed suit and have often addressed the phenomenon more comprehensively than Kwakye, for whom it is only a minor theme. Examples from Nigeria include Adichie's 2011 short story "Miracle," which was later incorporated into her novel *Americanah*, in which the mother of the protagonist converts from Catholicism to Pentecostalism and then changes churches several times,[22] and Okey Ndibe's 2014 novel *Foreign Gods, Inc.*, which—as discussed in chapter 6 of this book—engages Pentecostalism critically for its teaching of the prosperity gospel and its corruption of charismatic leadership. Examples from other parts of the continent are Zimbabwean writer NoViolet Bulawayo's 2013 novel *We Need*

New Names, which features a dramatic deliverance scene by a charismatic prophet-healer, and Ugandan writer Jennifer Nansubuga Makumbi's 2014 epic novel *Kintu*, which portrays the transition from the twentieth-century East African Revival to the late twentieth-century Pentecostal-Charismatic revival.

These titles are some indicative examples of what can be seen as a trend in African literature over the past two decades, of writing about Pentecostalism as part of contemporary African social life. One critical observation of this trend is that while African writers have not failed to adequately engage with recent developments in African Christianity, scholars have only expressed sparse interest in this productive and critical engagement. A telling illustration of this sparse interest is that the last book-length study of Christianity in African literature is from 1992, when the Kenyan theologian Jesse Mugambi published his *Critiques of Christianity in African Literature*. Mugambi's book, being over thirty years old, obviously does not engage with any of the developments in African Christianity, or the trends in African literature, over the past few decades. Yet exactly these recent developments and trends make the subject such a rich and exciting field of inquiry.

Decolonizing Christianities in Contemporary Nigerian Literature thus makes a timely intervention by addressing this lacuna in current scholarship and by demonstrating the diverse and fertile engagement with Christianity in contemporary African literature. Methodologically speaking, it significantly expands the scope of source material typically drawn upon in the study of African religions and world Christianity. Through a critical and constructive reading of Christian symbols and themes in contemporary literary texts, this book aims to reconstruct African religious and social thought as emerging from fictional writing. It does so with a particular focus on twenty-first century Nigerian literature, which arguably is one of the most vibrant and prolific branches of African literature today, the sheer volume of its output having been described as "intimidating."[23] Although Nigerian literature reflects a wide range of concerns, one recent and ongoing trend is the profound and substantial engagement with the diverse forms of Christianity flourishing in the country and shaping its cultural, social, and political spheres. Moreover, as Africa's most populous and economically powerful country, Nigeria offers a "magnificent template" for studying postcolonial Africa and its dynamic religious worlds more generally.[24]

Given the width and breadth of relevant source material available, and the steady flow of new texts being published, it is a surprise that contemporary Nigerian and more broadly African literature thus far have not been more systematically drawn upon in the study of Christianity, religion, and literature. Perhaps this is the downside of canonization, with many scholars continuing to work on a handful of classical texts from the mid-twentieth century and being reluctant to engage with recently published texts that have yet to prove their worth. It might also be the result of the policing of disciplinary boundaries; when speaking about this project to an audience of mostly Nigerian religious studies scholars, I could sense the initial reluctance in the room to seriously engage with literary texts—after all, as one of the attendees put it to me afterward, "We are not trained to do this," and "I hadn't realized that this approach yields so much fruit."

According to the ethicist Nimi Wariboko in his recent book on social ethics and governance in Nigerian writing, literature can make profound contributions "toward (re)constructing a philosophy of social transformation for a humane world."[25] The present book can be read as complementary to Wariboko's, but with a distinct focus on the ways contemporary Nigerian literary writings envision and engage the role of Christianity in that social transformation for a humane and more just world. It does so specifically in the light of questions of decolonization and decoloniality, which have become so pertinent in the study of Christianity in Africa and globally.[26] Where decolonization traditionally refers to the political process of former colonies becoming independent and forming sovereign nation-states, the concept of decoloniality has been coined to refer to modes of thinking and acting that are separated from "the colonial matrix of power"; decoloniality is therefore an epistemic, emotional, and aesthetic project.[27] In contemporary discourse, both terms are increasingly used interchangeably, as decolonization is understood to include an epistemological dimension—it is about "the right to think, theorize, interpret the world, develop own methodologies and write from where one is located and unencumbered by Eurocentrism."[28] In relation to Christianity, the quest for decolonization can then be understood as a twofold process: a critique of "the coloniality of faith, and Christian complicity with colonialism and its violent legacies" and the proposition of "decolonial options in the context of emergent Christianities."[29]

In the following sections of this introduction, I will first give an overview of the landscape of scholarship in which this book is located and that it seeks to advance. Second, I will introduce, and offer context to, the subjects of Nigerian literature and Nigerian Christianity, identifying some commonalities between the two. In doing so, I will also make a case for a reading that focuses on the connection between Christianity and social thought, which is typical of my approach to the selected literary texts. Finally, I will outline the structure of this book.

Research Landscapes: Christianity and African Literature

Decolonizing Christianities in Contemporary Nigerian Literature is an example of what the Africanist scholar Paul Zeleza has described as "cross-over interdisciplinarity," which is an approach in which "new fields are constituted from overlapping areas of separate disciplines," and which can also be described as transdisciplinarity.[30] The research I present in this book engages with, and borrows from, disciplines such as religious studies and theology, literary and cultural studies, and African studies, while aiming to constitute religion in African literature as an emerging subject of scholarly inquiry in its own right. As such, this book demonstrates and foregrounds the importance of inter- and transdisciplinary work in understanding and reflecting on the role of religion in African public life, specifically through the lens of literature.[31]

The book is located in, and contributes to, various fields of scholarship, including the study of African religions, specifically Christianity; the study of African literature; and the study of religion and literature. In each of these fields, there is some interest in, and work being done on, Christianity in African literature, but it is fair to say that this subject does not currently constitute a field on its own but is in fact rather dispersed over, and marginal in, various fields. Interestingly, scholars in each of these fields, as shown below, have underlined the need for a more systematic study of Christianity in African literary writing, and this book is a response to such calls.

Religion and Literature

Covering approaches that variably use religion as a lens for thinking about literary texts and use literature as a lens for thinking about religion, the field of religion and literature is broad and wide-ranging. Mark Knight has subsequently suggested that it should be thought of as a two-way "conversation," rather than as a "field," in order to highlight "the fluidity and movement between the disciplines" and the "continual state of flux" that characterizes the nature of their relationship.[32] Whatever terminology one might prefer, Susan Felch, as editor of *The Cambridge Companion to Literature and*

Religion, has argued that this field or conversation suffers from a "decided tilt towards texts and theories that are inflected by Western Christianity and its aftermaths," and she underscores the need for an engagement with Christianity in Global South contexts.[33] In the same volume, this task is taken up by Susan VanZanten, who, in a chapter titled "World Christianity," focuses on two African texts: a work of orature, Afua Kuma's *Jesus of the Deep Forest*, and a work of fiction, Adichie's *Purple Hibiscus*. She uses these texts to provide insight into the ways Christianity in postcolonial contexts is articulated and how the relationship between Christianity and culture in those contexts is negotiated.[34] In 2012, VanZanten also edited a special issue of the journal *Christianity and Literature*, about "African Narrative and the Christian Tradition," which includes several articles—about Chimamanda Ngozi Adichie's *Purple Hibiscus*, Uwem Akpan's collection of stories *Say You're One of Them*, and Ayi Kwei Armah's *Two Thousand Seasons*, among other, lesser-known, texts—that together examine "some of the ways in which the Christian tradition has informed and engaged this rich diversity of African texts."[35] In *The Routledge Companion to Literature and Religion* there is also a chapter on "global Christianity," by Colin Jager, discussing two novels by South African writers—Zakes Mda's *The Heart of Redness* and J. M. Coetzee's *Disgrace*—and exploring their "visions of reconciliation" in the postapartheid era.[36]

As important and welcome as these contributions are, it is probably fair to say that Felch's critical observation of a "decided tilt" toward Western Christian traditions and cultures by and large is still a valid characterization of the study of religion and literature today. For instance, the journal *Theology and Literature*, apart from one special issue on South African writing, published in 1999, has not dedicated any special issues to African literature and has only published a handful of articles on texts by African writers.[37] Addressing this imbalance is important, especially because literature is increasingly thought of as world literature, and Christianity as world Christianity, indicating the diverse global nature, scope, and reach of both subjects. Indeed, it is perhaps not a coincidence that, as the theologian Dorottya Nagy has observed, "parallel to the emergence of World Christianity discourses in recent decades, discourses on world literature, world philosophy, and world history have emerged as well." In her assessment, this indicates not only an emerging global perspective but also an increasing "world-mindedness" in the study of literature, religion, and other subjects in the humanities, which has as a starting point "the recognition of a shared humanity."[38] Acknowledging that African literature is a major part of contemporary world literature, and African Christianity of world Christianity, in this book I seek to expand the scope of literary engagement in the field of religion and literature by foregrounding contemporary Nigerian writing as a major resource enriching the understanding of Christianity as a global and ever-transforming religion.

Within the field of religion and literature, several methodological approaches have been identified. The approach most relevant for this book can be described as identifying and exploring "religion as a concern of literature (the texts and/or their authors)."[39] My key interest here is in how Christian beliefs and symbols, practices and institutions, emerge as a concern in contemporary Nigerian literary texts and how contemporary Nigerian literature offers a fascinating lens through which Christianity can be examined as embedded in present-day Nigerian lifeworlds. As much as the writers of the texts under discussion might have their own agenda in engaging religion as a concern, as a reader of these texts, I, too, bring my own perspective and interests to the process of reading and interpreting their literary representations of these concerns, as acknowledged in the preface to this book. Nagy's notion of "world-mindedness" in the study of world Christianity and literary scholar Chielozona Eze's notion of "ethics of openness" in the study of world literature convey the methodological, ethical, and political commitment that is at the heart of my approach of reading Nigerian literature and Christianity-as-a-concern-in-literature, in a quest for an affirmation of human flourishing and a transformation of social realities in our contemporary world.[40] However, different from some of my previous work, in this book I decided not to make the reflection on my own positionality explicitly part of my writing but rather to let the texts speak for themselves, and to read them in dialogue with the work of African thinkers.[41] The continuity with my previous work, however, is that in this book I continue to be interested in foregrounding and interpreting emerging counterdiscourses to hegemonic forms of Christianity and some of their problematic religious, social, and political impacts in contemporary African contexts.

African Religions and Theology

In the study of African religions and theology, Ezra Chitando observed in the first decade of the 2000s that scholars "have not devoted adequate time to analyse religious themes that run through most African literature," and he called for an increased engagement with literary writing for African religious studies to become "truly multidisciplinary."⁴² Writing in 2010, in his introduction to a special issue of *Studies of World Christianity* about "Religion in African Literary Writings," Afe Adogame reiterated this call as follows: "Scholars of literature and religion should begin to pay more attention to how and to what extent religion is embedded within African literary cultures; ways in which African literary scholars and their works are informed and illuminated—in their ideas and preoccupations, by religious traditions, imagery, ideas, and concerns; and how they engage with and reshape traditional and non-traditional discourses and repertoires."⁴³ The special issue in question includes articles about classical texts, such as Achebe's *Things Fall Apart*, Ngũgĩ's *The River Between* and *Weep Not Child*, and Armah's *Two Thousand Seasons*, as well as a more recent text like Kwakye's *The Sun by Night*.⁴⁴

Specifically with regard to African theology, Abraham Waigi Ng'ang'a several years ago observed an overall lack of engagement by African theologians with the works of African creative writers, which he argues is surprising because both share "deep affinity and common ground" in their quest for African identity in the postcolony.⁴⁵ Perhaps the exception is the work of Achebe, most typically *Things Fall Apart*, which has featured in several African theological texts, while Ngũgĩ's *The River Between* has also received some theological attention.⁴⁶ Ng'ang'a himself has engaged extensively with the works of the Nigerian writer and Nobel laureate in literature Wole Soyinka. Most recently, David T. Ngong's book *Senghor's Eucharist* has offered a profound political-theological engagement with the poetry of the Senegalese writer Léopold Sédar Senghor.

In a recent mapping of scholarship on religion and African literature, I asked what engaging with African literature brings to the table of the study of religion in Africa, and I identified three central and relevant concerns: "First, with the creative representation of religious traditions and dynamics; second, with the critique of religious beliefs and institutions and third, with the imagination of alternative religious possibilities."⁴⁷ Admittedly, these concerns and the ways they are reflected in literary texts often cannot be neatly distinguished and separated, as a given literary text may combine or move between them. Nevertheless, the three lenses of representation, critique, and (re)imagination are helpful for the purpose of this project, as I seek to examine how the diversity of Christianity and the role of Christianity in postcolonial society are represented in contemporary Nigerian literature; how literary texts engage in social and religious critiques of particular Christian beliefs and practices for the ways they constitute or reinforce problematic sociocultural norms and sociopolitical structures; and how these texts draw on Christian beliefs, texts, and symbols to explore the alternative world-making possibilities within Christian traditions that align with, and contribute to, a vision of social justice. In doing so, I seek to demonstrate the importance of contemporary literary writing as a source for studying, and thinking about, religion and cultural production in contemporary Africa, as well as in the context of world Christianity.

African Literature

African literary studies is firmly linked to, and shaped by, traditions of postcolonial criticism. This may be part of the reason why this field has not demonstrated much interest in Christianity, given this religion's close association with the history of colonialism in much of Africa. It is telling that a recent major handbook on African literature rightly has a chapter on Islam yet lacks a contribution on Christianity, while both faiths have a similar following and influence on the continent and also have profoundly shaped African literary traditions.[48] Islam and its African literary representation have also been the subject of at least two scholarly monographs, but there is no equivalent recent book-length study on African literary representations of Christianity.[49] Some attention is paid to Christian-related themes in a 2017 special issue of *Research in African Literatures*, edited by Jeanne-Marie Jackson and Nathan Suhr-Sytsma, about "Religion, Secularity, and African Writing," with the editors highlighting that "while Europe's status as Christian hegemon has waned... since the early twentieth century, sub-Saharan Africa has played an increasingly dominant role in Christianity's diffusion."[50] Suhr-Sytsma himself has recently published an insightful article on Christian-Muslim relations in Nigerian literature.[51] Two scholarly monographs—Mark Mathuray's *On the Sacred in African Literature* (2009) and Rebekah Cumpsty's *Postsecular Poetics* (2023)—use the much broader concept of "the sacred" to examine religion and spirituality in African literary texts; they do not engage with Christianity as a central subject of inquiry as such. Of course, the classic texts by Ngũgĩ, Achebe, and others have been widely studied in African literary scholarship, and one wonders whether these writers' postcolonial critique has positioned Christianity as unfashionable in the field.

Decolonizing Christianities in Contemporary Nigerian Literature capitalizes and seeks to deliver on the suggestion of Jackson and Suhr-Sytsma, in the introduction to their special issue mentioned above, that it is time to revisit the paradigm in which Christianity in Africa is constantly linked to the history of colonialism and imperialism, and to acknowledge and understand the central role that Africa plays in the postcolonial "diffusion" of Christianity. By the latter, I mean the process by which Christianity—if it ever was a purely "Western religion"—has become a Global South religion thriving in the postcolony, possibly because it gives its adherents a sense of agency, identity, and meaning in the ruptures and fissures of life in our contemporary, globalized, highly unequal world.

Earlier, I cited African theologians such as Kwame Bediako from Ghana and Lamin Sanneh from the Gambia, who, in the light of both precolonial historical trajectories and postcolonial developments, have made a case for thinking about Christianity as a non-Western, and indeed African, religion.[52] Although there is a clear demographic case for this, South African theologian Tinyiko Maluleke has argued that Bediako, Sanneh, and the like might have been too celebratory about Africa as "the new face" of global Christianity and failed to take "serious note of the tragic nature of Christianity in Africa"—a tragedy stemming, in his words, from "the violence of some of the methods with which it was transmitted, the violence of the colonial legacies, and the violence of the resulting conditions in which Africans find themselves."[53] Arguably, there is an important conversation to be had between African literature and African theology, engaging these questions about the dialectics of Christianity in the African postcolony. The Nigerian literary texts discussed in this book offer a rich starting point for such an interdisciplinary conversation. As much as these texts represent Christianity as part of the fabric of postcolonial society, they acknowledge and engage its problematic histories and legacies and explore alternative, decolonial possibilities within Christianity.

The decolonial theorist Sabelo Ndlovu-Gatsheni has described the quest for decolonization as "seek ye epistemic freedom first." His paraphrasing of a biblical verse can be seen as an allusion to the possible synergies between religious, specifically Christian, language and the intellectual and political project of decoloniality. As much as Ndlovu-Gatsheni acknowledges that during colonialism, and in the ongoing regime of coloniality, conversion to Christianity was "a form of epistemicide," as African indigenous knowledges were supplanted by European memory, he also implicitly suggests that seeking epistemic freedom, theologically speaking, is a project of eschatological significance, as it engenders what in the New Testament is called the Kingdom of God.[54] It illustrates the aforementioned paradox of Christianity in Africa and elsewhere in the majority world as simultaneously complicit with colonialism and its ongoing legacies and a resource for imagining and enacting "decolonial options."[55] Moreover, it subtly highlights the notion that decolonization is not about restoring a precolonial past and its indigenous knowledge systems—although a renewed appreciation of such knowledges can be part of it—but about envisioning new, liberatory African futures, potentially also through Christian imagination. This book examines the ways contemporary Nigerian literary writers grapple with this paradox while creatively exploring the decolonial options embedded in Nigerian Christianities. The word "decolonizing" in the title can be read both as an adjective and as a verb; together with the plural "Christianities," it signals that decolonization is an ongoing, dynamic, and pluriversal process with an ambivalent and complex but potentially productive relationship to Christian traditions as represented and reimagined in twenty-first-century Nigerian literary texts.

Limitations and New Directions

From the above review of relevant fields of scholarship, some observations can be made. Existing scholarship on Christianity and African literature, although dispersed and fragmented, has generated significant insights yet also has some serious limitations. First, it tends to focus on "canonical" twentieth-century texts, in particular by writers such as Achebe and Ngũgĩ—whose work is obviously worth studying—and consequently it tends to overlook more recent texts by younger writers, except perhaps for Adichie, whose work has enjoyed considerable attention. Second, as a result of the latter limitation, and as noted earlier, scholarship tends to be mostly concerned with the history of Christian mission in Africa and its links to European colonialism, which is a valid problem, yet fails to adequately acknowledge the postcolonial condition of Christianity on the continent. Third, there has been little sustained engagement with the ways African Christianity and its recent dynamics and transformations are represented in contemporary African literature and the new questions this raises. For instance, the enormous popularity of Pentecostal Christian movements and their representation in contemporary African literature have hardly been addressed.[56] Fourth, its emphasis tends to be on the critique of Christianity in African literature—as reflected in the aforementioned title of the only book-length study on the subject, by Mugambi. Subsequently it tends to overlook the ways a current generation of writers engage Christianity in creative ways, as they reimagine Christian faith and explore its relevance for thinking through current African issues.

Thus, as much as I have learned from, and build on, these various bodies of scholarship, *Decolonizing Christianities in Contemporary Nigerian Literature* aims to intersect, advance, and expand the fields identified above by focusing on contemporary writers and their twenty-first-century texts, which offer critical and creative literary representations of Christianity set in the postindependence period. A key example is Chimamanda Ngozi Adichie's 2003 novel *Purple Hibiscus*, which in its opening sentence makes a direct intertextual allusion to *Things Fall Apart*, but which narrates a Nigerian Christian world that is distinctly different from Achebe's classic. As I discuss in chapter 3 of this book, Adichie explores the possibilities of Catholicism taking root in a late twentieth-century Nigerian sociocultural milieu, including an apparition of the Virgin Mary in the local landscape. She counterbalances the dominant literary depiction of African Christianity as a product of European mission by including a narrative reference to a young Nigerian Catholic priest becoming a missionary in Germany, thus illustrating contemporary dynamics in global Christianity such as the phenomenon of the "reverse mission." The novel also mentions "mushroom Pentecostal churches" and their "fake pastors," a theme in Nigerian Christianity that Adichie further pursues in her second novel, *Americanah*, and that other writers such as Ndibe have also explored in recent texts (see chapter 6 of this book).[57]

My proposed focus on contemporary writers and their writings thus takes into account the aforementioned shifts and transformations, both in African literature and in African Christianity, and it allows for an innovative study of the ways contemporary literary writing engages with Christianity in modes that include, but are not limited to, critique. This is important, both because of the contested status—and simultaneous popularity—of Christianity in postcolonial Africa and because of the vital role of literature as "a lens for reading and thinking about religion."[58] Such a focus is also crucial in order to overcome, in VanZanten's words, "the historical myopia that associates Christianity solely with European Christendom" and to acknowledge that "world Christianity today spans multiple continents, theological traditions, nationalities, ethnicities, and cultures." Moreover, it acknowledges specifically that Africa has become home, in the words of the missiologist Andrew Walls, to "potentially *the* representative Christianity of the twenty-first century."[59] Although focusing on the specific subset of Nigerian literature, my broader aim in this book is to demonstrate that religion, specifically Christianity, and African literature is a fascinating subject of inquiry yielding rich fruits and that it can become a transdisciplinary field of study in its own right. I do so by foregrounding literary writing as a critically important and innovative lens for understanding and reflecting on the sociocultural and sociopolitical roles of Christianity in Africa and foregrounding Christianity as a central concern and creative theme in contemporary African literature.

Intersecting Nigerian Literature and Nigerian Christianity

Both the literary scene and the Christian scene in twenty-first-century Nigeria demonstrate a high level of vibrancy and vitality, with commentators widely recognizing their respective reach, impact, and influence within Nigeria, across the continent, and indeed worldwide. Both subjects have also received a considerable amount of scholarly interest, with the study of Nigerian literature and of Nigerian Christianity having become flourishing research areas on their own. With these two subjects being largely studied separately, *Decolonizing Christianities in Contemporary Nigerian Literature* aims to put them in a productive and exciting interdisciplinary conversation. To begin that conversation, I identify and discuss in this section some common characteristics.

The Colonial Connection

Historically speaking, Nigerian literature and Nigerian Christianity are to a considerable extent byproducts of British colonialism, which started in the mid-nineteenth century and lasted till 1960, when Nigeria gained independence. Admittedly, in the territory now known as Nigeria, there were literary cultures in various forms and in diverse languages pre-dating the arrival of the British or other Europeans. Some of these, such as Hausa literature in northern Nigeria, have continued to thrive. Yet colonialism "succeeded in transforming literary cultures in diverse ways. The introduction of English as an official language in the region diminished the importance of local vernaculars, yet literacy in English inspired new forms of literature that coexisted with the dominant cultural traditions of the spoken arts."[60] Obviously, schools established by European missionaries were key to this introduction and promotion of English, and, as such, Christian missions have been instrumental to the birth of Nigerian literature in English, while this literary production simultaneously became a way to "write back" to the colonial and missionary (mis)representation of local cultures and traditions.⁶¹ With regard to African literature more generally, Gikandi argues that it "can be considered to have been a product of the Christian mission," because the major African writers of the twentieth century were educated in mission schools where they encountered European literary traditions and because missionary printing presses "were the places in which African literature was first materially produced."⁶² Thus, somewhat paradoxically, as much as literary writing in the twentieth century gradually became a vehicle of nationalist agitation against colonialism and mission, it was also indebted to them.

With regard to Christianity, European missionaries were active in the region now known as Nigeria before British colonialism. Notably, the first missionaries on the West African coast were Portuguese; they arrived as early as the fifteenth century, alongside explorers and traders from the same country, although their effort is generally seen not to have had a lasting effect. Yet a second, and more enduring, missionary effort came in the nineteenth century, with the first Protestant missions being set up in Yorubaland in the 1840s, followed a few decades later by the Catholics, who became particularly active in Igboland.⁶³ This initiated a complex process of conversion and religious change, which was directly linked to broader social, economic, and political transformations in the region, brought about by colonialism and the subsequent reconfiguration of power and identity during colonial modernity.⁶⁴ In the first half of the twentieth century, southern Nigeria, which was under direct British colonial rule, was gradually Christianized, while northern Nigeria, which was under indirect rule, remained overwhelmingly Muslim because Christian evangelism was restricted there. This laid the basis for a religious divide that continues to define and trouble the country to date (see chapter 5 in this book).

Although the relationship between mission Christianity and colonial administration was complex and sometimes fraught, overall, they benefited from each other. As the Africanist historian Olufemi Vaughan puts it: "Christian missionaries and colonial administrators worked creatively to deploy complementary doctrines of Western training and enlightenment to advance colonial imperatives."⁶⁵ Especially through the provision of education and health care, the missions were able to establish themselves in local communities and have a far-reaching impact. The emergence of African-initiated churches, often referred to in Nigeria as *aladura* (a simplification of the Yoruba word *aláàdúrà*, meaning "one who prays"), in the early twentieth century heralded a new and significant chapter in the local appropriation of Christianity outside of European missionary structures.

They brought about a "unique synthesis" of biblical tradition, Christian liturgy, and indigenous religious concepts and rituals, thus "shaping a new version of Christianity" with charismatic features and local resonance.[66]

Postcolonial Vitality and Diversity

The historical connection to colonialism did not stop Nigerian literature, or Nigerian Christianity, from flourishing in the postcolonial era, leading to increasingly diverse and dynamic fields that scholars have attempted to categorize and structure.

As for Nigerian literature in English, several genres have emerged and proliferated, including fiction, poetry, and theater, together forming a "corpus of impressive bulk and astonishing variety."[67] A common, though contested, method of categorizing Nigerian (and, more generally, African) Anglophone literature has been generational. In this model, writers such as Achebe and Soyinka are typically seen as part of the "first generation" that used literature for a project of "cultural nationalism," while subsequent writers are seen as part of a second generation, characterized by a "disillusionment with the failings of the postcolonial state," and a third generation is associated with "an opening up in terms of thematic concerns and narrative experimentation."[68] Most recently, a fourth generation has been proposed to refer to writers "characterized by a new set of literary trends that have developed since the beginning of the twenty-first century."[69] Although this generational model has been critiqued for "its over-reliance on age-similarity, social, bio-psycho, historical, and artistic convergences (and divergences)," it offers one way of acknowledging and interpreting the development of, and trends and innovations within, Nigerian literary cultures.[70] As such, the model—and its continued prevalence and expansion—illustrates the vitality of Nigerian literature in English, which has now become an "orchestra of pluralities."[71] The writers whose work is featured in this book are generally associated with the third and fourth generations. They are part of what has been described as "an unprecedented wave of African writing that moves beyond the 'writing back' of previous generations who sought to redress colonialism and its aftermath."[72] Acknowledging this generational shift, I question how these contemporary writers engage with Christianity as part of their experience and representation of postcolonial Nigeria.

As for Nigerian Christianity, and for African Christianity more generally, the religious studies scholar Asonzeh Ukah has argued for the use of the plural "Christianities" to acknowledge the existence of "different strands or traditions that may or may not be compatible one to another."[73] This pluralization is characteristic of what Martha Frederiks has called a "World Christianity approach," in which Christianity is conceptualized as an "inherently plural, cumulative tradition" with complex and changing entanglements with its multiple sociocultural and sociopolitical contexts.[74] Ukah, like many other scholars, distinguishes three broad categories of the forms of Christianity practiced in Nigeria, in a model that is also somewhat generational: first, the historical mission (sometimes also referred to as mainline) churches, which have their origins in nineteenth-century Catholic and Protestant (e.g., Anglican, Methodist, Presbyterian) missionary activity; second, the independent or indigenous churches, which emerged in the late nineteenth century and in the first half of the twentieth century as local Christian initiatives outside of the mission churches, including the aforementioned Aladura churches, which grew rapidly in the 1920s and later decades, attracting followers with their strong emphasis on prayer, healing, and prophetic visions; and third, Pentecostal churches that emerged in the mid-twentieth century, some of which are historically linked to North American classical Pentecostal movements (e.g., the Assemblies of God), while others emerged as local initiatives, and with a new wave, around the 1980s, often referred to as Pentecostal-Charismatic or neo-Pentecostal churches.[75] The latter subcategory has become enormously popular in recent decades, thanks to its teachings and practices of prosperity, deliverance, and spiritual warfare.

This threefold categorization is useful to acknowledge some of the historical, sociological, and theological differences between various churches and movements. However, it should not be interpreted as a rigid frame, as the boundaries between the various categories are fluid. For instance, the Redeemed Christian Church of God was founded in 1952 as an Aladura church but soon reinvented itself in Pentecostal style and today is often seen as a typical example of Nigerian neo-Pentecostalism.[76] The historic mission churches also have incorporated many practices typically associated with Pentecostalism, such as charismatic worship, healing, and deliverance, in an attempt to retain a following. Thus, denominations such as the Anglican and Catholic churches have sizable charismatic renewal movements in their midst, and scholars speak of the "Pentecostalization" of Christianity at large.[77] As the total Christian population of Nigeria has grown tremendously, churches across the spectrum are thriving in what has become a

INTRODUCTION

diverse and dynamic Christian landscape and a highly competitive and innovative religious market.⁷⁸

A Global Outlook

As part of their flourishing in the postcolonial period, both Nigerian literature and Nigerian Christianity have become globally significant phenomena, firmly embedded in Nigerian diaspora networks and in global sociocultural flows. Many contemporary Nigerian writers, including a range of authors discussed in this book, are based, or spend a significant part of their time, in North America and Europe; they often produce their work from those contexts, publish it internationally, and build their reputation through international awards and other forms of recognition. Literary scholars, such as Madhu Krishnan, in her book with the telling subtitle "Global Locations, Postcolonial Identifications," are debating why this "decidedly migratory African identity" has become representative of Nigerian (and, more generally, African) literature and how it affects and reflects in the resulting literary works.⁷⁹ It has been suggested that some of the internationally acclaimed diaspora-based African writers, because of their geographical location, their diasporic perspective, and their writing for a global market, could be described as "equally non-African" or "part-time Africans" producing an "Africa-lite" literature.⁸⁰ Other scholars have drawn on notions of pan-Africanism and, more recently (as well as more controversially), Afropolitanism to foreground the fact that African literature in the postcolonial period has come "to be located in a unique global moment" and to propose a conceptualization of African identity in a globalized world that is not limited to identification with one nation or continent but acknowledges "the fluidity of African self-perception and visions of the world."⁸¹

I do not seek in this book to contribute to these debates as such. As much as I recognize that several of the authors featured in the following chapters are based in or publish their work from North America or Europe, what matters here is that they write about Nigeria as "this our country." *Of This Our Country* is the title of a recent collection of essays by well-known Nigerian writers, including Chimamanda Ngozi Adichie, Okey Ndibe, and Chigozie Obioma, who each are discussed in this book and who are based in the United States; the various essays demonstrate insightfully how these writers, regardless of their geographical location, consider Nigeria as central to their sense of home and belonging, identity, and culture.[82] More specifically, as will be explored in the chapters of this book, Christian beliefs, practices, texts, and symbols take center stage in their writing about Nigeria, demonstrating how Christianity is part of their representation of Nigerian society. Even when originally published in the Global North, books by Nigerian writers do still circulate in Nigeria. When I visited a bookshop in Abuja, in May 2024, I found copies of almost all the titles discussed in this book, in several cases locally published versions of titles originally published in the United Kingdom or the United States.

Nigerian Christianity, too, has become a global phenomenon. As a result of migration, Nigerian Christians are influencing religious cultures and communities in other parts of the world. Moreover, Nigerian churches, of various types, have also actively embarked on a strategy of continental and indeed global influence and expansion. Thus, Nigeria is a major part of what Adogame calls the "African Christian diaspora" and is transforming Christianity in the West and globally.[83] Discussing "the Nigerian factor in global Christianity," the missiologist Allan Effa identifies three key arenas in which this transformation is visible.[84] First, in the arena of what he calls "mainline Christianity"—that is, the historic Catholic and Protestant denominations that through missionary activity were transplanted to Nigeria. Due to church growth in Nigeria, and ongoing processes of secularization and church decline in the West, Nigerian churches in this category have become important players in their respective global denominations. This is visible, for instance, in the worldwide Anglican Communion, where Nigerian bishops play a leading role in what has become known as the crisis about issues of homosexuality, and in the worldwide Catholic Church, where there is an increasing dependence in Europe and North America on priestly vocations from Nigeria and other parts of Africa. Second, in the arena of "evangelical world missions," Nigerian missionaries are actively involved in evangelism and church-planting initiatives, especially in Muslim-majority countries. Third, in the arena of "reverse mission," Nigeria-founded and -led churches, especially of the Pentecostal type, embark on a vision of "bringing back" the Christian faith to secularized countries in Europe, North America, and other parts of the world. The extent to which these churches succeed in converting autochthonous people or mostly cater to diaspora communities is debatable, but it is a fact that originally Nigerian churches, such as the Redeemed Christian Church of God, are helping keep Christianity alive in countries in the Global North.

None of the novels discussed in this book engage with the diaspora dimensions of Nigerian Christianity, as they are all set in, and focus on,

Nigeria itself.⁸⁵ Yet the global outlook of Nigerian Christianity does underscore the importance of understanding Christianity in the Nigerian context, which is what I seek to contribute to. Thus, in light of Nigerian Pentecostal churches preaching versions of the prosperity gospel globally, Ndibe's novel *Foreign Gods, Inc.* is worth reading as an example of how this religious culture is represented and critiqued within Nigeria. And in light of the aforementioned Nigerian Christian politics of homosexuality, Chinelo Okparanta's novel *Under the Udala Trees* offers a worthy insight into how alternative Christian understandings are imagined from a Nigerian perspective.

A Public Role

Lastly, both Nigerian literature and Nigerian Christianity play important public roles, meaning that their significance and relevance exceed their respective literary and religious domains narrowly defined. As for the public role of literature, already during, but especially after, the colonial period, Nigerian writers contributed significantly to the narrative invention and imagination of the nation, or what the historian Toyin Falola calls "the nationhood project."⁸⁶ Thus, they engaged, and continue to engage today, in critical sociopolitical thought—for instance, addressing questions of citizenship, democracy, social justice, and human rights.⁸⁷ This frequently put them at odds with the government of the day, especially during the military regimes that ruled the country from 1966 to 1999 (with a democratic interval from 1979 to 1983). For instance, Soyinka, one of Nigeria's most illustrious writers, was a political prisoner in the late 1960s, after being accused of siding with the Biafra nationalists during the Nigerian Civil War, while the internationally renowned writer and environmental activist Ken Saro-Wiwa was imprisoned and hanged in 1995, at the height of his campaign against environmental degradation by the petroleum industry. It is perhaps no coincidence that the current vibrancy of Nigerian literature is associated with the postmilitary dictatorship period following the transition to civilian rule in 1999, when writers were able to work in relative freedom.⁸⁸

One way literary writing performs a public role is by holding up a mirror to readers, and to society more generally, stimulating awareness of, and critical reflection on, injustices and other social concerns. Thus, Nigerian writers, as African writers more generally, in the words of the Africanist scholar Wale Adebanwi, are "social thinkers," who use their creative writing for what the literary scholar Ato Quayson has conceptualized as "a calibration of the social."⁸⁹ Several of the novels discussed in this book demonstrate this concern with social issues, be they in the realm of gender, such as Adichie's addressing of gender-based violence in *Purple Hibiscus*, or in the realm of sexuality, such as Okparanta's interrogation of same-sex relationships in *Under the Udala Trees*, or in the realm of ecology, such as Obioma's engagement with environmental degradation in *The Fishermen*. What stands out in each of these examples, as I will show in the relevant chapters of this book, is how these writers engage these social issues in relation to religion, and specifically Christianity. Thus, the writer as a social thinker also frequently appears to be a religious thinker, precisely because social and religious domains are closely intertwined. My interest in this book is in how contemporary Nigerian literary writers think about, with, or against Christianity as part of their critical, creative, and imaginative engagement with contemporary sociocultural and sociopolitical issues. Inspired by Quayson's notion of "reading *for* the social"—that is, "using the literary as a means toward social enlightenment"—I will be reading the religious dimensions of literary texts as intricately linked to their social dimensions, and I will explore how the texts seek to engender social and religious "enlightenment."[90]

Christianity, too, plays a prominent public role in Nigeria, as elsewhere in Africa, meaning that Christian idiom and practice have been appropriated "beyond the boundaries of religious expression" in a narrow sense.[91] Where in Western contexts there is a secular tendency to consider religion as part of the private sphere and relegate it to the margins of society, in much of Africa (and indeed many parts of the world) religion is a highly public phenomenon, manifesting itself in social, political, and popular cultural domains. Nigeria is a key example of a country where Christianity—especially, but not only, in its Pentecostal form—is a public religion. Recent studies have argued, for instance, that Nigerian Christianities constitute, in the words of the political theorist Ruth Marshall, a "political spirituality" and transform the country, in what the sociologist Ebenezer Obadare has called a "Pentecostal republic," while also shaping the popular cultures of the local movie and music industry and structures of socioeconomic development.[92] Precisely because Christianity has become part of the fabric of Nigerian society, Christian beliefs, rhetoric, ritual, and symbols also influence social and political attitudes toward issues of public concern, such as in the realms of gender, sexuality, human rights, and democracy.

According to the character Obierika in *Things Fall Apart*, missionary Christianity in the colonial period was like "a knife on the things that held us together," as a result of which "we have fallen apart." Following from this, one wonders what the role of Christianity has been in the postcolonial period and how this is represented in contemporary literary texts. Thus, my interest in this book is in the ways Christianity, as a public religion, itself is engaged publicly in literary texts and how literature opens up an interface for thinking about the public role of Christianity in Nigerian society today. According to the literary scholar Abiodun Adeniji, among the main social issues in postindependence Nigerian literature is the question of religious hypocrisy. Referring to texts such as Soyinka's 1964 play *The Trials of Brother Jero*, he points out that "the misuse of religion as recorded in Nigerian literature almost always comes in the form of satire on the hypocrisy of the priests of such religions. These are portrayed as Janus-faced characters who preach holiness, righteousness, and contentment . . . but exhibit worldliness, rapacity, and duplicity in their off-the-pulpit dealings with their fellow men and women."[93] This is still a central concern in twenty-first-century texts, some of which are discussed in this book, such as Okey Ndibe's *Foreign Gods, Inc.* and Elnathan John and Àlàbá Ònájìn's *On Ajayi Crowther Street*, which both use satire to expose religious hypocrisy among pastors, specifically in Pentecostal settings. However, this is certainly not the only, and not necessarily the most dominant, way contemporary Nigerian writers engage with religion. As I will show in subsequent chapters, literary writers think not only against but also *with* Christianity, drawing on symbolic and textual resources from within Christian traditions to engage in social thought and political imagination. Thus, Nigerian literature, as a mirror to society, allows for grasping the complexity and ambiguity of Christianity as a public religion in contemporary Nigeria.

The Organization of This Book

The literary texts I discuss in *Decolonizing Christianities in Contemporary Nigerian Literature* are all from the twenty-first century, with Adichie's *Purple Hibiscus* (2003) being the oldest text. They are written by authors from the postindependence generation, with Okey Ndibe (born in the year Nigeria gained independence, 1960) being the most senior and Chigozie Obioma (b. 1986) being the youngest. Each of the fictional narratives is also set in the postindependence period. In this threefold way, the selected texts offer a rich insight into how contemporary Nigerian literature represents and engages Christianity as part of the fabric of postcolonial society.

My selection of texts does not claim to be comprehensive but is illustrative, I believe, both of the diversity in Nigerian Christianities and of the diverse treatment of Christianity in contemporary Nigerian literary writing. Admittedly, the selection unintendedly turned out to feature many texts by authors of Igbo decent—the only two writers from a different ethnic background are Uwem Akpan and E. E. Sule (discussed in chapter 5). This is indicative of the significant contribution of Igbo writers—described as being among "the most prolific writers in Africa in terms of output and attention given to their novels"—to contemporary Nigerian literature in English.[94] It is also illustrative of the enthusiastic reception of Christianity among the Igbo since the missionary era and the colonial period, which was further intensified in the postcolonial period, when Igboland witnessed a strong Christian revival in the aftermath of the Biafra War (1967–70).[95] The texts discussed in this book are all set in the period during and in the decades after the war, and many of the writers featured have family histories directly shaped by the war. These factors may explain why Christianity emerges as a central theme specifically in contemporary Igbo-Nigerian literature.

The selection also turned out to have a bias toward bildungsromans, which are featured in all chapters of this book but chapter 6.[96] Although a term derived from German, the bildungsroman has become a dominant genre in African literary writing, where it distinguishes itself from its European counterpart, among other characteristics, by narrating "the ongoing remediation of colonialism's traumatic legacy" and its postcolonial aftermath "throughout the self-maturation process."[97] Given that Christianity is a central part of the legacy of colonialism and of the postcolonial condition in much of Africa, including Nigeria, it is perhaps no surprise that it is a common theme in many bildungsromans by contemporary Nigerian writers. In these novels, Christianity is critically discussed in relation to other issues closely linked to (post)colonialism, such as civil wars, patriarchy, homophobia, environmental degradation, and interreligious violence. In the selected texts, as we will see in the main chapters of this book, Christianity variably emerges as a symbolic resource to make sense of (post)colonial trauma, as a problem that protagonists must contend with in their quest for identity and maturity, and as a terrain for renegotiation and creative appropriation.

The discussion of the selected texts is embedded, in each chapter, in a review of their broader literary and religious landscapes, providing context and depth to the analysis. Reading religion as a concern in the selected texts, I will examine and explore this concern with the help of relevant thinkers—theologians, philosophers, and social theorists—for which primarily and principally I draw on Nigerian and other African scholars. Making their work part of the conversation allows me to further elucidate key themes and critical questions regarding the status of Christianity as part of social life in contemporary Nigeria, and to reveal and expand on the critical and constructive religious and social thinking that is embedded in the literary texts under discussion. This also enables me to acknowledge the theologizing that happens within, and emerges from, these texts, reading them as contextual theologies in the making—however incomplete and partial they may be.

The six chapters of *Decolonizing Christianities in Contemporary Nigerian Literature* are organized thematically; in each chapter I read one or more selected literary texts, analyzing the engagement with Christianity in relation to a specific area of social concern. The title of each chapter is a keyword of Nigerian Christian idiom emerging from the text under discussion and capturing the ways religious and social thought are intertwined. Each chapter can be read independently, but the chapters are interconnected and speak to one another in various ways. For the purpose of presenting them in this book, I have contemplated various possible structures. In the end, I settled for an ordering in terms of the historical context of the literary texts under discussion, which was the most unambiguous. Thus, the first chapters of the book focus on texts set during, or in the aftermath of, the Nigerian Civil War, while the subsequent chapters are concerned with, or refer to, more recent events and contexts.

The Nigerian Civil War, also known as the Biafra War, was fought from July 6, 1967, to January 15, 1970, between the federal Nigerian state and the short-lived secessionist state called the Republic of Biafra, which had been launched by Igbo nationalists after years of rising tensions between the Igbo and other ethnic groups in Nigeria. The significance of this war, during which an estimated five hundred thousand to three million people died, for Nigerian postcolonial history and nationhood cannot be overstated. Achebe has even claimed that the Biafra War not only "changed the course of Nigeria" but was a "cataclysmic experience that changed the history of Africa."[98] The suppressed memory and trauma of the war has led to the emergence of a literary tradition of "writing the Nigeria-Biafra war," which includes not only historical fiction about the war itself, the events leading up to it, and its aftermath but also texts that use the war as a background of social and historical meaning.[99] As such, the civil war features in several of the literary texts discussed in this book, although it is not the central theme in any of them.

In chapter 1, "Forgiveness," I discuss two novellas, Chris Abani's *Song for Night* and Uzodinma Iweala's *Beasts of No Nation*. Neither text explicitly mentions the war, yet Abani includes narrative pointers that allude to it, while Iweala has claimed to have been inspired by the history of the war. Both novellas can be seen as part of the tradition of "writing the Nigeria-Biafra war" broadly defined, which they combine with another tradition or genre in West African literature: child soldier narratives. As I will demonstrate by analyzing the literary representation of material religion and theopoetics, both novellas seek to process postwar memory and trauma by drawing on Christian objects, texts, and symbols and by addressing the ethical and theological question of the possibility of forgiveness. Thus, I read these novellas as texts of religious imagination in the context of conflict-induced Nigerian and West African postcolonial trauma.

In chapter 2, "Deliverance," I focus on Chinelo Okparanta's novel *Under the Udala Trees*. Although the novel opens with the war, and most of its story unfolds in the immediate postwar period of the 1970s, war memory is not its central theme. Instead, Okparanta uses the war as a historical background for a story about what has become another battleground in contemporary Nigeria: same-sex relationships. By juxtaposing these two battles, the novel makes a narrative connection between ethnicity and sexuality, suggesting that both categories can be equally divisive and the cause of conflict, violence, and human rights offenses. I read *Under the Udala Trees* as a major contribution to the emerging genre of queer Nigerian literature, specifically examining its creative negotiation of Christianity in relation to the quest to affirm diverse sexualities. Using the key term of deliverance—derived from Pentecostal discourse—as a lens, I examine how religiously violated and demonized queer bodies are written in this novel into an affirmative space of freedom.

In chapter 3, "Apparition," I discuss Chimamanda Ngozi Adichie's *Purple Hibiscus*, which is set in the 1980s but includes some references to the civil war. It has been suggested that through its main protagonists, Kambili and Jaja, Adichie "pays homage to the silent children of Biafra" and that the novel reflects a deliberate effort to reclaim Igbo cultural identity in the postwar era.[100] As part of that effort, it explores whether and how Christianity, specifically Catholicism, links to that quest for Igbo identity. In doing so, the novel offers a narrative account of the changes in Catholicism in Nigeria, as a formerly colonial form of religion becomes rooted in its local context. My reading focuses specifically on issues of gender that are prominent in the novel, and which Adichie links creatively to the theme of Marian devotion, culminating in an apparition of the Virgin Mary.

The subsequent three chapters focus on texts that move away from the civil war as a historical background or point of reference. In chapter 4,

"Prophecy," I focus on Chigozie Obioma's *The Fishermen*, alongside a brief discussion of Nnedi Okorafor's *Lagoon*. Set in the late 1990s, *The Fishermen* has often been read against the political turmoil in Nigeria at the time and as an allegory of Nigeria as "a dwindling nation." However, I offer an ecological reading of the novel, which explores its engagement with environmental issues in relation to Christianity. *The Fishermen* shares this thematic interest with the futuristic novel *Lagoon*, yet each text approaches the subject quite differently. Where the latter novel offers a blunt ecological critique of Christianity, specifically in its Pentecostal form, the former complements such critique by narratively foregrounding the environmental referentiality of indigenous churches, specifically the Celestial Church of Christ, and by drawing on broader Christian biblical and hymnal texts to engage in ecotheologizing. *The Fishermen*'s plot centers around a prophecy that turns out to be a curse; however, my reading also foregrounds how, on a different level, the novel can be read prophetically, as it calls for ecological justice in the context of Nigerian Christianity.

In chapter 5, "Spiritual Warfare," I discuss three texts—two novels and a novella—that together cover the period from the 1990s to the 2010s. Set in different decades, each text speaks to a particular stage or major incident in the increasingly tense interreligious climate in Nigeria—specifically, the unfolding tensions and violence between Christians and Muslims. Thus, in historical order: E. E. Sule's novel *Sterile Sky* opens with a horrifying story of mob violence by Muslims against Christians that was incited by a crusade of the German evangelist Reinhard Bonnke in Kano, which took place in October 1991. Akpan's novella *Luxurious Hearses* is set in the immediate aftermath of the Sharia crisis, which broke out in February 2000 after the Kaduna state governor legalized Islamic law. The story is located in a fictional city called Khamfi, which resembles Kaduna. Lastly, Adaobi Tricia Nwaubani's novel *Buried Beneath the Baobab Tree* was directly inspired by the 2014 Chibok crisis, during which 276 mostly Christian schoolgirls were kidnapped by Boko Haram. Drawing attention to discourses of spiritual warfare against Islam, which can be found in some Nigerian Christian circles, my reading explores the different ways these texts seek to overcome the politics of alterity in which the religious Other is seen negatively, as an existential threat, and even as demonic, and how instead they seek to promote interreligious recognition.

Finally, in chapter 6, "Prosperity," I focus on Okey Ndibe's novel *Foreign Gods, Inc.*, which is set in the first decade of the 2000s in a transnational context of migration, globalization, and neoliberal capitalism. Of all the texts discussed in this book, Ndibe's novel offers the most in-depth engagement with Pentecostalism, a strand of Nigerian Christianity that has become enormously popular since the late twentieth century. It is also a key example of literary critique of popular religion, deploying satire to interrogate some of the critical issues in Nigerian Pentecostalism, such as its tense relationship with indigenous religions, its propagation of the prosperity gospel, and the corruption of charismatic leadership. My reading argues that *Foreign Gods, Inc.* offers an important mirror to a society where Christianity has become deeply Pentecostalized and, as part of that process, has become deeply intertwined with money, power, and popular culture, with all the risks that entails.

Together, these six chapters offer a rich array of diverse Christian traditions in Nigeria and insight into the ways these Christianities intersect with a range of current social concerns. *Decolonizing Christianities in Contemporary Nigerian Literature* demonstrates the deep insights that literary writing offers to the study of Christianity and social thought. As captured in the epigraph of this book, the Nigerian literary writer and public intellectual Wole Soyinka has suggested that the key question for our times is whether religion can "peacefully cohabit with humanism" and indeed whether it can "cohabit with humanity itself." Soyinka, as a well-known religion skeptic and as someone who has broken with his Christian upbringing, appears to answer this in the negative, especially in relation to monotheistic religions such as Christianity and Islam, which, in his assessment, "threaten the very fabric" of the African continent because of their evangelizing zeal and intolerant moral-political agenda.[101] I do not read the selected literary texts in a direct conversation with Soyinka. Yet I do show that contemporary Nigerian writers, inasmuch as they share some of Soyinka's concerns and reservations about religion, and specifically Christianity, continue to explore critically, creatively, and constructively its possible contributions to a humane society. *Decolonizing Christianities in Contemporary Nigerian Literature* invites other scholars to follow suit by offering alternative readings of the texts I have discussed, as well as readings of other texts by Nigerian writers that I did not include, and of literary texts from other parts of the African continent. May the conversation between literature and Christianity in Nigeria, and Africa, thrive, as a reflection of the vitality of its two subjects, and as a stimulus to critical and creative social and religious thought.

Chapter 1

FORGIVENESS

Christianity, Civil War Trauma, and Religious Memory

Nigeria's postcolonial history has been a violent one. The 1967–70 Nigerian Civil War, between the federal government and the newly founded and short-lived Republic of Biafra, is widely recognized as a particularly violent eruption, the shadows of which continue to shape the country's political, as well as literary, history. Centered around two of the most critical issues in postcolonial Nigeria—ethnicity and the distribution of resources—this war has led to the emergence of a subgenre in Nigerian literature narrating the memory and ongoing trauma of this conflict.[1] The Nigerian Civil War does not stand alone, as West Africa more generally has witnessed several civil wars in recent decades, in countries such as Liberia, Sierra Leone, and Ivory Coast. Some of these wars, including the Biafra War, have been widely associated with the deployment of child soldiers, which has subsequently generated another subgenre in West African literature: child soldier narratives. The two novels (or novellas, given their relatively short length) under discussion in this chapter, both written by writers of Nigerian descent and centering around child soldier protagonists, blend these two subgenres creatively. As the literary scholar Alexander Hartwiger has observed with reference to these novels, "The child soldier narrative as a form provides an ideal space to engage with transitional justice practices in the wake of the Nigerian Civil War because this genre moves the consideration of the pain and trauma of the war from the space of private memory into public consideration without assigning political responsibility."[2] As part of this quest for transitional justice, the novels articulate the burden of a past that continues to haunt their protagonists and from which they seek release. In doing so, they express a profound need for forgiveness and explore related ethical-theological questions, such as redemption and reconciliation, which in both texts is mediated by language and imagery of Christian faith.

Uzodinma Iweala's *Beasts of No Nation* was published in 2005, its title being derived from an album by the Nigerian music legend Fela Kuti.[3] The book offers a deliberately delocalized account characterized by "geographical indeterminacy," avoiding direct identifications with particular historical, social, or political settings.[4] As Iweala himself has recounted, he was trying to write about "something that perhaps was a little bit abstracted from the specifics of any particular country's politics." Although he admits to having taken his inspiration from the Nigerian Civil War, the memory of which is part of his family history—"You can't be Igbo from Nigeria and not hear stories about the civil war and how it affected families"—the book does not explicitly engage with this history.[5] Yet it is noteworthy that the protagonist, Agu, has an Igbo name; also, the "no nation" in the title can be seen as a reference to Biafra, which, after all, did not survive as an independent nation. Chris Abani's *Song for Night*, published in 2007, also avoids directly engaging with the tradition of "writing the Nigerian-Biafra war," yet it does include several narrative details that clearly locate the story in Nigeria and link it to the civil war.[6] This includes a reference by the protagonist, My Luck, to "three years of a senseless war" and the story about "pogroms against the Igbos" by Hausa people in the northern part of the country (*Song*, 9, 74).

Both authors have family histories connected to the civil war, which formed part of their motivation and inspiration for writing these gripping texts.[7] Their novels have been studied widely, both individually and alongside each other (as well as other texts, like Adichie's *Half of a Yellow Sun*, which also is about the civil war and includes a child soldier character).[8] Several readings have drawn attention to the spiritual dimension of these texts and how this relates to the quest for the healing of trauma, and for transitional justice, that the authors engage in. As the literary scholar Allison Mackey points out, "the apparition of various kinds of spirits, beasts, ghosts, and zombies draws attention to that which has been elided or repressed. These decidedly not-quite-human figures force the reader to think about what 'rehumanization' might mean in terms of the reintegration of child soldiers."[9] However, most critics seem to gloss over the Christian symbolism embedded in these narratives. By foregrounding this aspect, I read both texts in relation to broader questions concerning Christianity, memory, and postcolonial trauma in Nigerian and more generally African contexts. As the religious studies scholar Afe Adogame has argued, African religions, and specifically African Christianity, are a central but understudied part of the "narratives of articulation" through which the memory of traumatic events in postcolonial African societies is kept alive and given meaning.[10] Thus, in this chapter I adopt the lens of material theopoetics to explore the role of Christian symbols and imagery in *Beasts of No Nation* and *Song for Night*, reading these novels as texts of religious imagination in the context of conflict-induced Nigerian, and more broadly West African, postcolonial trauma.

By exploring the profound questions about the possibility, or impossibility, of forgiveness raised in both novels, I also read these texts as contributing to the discourse about the politics of forgiveness in contexts of postcolonial African trauma, specifically in the context of post–civil war Nigeria.[11] What emerges from my reading is a sense of forgiveness that is messy and incomplete, probably more so than any systematic Christian theological treatise would have it. This messiness is reflective of, and meaningful in, the complex historical, political, and moral-theological contexts in which the stories are set, thus demonstrating the distinct nature of religious imagination and meaning-making that literary texts can perform.

Haunted Landscapes of Trauma

Both *Beasts of No Nation* and *Song for Night* center around a male child soldier protagonist, of twelve and fifteen years old, respectively. *Beasts of No Nation* offers a narrative account of Agu's experiences in the rebel army that he was forced to join after his village had been raided. Narrated in a first-person present tense and in simple language that is somewhat reminiscent of the "rotten English" used in Ken Saro-Wiwa's child soldier novel *Sozaboy*, the novel is interspersed with flashbacks to Agu's childhood memories of growing up in a Christian family. In a way, Iweala's novel follows but simultaneously disrupts the pattern of a typical bildungsroman, with the story showing how the coming-of-age of its protagonist is stilted by the brutal experiences of violence, thus thematizing "distorted personal development as a result of war."[12] The narrative landscape of *Beasts of No Nation* is characterized, as the literary scholar Cecilia Addei has argued, by "the grotesque," including references to spirits and ghosts, through which the novel conveys its protagonist's gradual loss of humanity and the broader dehumanizing effects of war.¹³ For Agu, even the distinction between humans and spirits, and between life and death, is becoming blurred, such as when he comments: "What if they are not seeing us? What if we are dying and becoming spirit? What if they are spirit because they are all looking the same?" (*Beasts*, 126–27). Yet the novel's ending, with Agu escaping the rebel army and finding himself in a rehabilitation camp for child soldiers, suggests "the (uncertain) possibility" of his rehumanization and a return to the social world, honoring his quest for forgiveness.¹⁴

Song for Night engages similar themes of haunted landscapes and makes it even more prominent as a narrative frame. The novel sets up a narrative ambiguity concerning whether the first-person narrator is still alive, has died, or is in a liminal space between life and death. Early on, the text creates the suggestion that My Luck has survived the explosion of a land mine that killed one of his fellow soldiers and that the following story narrates his search for the other surviving members of his platoon, who left him behind assuming that he was dead. After all, the reader is told that My Luck "just regained consciousness" (but what state of consciousness?) after hearing the blast (*Song*, 11). However, as the story unfolds, it gradually emerges that My Luck is actually on a journey into the spirit world through which he rejoins the ancestors and, on the final page, is reunited with his deceased mother. According to Mackey, *Song for Night* can subsequently be seen not as a bildungsroman but as an "anti- or failed coming-of-age story," as the protagonist "is absolutely refused reentry into his social community and his backward-moving journey only ends when he is, instead, reunited with his mother in death."¹⁵ A more positive reading is given by Sam Durrant, who observes that while "there may be no hope for My Luck as a discrete human soul . . . there remains an infinite amount of hope for him as a transcorporeal, post-sovereign assemblage."¹⁶ Perhaps this ambiguity is typical of postcolonial African bildungsromans, which are often characterized by "inherent conflict."¹⁷

For much of the novel, My Luck finds himself in a liminal space, symbolically captured in the story about him being stranded on a sandbank in the river, a river that itself is a metaphor for life and death; he is kept on that sandbank "by some spirit's still unfulfilled wish" (*Song*, 57). This liminality is linked to the indigenous belief that the spirits of those who die suddenly are confused and need to be eased to the other side. My Luck's journey, from that perspective, is one of spiritual healing, through which ancestral ties are restored and through which he is "absorbed back into a larger political community."¹⁸ Yet the liminality of the space My Luck inhabits is also narrated in a way that somehow resembles the Catholic idea of purgatory, which is the process of purification through which the souls of those who have died are prepared to enter into heaven. One fascinating scene merges the figure of Saint Peter, who according to Catholic tradition holds the keys to heaven, with the figure of an indigenous religious priest who uses the smoke of smoldering herbs to help the souls of dead soldiers cross into the world of the ancestors. When My Luck is confused about the man's appearance, the latter mysteriously responds by saying, "The conflict is never in the truth, only in how we receive it" (*Song*, 90). This can be interpreted as a narrative suggestion that Christianity and indigenous spirituality are not mutually exclusive traditions of truth, and also that My Luck is on his way to a realm that blurs the Christian concept of heaven and the indigenous concept of the spirit world.

Christianity as Memory

As the above already indicates, both novels include references to Christian texts, beliefs, and symbols, which are naturally blended with references to indigenous mythology and worldviews. Although neither of these texts engage with Christianity in an explicitly denominational way, the Christian cultural and religious frame of reference is in *Beasts of No Nation* broadly Protestant and in *Song for Night* broadly Catholic.

In *Beasts of No Nation*, Christianity is mostly presented as a central part of the narrator's childhood memory, as Christian faith was an integral part of life in the family and village Agu grew up in, seemingly without much tension with the ongoing practice of traditional ceremonies. For instance, there is a flashback about the masquerade festival happening in the village as part of the annual initiation ceremony, with masked and costumed dancers performing traditional dances, such as the Dance of the Warrior and the Dance of the Goddess. Agu's devout Christian mother used to grumble about it every year, but nevertheless she would join the other women in the village cooking and singing the song of the river goddess, while Agu's father would calm her nerves by saying, "God is knowing that we are only worshipping him truly, but there are other spirits that we must also be saying hello to" (*Beasts*, 66). This scene illustrates how in Igboland and other parts of Nigeria and West Africa, masquerade practices are being preserved to this day, with Christians participating in them, despite missionaries having declared these practices to be "pagan fetishes."[19] In another flashback, Agu recounts how his mother used to read Bible stories to him every evening:

> She is coming to the bookshelf and pretending to search for just the right book. The shelf was having many books of different size and different colour—some red, some yellow, some blue, and some brown, but the one I am always wanting her to pick, the only one that I am wanting to hear is the one that is holding all of the other books up, the big white Bible. I was so small and the book so big that I am almost not even able to be carrying it. But I was enjoying how the cover is so soft, and how the letter saying HOLY BIBLE was made of gold. This was my favourite book because of how it is looking and because of all the story inside of it. . . . My mother is reading very very slowly because she is not schoolteacher like my father . . . but she was always saying, I am knowing enough to read the only book that is mattering. (*Beasts*, 31)

Although the novel is not explicitly set in an Igbo context, this passage can be read as an illustration of the point that "the Bible has an important role in the life of the Igbo family," with daily prayers, Bible readings, and religious discussions being a common feature of family life.[20] The Bible in question might well be the Igbo Union version, translated early in the twentieth century by the Anglican clergyman Archdeacon Thomas J. Dennis, known for its large size and heavy weight. According to the biblical scholar Anthony Nkwoka, this version cultivated a strong Bible-reading culture among Igbo Protestant Christians. The above passage also suggests that much of the family devotion depends on women, who—even when they are less educated and less well-read than their husbands—may take the task of reading the Bible to their children as their personal responsibility. Agu's love for the Bible was further stimulated at Sunday school, as captured in the following flashback:

> I am always going to Church every Sunday where I am first going to the Sunday school to be sitting outside under the shade of one big tree in the church compound with all of my mate [sic] . . . to be listening to the women reading us more story from The Bible . . . and telling us that we should watch out so that we are taking the hard road and not the easy road. And then we are saying prayer for forgiveness and the Our Father and also singing many song because God is liking music more than just talking. (*Beasts*, 36–37)

The reference to prayers for forgiveness in this passage is significant, as it is the first mention of this theme, which, as discussed later, is central to the novel's moral-theological quest. Likewise, the reference to the choice between the hard or the easy road alludes to a popular theme in evangelical Protestant literature, where discipleship—the life of a Christian as a follower of Jesus—is imagined as following a narrow, or hard, road characterized by Christian virtues, in contrast to the broad, or easy, road followed by nonbelievers who give in to sin and the temptations of the flesh. Derived from Jesus's teaching in the Sermon on the Mount, and popularized by English Puritan clergyman John Bunyan's classic *The Pilgrim's Progress* (which was disseminated in Nigeria from the early 1900s), the metaphor of life as a moral choice between two paths—of good and evil—is widespread in Protestant Christian cultures and is commonly used in evangelical children's and youth education.[21] In the above quote, it is significant that praying for forgiveness is linked to taking the hard road—forgiveness is not an easy forgetting of the wrongs one has done but instead involves an existential and spiritual sense of remorse.

Notably, the flashbacks of his mother's Bible reading and of the Sunday school lessons are woven into the story as part of a chapter that opens with a scene where Agu tries to convince himself that, despite the killing and raping he is involved in, he is not a "bad boy" because he is simply doing his job as a soldier, as if that makes him morally unaccountable and without need of forgiveness. Yet these attempts to salve his conscience constantly fail: "It is never working because I am always feeling like bad boy" (*Beasts*, 30). The reason for this failure, the novel suggests, is that his conscience has been shaped by the moral ideas from his Christian upbringing, which Agu has internalized. These ideas are the reference frame for Agu's religious-ethical reflection on his life as a child soldier, making the question of forgiveness so pertinent.

Critically, the novel also subtly alludes to the moral ambivalence of the Bible itself in relation to violence. For instance, in the flashback to his mother's Bible reading, Agu recounts: "She is reading to me about how Cain is killing his brother Abel, and how God is visiting Abraham, and about Jonah living in the fish. She was also reading about how God is making Job to suffer very much, but how he is rewarding him at the end, and how David is killing Goliath" (*Beasts*, 31–32). The intertextual reference to the story of Cain and Abel is particularly significant, because this is a biblical story of fratricide that in the Nigerian context is frequently invoked to thematize both interreligious tensions between Christians and Muslims and interethnic tensions between Igbo, Yoruba, Hausa, and Fulani communities. For instance, referring to the national trauma of the civil war, the theologian

Ikenna Okafor writes that Biafra, "like the story of Cain and Abel, is also a story of fratricide—a war that sadly pitted brother against brother—African brothers, who once lived peacefully."²² Ironically, in the biblical story, Cain's jealousy of Abel, which leads to the latter's murder, is informed by the fact that God appears to favor Abel, thus putting (the perception of) divinely sanctioned unequal treatment of people at the heart of the problem of violence. The story of David and Goliath also plays a dominant role in the memory of the civil war, with the Biafrans (Igbo people fighting for an independent state) identifying with David, the young and small but courageous shepherd-cum-warrior who believed that, with God on his side, he could take on the giant, Goliath.²³

Without directly invoking the ethnopolitical afterlives of these Bible stories in postcolonial Nigeria—after all, Iweala deliberately avoids writing *Beasts of No Nation* as a Biafra War story—the novel nevertheless subtly alludes to them, as if to highlight how biblical stories can become part of economies of war and be used to justify violence. One of the flashbacks in the novel tells us that the story of David and Goliath spoke to Agu's childhood imagination and instilled in him the wish to become a warrior, fighting a similar battle of good versus evil. However, when he finally becomes a soldier (not by choice but by circumstance and force), Agu increasingly realizes that the war he is involved in is a senseless one and that the violence he is part of is not justified but is violence for its own sake. That is why being a soldier is turning him into a "bad boy" committing serious wrongs: "To be a soldier is . . . to have people making you do thing that you are not wanting to do and not to be doing whatever you are wanting" (*Beasts*, 38). This also explains why, in another flashback, the memory of a prayer they used to pray at school every day—"Please God help me to use what I have learned for the good of all"—makes him feel sad: Agu is painfully aware that, instead of contributing to the common good, he is on a destructive path (*Beasts*, 132).

By narrating Agu's Christian childhood through flashbacks, *Beasts of No Nation* deploys Christianity, despite the ambiguity of some biblical stories, as a vital part of Agu's memory that shapes his moral framework and that, as discussed later, drives his consciousness of guilt and quest for forgiveness. *Song for Night*, too, includes flashbacks about the protagonist's religious upbringing, which, in this case, is of an interreligious nature. Both of My Luck's parents are Igbo from Christian families: His mother is a practicing Catholic, while his father converted to Islam as a teenager and became an imam in "the foreigner's ghetto" (Sabon Gari) in a city in the Hausa north of the country, thus making him a "hybrid." As the narrator explains: "It is a terrible thing in this divided nation, even in its infancy, for an Igbo man to be Muslim" (*Song*, 73).[24] As an Igbo mixed-faith family, they became natural targets during the outbursts of interethnic and interreligious violence (referred to as "pogroms" in the novel), with both of My Luck's parents being murdered and My Luck himself barely managing to escape. While growing up, My Luck never understood why his father converted and moved to the north, and he hated him for these decisions that made them outcasts in their own family and in the city where they lived. Certainly not identifying as Muslim himself, he also did not take to the Catholicism of his mother. Instead, he remained "undecided" and realizes: "Nothing I know of the world came from my Catholic mother or my Muslim father. All I know comes from the stories Grandfather told me" (*Song*, 88).

Indeed, memories of Igbo myths and folktales told by his grandfather are woven throughout the novel and serve as a frame of meaning through which My Luck tries to make some sense of the happenings in his life. Yet, on another level, Christianity, specifically Catholicism, plays a prominent role in the novel, much more than Islam. As discussed in the next section, Catholic symbols and imagery are part of the lifeworld that My Luck and his fellow soldiers inhabit, but they are also deployed as a meaning-making device by the author in this story of violence and trauma. This is perhaps not a surprise, given that Abani was once trained to become a Catholic priest.[25] In the novel, it appears as if some of the things that My Luck knows of the world do come from his Catholic mother, more than from his Muslim father, and that Catholicism serves as some form of moral compass, especially when the question of forgiveness comes up.

Material Religion and Theopoetics

A striking aspect of *Song for Night* and of *Beasts of No Nation* is the materiality of religion—that is, the narrative references to material religious objects and the role these objects perform in the texts. As part of their engagement with Christianity, both novels feature objects that, in the Christian world of the text, are held sacred. In doing so, they offer a literary representation of Nigerian Christianity as a lived religion with a rich material culture, but more than that, the texts also creatively draw on these sacred objects as meaning-making devices in situations of violence and brutality. In my reading, the references to material religion represent a literary form of "material theopoetics." I derive this term from the American pastoral theologian Michelle Walsh, according to whom "theopoetics in material form represent first-order expressions of our felt relationship to hope, grace, transcendent connection, transformation, and the divine. Such performative material creations cannot be dismissed or minimized as 'merely' material religion. In human hands made in the *Imago Dei*, matter becomes fiercely living and transformative as theopoetical testimony and witness to life after violent trauma."[26] Walsh is writing about her experience in pastoral ministry to people who have survived homicide and for whom material objects with religious meaning engendered resilience in the face of trauma and enabled living in a wounded world. Transferring this notion to the literary texts under discussion here, I explore in what follows, first, the narrative depiction of the use of Christian sacred objects for protective purposes in the context of violence and, second, the narrative deployment of sacred objects in the quest for divine redemption in the face of the brutality of war and subsequent human suffering.

A Material Poetics of Spiritual Protection

Both novels allude to the ways sacred objects, in a West African Christian context, are believed to be imbued with protective powers. Thus, in *Beasts of No Nation*, we read that one of the soldiers in Agu's platoon, nicknamed Preacher, carries a Bible with him: "Preacher is having Bible that he is using as pillow sometimes. That is why we are calling him Preacher. His Bible is so tattered that it is not even staying together by itself anymore and he is having to hold it together with piece of old shirt. He is keeping it in his pocket with his knife and his extra bullet" (*Beasts*, 98). Sleeping with the Bible as, or under, one's pillow is a practice that reflects a belief in evil spirits as being particularly active at night. Keeping the Bible alongside a knife and bullet illustrates its conception as a weapon in spiritual warfare. Thus, this passage illustrates what the Ghanaian theologian Mercy Amba Oduyoye has described as "using the Bible as a talisman," with the holy book itself, as an object, believed to represent God's protective presence and power that keeps away malevolent spirits and other sorts of evil. Somewhat to her surprise, Oduyoye found this to be a common practice among well-educated Christians in Ghana and Nigeria.[27] Where European missionaries had prohibited the use of traditional ritual and material measures of spiritual protection, converts to Christianity adopted symbols from their newfound faith to combat evil. As the Nigerian biblical scholar

David Adamo puts it with reference to worshippers in indigenous churches: "They approach the Bible and use it with the same method that the indigenous African people used to deal with the problem of enemies and seek protection against enemies. They used the entire Bible as potent words, charms, and medicine to combat evil forces and protect them against such forces of evil."[28]

Where the use of the Bible as an object of spiritual power is mostly found in Protestant circles, *Song for Night* demonstrates that in the Catholic world of this text other material objects are used for a similar purpose. We read about the soldiers of the platoon carrying "crucifixes, scapulars, and other religious paraphernalia to keep us safe" (*Song*, 10). These sacred objects are a key part of their equipment, alongside rifles and machetes, illustrating how spiritual and profane weapons are seen as complementary and essential. Later in the story, we read about a medallion of Saint Christopher that Agu had received from his fellow soldier and girlfriend, Ijeoma, just before she died: "She said it would protect me for sure now, especially as it had already claimed one victim" (*Song*, 39). Notably, Saint Christopher is traditionally associated with protection against danger and sudden death. In Catholic Christianity, the crucifix symbolizes the redemptive death of Jesus Christ on the cross; devotional scapulars are pieces of cloth usually bearing images of saints and worn over the shoulder, while medallions usually also have images of saints and are worn around the neck. These material religious objects are popular in Catholicism as a lived religion in Africa, where they are frequently invested with protective or healing powers and are carried as an amulet on the body.[29] Importantly, the use of these sacred Christian material objects for protective purposes reflects a continuity between Christianity and indigenous religions, where sacred objects such as charms and amulets represent "worlds of power" and have long been used for protection against witchcraft, spells, and evil spirits.[30] Although the specific objects may have changed, the underlying worldview of spiritual power affecting one's physical and personal well-being has remained intact. Thus, both novels provide a subtle but fascinating insight into the intersections between material religious cultures and cultures of violence in a West African context.[31]

A Material Poetics of Divine Presence

Both novels demonstrate an engagement with Christianity, material religion, and violence on another, deeper level—that is, as part of their quest for meaning-making in the face of the brutality of war, specifically the quest for divine redemption. This question is explicitly alluded to in *Song for Night*, which features a figure like Preacher in *Beasts of No Nation*, who is named Isaiah and described as "our prophet," because he often quotes from the Bible, in particular the book of Psalms. His favorite lines include phrases such as "I have longed for your salvation, O Lord" and "He will never forsake his children," reflecting a deeply rooted hope for, and trust in, God's redemption in the midst of war (*Song*, 106). However, how can such redemption be imagined in a profound and meaningful way, without reproducing Christian platitudes?

Discussing two examples, one from each novel, of material theopoetics, I will explore the theological significance of the invocation of sacred objects in *Song for Night* and *Beasts of No Nation*. As such, I read these novels as a response to the Cameroonian theologian David Ngong, who recently underlined the need for African theology to make the question of African suffering a central problem.[32] I suggest that the material theopoetics in both texts offers an alternative language to grasp the problem of human suffering in the context of the memory and trauma of war and violent conflict, and an alternative imagery to engage the question of divine presence in the midst of such suffering. Given that the suffering narrated in these texts is human induced, with the protagonists being directly involved in it and struggling with the subsequent unresolved guilt, the question of forgiveness inevitably emerges from these narrative accounts of African suffering, as will be discussed later.

One of the scenes in *Song for Night* that perhaps most evocatively captures the brutality and absurdity of war is where My Luck recollects an event that has been traumatizing him ever since. His platoon, making their way through the forest, stumbles upon a half-collapsed church with a few people rescuing statues from the rubble, intending to transport them to safety with a battered pickup truck: "In the shadow of the bombed-out church, two women were washing a statue of the Virgin with all the tenderness of a mother washing a child. A seven year-old girl played in the gravel by their feet. I stared at that sight unbelievingly. Of all the things they could have salvaged, I remember thinking. Just then, a man came around the corner carrying a statue of Jesus, cradled like a baby. I fought tears. There was something matter-of-fact about it all that was heartbreaking" (*Song*, 26). These sentences intimately narrate the way the people in this church tableau attend to the sacred statues of Jesus Christ and the Virgin Mary with great care and attention. If these statues symbolize the sacred in the midst of the profanity of war, and if they mediate divine presence in the midst of violent conflict, then rescuing these statues and bringing them to a place of safety can be seen as an act not only of lament but also of hope and faith: lament for the suffering of the victims of this violence, hope that one day this war will be over, and faith in God's abiding presence even in the current atrocities. Thus, these statues can be seen as performing a material theopoetics through which imagining, and thinking about, divine presence is rendered possible.

Yet, as the narrative continues, this possibility is brutally called into question. The intimate scene of tender care for sacred statues is followed by a horrific scene in which the young girl—unaware of any danger—runs toward the approaching soldiers and is lifted up by the major in charge of the platoon, named John Wayne, who turns toward his soldiers, saying, "This one is ripe. I will enjoy her" (*Song*, 26). Realizing that his superior has lost any sense of humanity, My Luck lifts his AK-47 to kill the major, but, tragically, the shot also kills the little girl he sought to protect. Capturing the absurdity of war, and the horror of sexual violence against children, this scene sharply contrasts with the tableau of the church people caring for the sacred statues—a contrast that evokes the question whether God is present at all. We learn that the name of the girl is Faith. Thus, literally, this scene narrates the tragic end of faith in the face of the brutality of war. As My Luck recollects his memory: "I was numb to John Wayne's death. Gladness would come later. For now, all I could think of was that the only real casualty was Faith" (*Song*, 27). One might well conclude that this scene conveys the point that hope and faith are lost—unless one attaches a theopoetical significance to the priest who jumps from the pickup truck to say a prayer over the dying girl, kissing her forehead, and making the sign of the cross, or to the man carrying the statue of Jesus who, when everyone scatters for cover at the moment of shooting, is said to be "still carrying Jesus" (*Song*, 27). What does it mean that this man, seemingly helplessly, is carrying Jesus at the moment Faith is accidentally killed? It is a reversal of the popular Christian belief that Jesus Christ, or God, will carry the faithful in times of need. In a theopoetical reading of this heartbreaking scene, its meaning might well be that divine presence in a brutal world is not of a miraculous nature, with God intervening in the mess of human affairs, but is cruciform, vulnerable, and fragile, with the divine sharing in human suffering to the fullest.

Later in the novel, My Luck again passes the place in the bush where he and other members of his platoon rested overnight, shortly after the church incident. His sense that the place looks familiar and that he might have been there before is confirmed when he finds the statues that were rescued from the church and had been hidden away here. The wooden statue of Jesus is missing one leg, as they had needed firewood that night. The originally white-painted concrete statue of Mary has turned green and is "mottled from the bullet holes we inflicted with target practice" (*Song*, 41). Manifesting their fragility, these sacred statues bear the scars of violence and war, as stigmata inscribed onto their divine bodies. If these statues symbolize the sacred and represent the divine in the midst of the profanity and brutality of war, *Song for Night* conveys a theopoetics of vulnerability, according to which "the vulnerability of humanity before the Lord is matched with the vulnerability of God."[33] Another literary example of this can be found in the short story "My Parents' Bedroom," by the Nigerian writer Uwem Akpan. Set in the context of the Rwandan genocide of 1994, the crucifix that is part of the family altar plays a central role in the story. In a critical scene, when the house of the child protagonist, Monique, is invaded by Hutu neighbors looking for her Tutsi mother, we read that "Christ's body breaks from the cross, crashing to the floor"; Monique is barely able to pick up the broken crucifix and run outside before the house is put on fire.[34] This story, like *Song for Night*, alludes to God sharing in the brokenness of this world.

A similar theopoetics is conveyed later in *Song for Night*, not in a material but in a ritual form, where My Luck has a vision—or a dream, or a memory?—in which he and his lover, Ijeoma, are on a battlefield when the church bells ring to call for the Angelus. The Angelus is a prayer central in Catholic devotional life, prayed by both religious and laity three times a day. In some parts of Nigeria, especially in Igboland, which has a strong Catholic presence, the Angelus is commonly prayed in public—for instance, at marketplaces—and is recited daily on public radio.[35] *Song for Night* captures this part of lived Catholicism in the context of war as follows:

> I am in the middle of a battlefield.
> The Angelus rings and I stop and lower my head. Before me, Ijeoma does the same. Behind us and all around but invisible in the shadows are the sounds of wings, a host of unseen. Ijeoma and I mouth the prayer together, lips folding greedily around words we can never utter: *The angel of the Lord appeared unto Mary . . . Hail Mary . . .* the words burn in us, like the love we still share. I finish and look up smiling. (*Song*, 119)

Deriving its name from the biblical story where the angel Gabriel appears to Mary to announce that she will be the mother of Jesus Christ, the Angelus prayer is a central part of Marian devotion that, in the words of the Nigerian theologian Agbonkhianmeghe Orobator, "has caught on like a bushfire in the harmattan across the Catholic landscape in Africa."[36] The prayer includes a petition for Mary's intercession: "Pray for us, O holy Mother of God." At its heart, the Angelus is concerned with commemorating the Incarnation—that is, the belief that God became human in the person of Jesus Christ. The prayer includes a quotation from the Gospel of John, "The Word was made flesh and dwelt among us," which captures the mystery of the Incarnation. Although these words are not cited directly in the novel, they immediately come to the minds of attentive readers familiar with the prayer. An intertextual reading of the prayer in the narrative context of the novella shows how the passage above alludes to the reassuring effect that praying the Angelus, asking for Mary's intercession, and commemorating the Incarnation of Christ can have: It makes My Luck smile, and it makes him and Ijeoma aware of the comforting presence of angels as invisible forces surrounding and protecting them.

Thus, *Song for Night* subtly explores the fundamental question of God's presence in the middle of war, using material and ritual poetics to suggest that the divine shares in the human tragedy of violent conflict and is equally affected by it; this divine presence in vulnerability does not solve the problem of evil or magically redeem humans from it, yet it can be a somehow reassuring, comforting, and hopeful presence nevertheless. The Ugandan theologian Emmanuel Katongole has pointed out that the idea of a vulnerable God is not popular in African theologies, as it goes against the widespread idea of God as a powerful being actively intervening in human affairs. Yet he argues—and *Song for Night* points in the same direction—that a belief in, and awareness of, God's vulnerability "opens up a huge arena of passionate, pastoral, and practical engagement," especially in situations of conflict and oppression, as it recognizes the experience of "the crucified ones in history."[37] The question remains, however, how this idea of a God suffering with the victims of war relates to the hope for God's salvation from war, expressed in *Song for Night* by Preacher's quoting from the book of Psalms. The sacred-but-scarred statues of Jesus and Mary that My Luck finds in the bush are perhaps also a reminder of this possibility of redemption—a reminder that, regardless of the scars caused by the violence of war, one may survive and be salvaged.

The same question of God's presence is also touched upon in *Beasts of No Nation*, but in a theologically more conventional way. We read that Agu, at that moment still staying with his family while the rebel fighters are approaching their village, asks his mother whether she is afraid, to which his mother responds: "Why should I be fearing Agu? . . . Aren't you remembering that the Lord is protecting everybody and making sure that nothing bad will ever be happening to us? Now go and get ready for bed okay. And don't be forgetting to pray. No matter what is happening remember that God is only remembering those who are praying" (*Beasts*, 82). This typical answer of a devout Christian mother reassuring her child is one of the last memories Agu has of her, because the next day the family is separated: The UN escorts his mother and sister from the village, while Agu and his father remain. Later, when Agu has been adopted into the rebel army, has killed and seen death, has raped and has been raped, he still remembers his mother's words but can no longer believe in them: "I am thinking that we should not even be asking God for anything because it is like He is forgetting us. I am trying to forget Him anyway even if my mother would not be happying with me. She is always saying to fear God and to always be going to church on Sunday, but now I am not even knowing what day is Sunday" (*Beasts*, 55). Even when he tries to pray, it feels like his words are going to the devil. Agu even starts wondering whether the demonic curses that some of his victims cast on him—"Devil bless you! Devil born you!"—might have come true: "I am thinking maybe Devil born me and that is why I am doing all of this" (*Beasts*, 59). When one woman, who together with her daughter has been caught and is about to be raped and then killed, is praying to God in despair, Agu can only laugh, "because God is forgetting everybody in this country" (*Beasts*, 60). Clearly, the narrative suggests that the words of Agu's mother about the Lord protecting everybody prove to be hollow and meaningless in the face of the dehumanizing brutality of war. Notably, the novel does not so much call into question the existence of God as an abstract concept as it thematizes the experienced absence of God as conveyed in the question whether "God is still alive *in this place*" (*Beasts*, 174–75; emphasis mine).

Yet a residue of faith in God remains present, not only in the form of Agu's memories of his mother's simple but strong faith but also in the character of Preacher, one of Agu's fellow soldiers, who in his sleep sings: "Thou art worthy. Thou art worthy oh Lord." This gospel song, made popular in Nigeria by artists such as Stella Nadis, is inspired by the biblical book of Revelation (4:11), where it is sung as part of a heavenly vision of eternal praise for God as creator.[38] This heavenly vision, and specifically the line in the lyrics that states, "And for Thy pleasure they [all things] are created," stands in sharp contrast with earthly reality, in which the world has turned into a battlefield and human lives are worthless. Agu recognizes this otherworldly dimension opened up by Preacher's singing, the repetition turning the song into a mantra: "It is sounding like it is coming from nowhere, from spirit" (*Beasts*, 98). The theopoetical significance of this gospel song in the broader context of the novel is in its allusion to another world possible—a world where humans live together, not as beasts or devils but in peace and harmony, for the pleasure of God.

The Im/Possibility of Forgiveness

As already alluded to above, both novels address the key moral-theological theme of forgiveness, demonstrating the existential nature of this question in the context of horrific war crimes. The quest for forgiveness is narratively associated with guilt and remorse for committed wrongs, especially in the context of a "senseless" war and violence for the sake of violence, which has dehumanized the protagonists.

Forgiveness, here, emerges primarily as a religious category—both protagonists raise the question of forgiveness from God—more than a social or interpersonal category—no effort is made to seek forgiveness from their victims. On one level, this is because, in the context of the stories, the victims did not survive, although clearly their spirits are haunting the protagonists. Yet, on another level, it also thematizes a point made by Katongole that, in the context of African civil wars, one of the effects has been the blurring of "the distinction between victim and perpetrators, since many of the fighters were the so-called child soldiers who were either abducted or forcefully recruited into the rebel forces."[39] *Beasts of No Nation* renders the victimhood of the child soldier explicitly visible in the story about Agu being subjected to repeated rape by the Commandant. Strika tries to comfort Agu by saying that "God will punish" the Commandant for this, yet, of course, the idea of a God who punishes moral wrongdoings instills a fear in them, too, because they themselves have also committed acts of sexual violence (*Beasts*, 106).

The theme of seeking forgiveness is most prominent in *Beasts of No Nation*. Earlier in this chapter, I mentioned Agu's recollection of Sunday school, as he remembers how they used to be told Bible stories, sing songs, and say prayers for forgiveness. Later in the novel we read how Agu, by then a child soldier who has committed many atrocities, is contemplating the end of the war and, being reminded of his Sunday school classes, realizes that he is in desperate need of forgiveness. Centering a material sacred object—a statue of Jesus—the following passage can be read theopoetically as capturing the existential moral and spiritual quest for divine mercy:

> Then I will go back to church. I will go back to church to ask God for forgiveness every day. And I will go back to church and sit on the bench under the fan that one day will just be falling and crushing me and I will not even be minding the splinter that is chooking into my leg because I will be paying attention to Jesus. I won't even be moving my eye from the statue of Jesus and instead I will just be sitting there watching him and watching him until one day he will be telling me that it is okay. (*Beasts*, 95)

The statue of Jesus here becomes the focal point of a poetics of repentance and forgiveness in which Agu wrestles with moral guilt. Crushed by the memories of committed atrocities, he projects his hope for a new, clean start onto this statue, waiting—perhaps against all odds—to receive absolution. Dreaming of becoming a doctor, he also hopes that by "helping people instead of killing them . . . maybe I will be forgiven for all my sin," thus reflecting the notion that doing good deeds is a penitential practice inherently part of the quest for divine forgiveness and reconciliation (*Beasts*, 94).

At this stage, the reader has already been given some insight into Agu's moral considerations, such as when he unsuccessfully tries to convince himself, after killing someone with a machete, that he is not "a bad boy" or born from the devil because he is a soldier, and killing is part of a soldier's profession (*Beasts*, 29, 59). He fails to convince himself because there are too many other voices in his head telling him otherwise. In the novel's final chapter, we find Agu in a rehabilitation camp as he has managed to escape the war. The priest there advises him to "turn to God . . . so he can be forgiving you," yet by then, the big words of confession, forgiveness, and resurrection are "not making any sense" to Agu (*Beasts*, 174). Having witnessed and having committed "too many terrible thing," Agu comes closest to experiencing a sense of forgiveness when he admits that he might be "some sort of beast or devil" while adding that "I am also having a mother once, and she is loving me" (*Beasts*, 176–77). In this touching closing sentence of the novel, the memory of his mother's unconditional love appears to supplant, but can also be seen as substituting for, the experience of God's forgiveness. After all, virtually everything that Agu knows about God is what he has learned from his devoutly Christian mother. Thus, in my reading, the novel's narrative suggestion is not so much that psychological and spiritual healing "might come outside the context of Western religious and moral frameworks" such as Christianity, as one critic puts it.[40] Instead, I suggest that Christianity is intricately and intimately part of the narrator's religious and moral framework, which he has internalized from his upbringing, and from within which he embarks on a journey of healing, of which the quest for forgiveness is a crucial part.

A brief reference to Igbo mythology is woven into the ending of the novel, when Agu tells about his dream that "one Iroko tree will be growing from my body, so wide that its trunk is separating night and day, and so tall that its top leaf is the moon until the man living there is smiling" (*Beasts*, 176). The iroko tree, which can live for hundreds of years and grow up to fifty meters tall, is central in West African, including Igbo, ecospirituality, where it is considered sacred, believed to be inhabited by spirits and gods, and linked to the ancestors and beliefs in reincarnation.[41] Capturing the moral-restorative significance of Agu's dream, the literary scholars Sam Durrant and Ryan Topper write: "Day and night, right and wrong, have become confused in and by Agu's experience. To dream of seeding an iroko tree is to dream of restoring such distinctions." Yet Agu dreams not only of seeding an iroko tree but of this tree reaching the sky and making "the man up there" smile. This can be read as an allusion to the hope for a divine smile that would affirm that God, like Agu's mother, has forgiven him and still loves him.

Song for Night also narrates in some detail how its protagonist wrestles with his sense of guilt. In one passage, we read how the road My Luck is walking on suddenly ends in a cliff, from the edge of which he stares into an "impenetrable darkness" (*Song*, 125). Interpreting this cliff metaphorically, he tells himself that "this is only the shape of my guilt: guilt for all the lives I've lost or taken, guilt for letting my platoon down, guilt for losing my mother, for leaving her to die for me while I hid in the ceiling like a little coward." Clearly, at this point he is tormented by remorse and asks himself how his sin can be "so luminous" (*Song*, 129). In an earlier scene, this guilt is suggested to be worked by Mami Wata, the water deity who is usually associated with wealth-related morality but who apparently can also deal with weightier moral issues such as rape and murder.[42] Encountering a woman on the riverbank, her appearance reminds My Luck of the first woman he raped, and in a state of confusion he wonders "if she is real or if she is a ghost, an apparition drawn by the river goddess mami-wata [sic] from my guilt; to punish me" (*Song*, 65). It suggests that one continues to be haunted by ghosts of the past as long as forgiveness is an unresolved business. In another scene, My Luck links his sense of remorse to the question of forgiveness from God: "I have killed many people during the last three years. Half of those were innocent, half of those were unarmed—and some of those killings have been a pleasure. But even with all this, even with the knowledge that there are some sins too big for even God to forgive, every night my sky is still full of stars; a wonderful song for night" (*Song*, 60). The knowledge that his sins might be too big to be forgiven clearly weighs heavily on him, yet the stars in the sky reassure Agu that forgiveness may still be possible: "Even if water won't wash me clean, hope might" (*Song*, 114).

Similarly to *Beasts of No Nation*, *Song for Night*, too, closes with a scene where the protagonist is welcomed and affirmed by his mother. Although the whole story is about My Luck attempting to find the fellow soldiers in his platoon by following the river, on the closing page, he finally crosses the river—seemingly a metaphor for life, implying that he is no longer alive—and drops his gun and machete because he decides that he "can't do this anymore." At that moment, as in a dream, he sees a woman whom he recognizes as his mother, and who welcomes him by saying, "My Luck, My Luck. You are home" (*Song*, 138). The prominent place of mothers in the endings of both novels is significant, and it illustrates the importance of motherhood in the narratives of traumatized child soldiers. As mentioned earlier, in *Beasts of No Nation*, Agu's memory of his mother's unconditional love can be seen as somehow symbolizing the experience of God's forgiveness. In *Song for Night*, one could read My Luck's vision of his mother in relation to the Virgin Mary. After all, only ten pages earlier we have read that his mother was deeply involved in Marian devotion herself, seeking the Virgin's mercy and pleading for her to intercede. Modeling Mary's example of sacred motherhood, My Luck's mother here becomes a symbol of divine mercy herself, welcoming her lost son back home, upon which his voice—literally cut out early in the war—returns. Such a reading goes against Mackey's earlier-quoted suggestion that My Luck is on a "backward-moving journey" because he is "refused reentry into his social community." After all, his mother, as the most important figure in his social community, rehabilitates and reintegrates him, honoring his quest for forgiveness and reconciliation. The story's ending thus suggests that My Luck is reunited with his ancestors, represented by his mother, and also that his soul has passed through purgatory and is accepted into heaven, which, spiritually speaking, is a new journey forward.

Raising the question of forgiveness in the context of postcolonial conflict and brutal violence, both novels draw on religious imagination to subtly allude to the possibility of forgiveness as key to the rehumanization and rehabilitation of child soldiers. Yet they do so without developing any systematic treatise on the moral and theological intricacies of the politics of forgiveness in Nigerian and other postcolonial African contexts. In doing so, they demonstrate the ability of literary texts to do justice to the complexities of forgiveness—it remains fragmentary and does not erase a broken past—precisely by avoiding conclusive answers. As the American theologian Matthew Ichihashi Potts has argued in his recent book about forgiveness in literary texts: "Literary fiction doesn't expect to speak conclusively of forgiveness, it only wishes to speak at all. It looks for—but does not ever conclusively find—meaning in its fraught scenes of forgiveness, and in so doing it in fact mimes the meaningful movements of forgiveness itself, which is also provisional and fragile, a habit of continued survival rather than a conclusive feat of sanguine understanding or triumphant resolution."[43]

Conclusion

The genres of both civil war literature and child soldier literature raise complex sociopolitical and moral-theological questions, such as those regarding reconciliation and restorative and transitional justice. The novels under discussion specifically focus on the aftermath of the Nigerian Civil War, the memory of which is "still wrapped in a formal silence," as Chimamanda Ngozi Adichie has put it.[44] Hartwiger has observed that both novels have indeterminate endings, which enables the authors "to provide a space for posing specific questions about the type of conversation still needed" in post–civil war Nigeria.[45] As several critics have argued, *Beasts of No Nation* and *Song for Night* are not so much concerned with the historical, political, and legal debates about the civil war and its aftermath—both texts deliberately avoid engaging such debates. Instead, through intimate first-person narratives, they bring the war and its trauma back to a human and communal level, and they foreground the spiritual and psychological healing that is needed. Importantly, and generally overlooked in discussions of these texts, this quest for healing is imagined to a significant extent by drawing on Christian symbols and imagery and by engaging a moral-theological conversation about the complex questions of divine redemption and forgiveness.

As for salvation during and from the suffering of war, the novels capture three possible interpretations. One is represented by Agu's mother, and it is perhaps most typical of many Nigerian and other African Christians: the simple faith that "the Lord is protecting everybody" and that therefore "nothing bad will ever be happening to us." This belief is expressed in a material form through the use of sacred objects, such as Bibles, crucifixes, and medallions of saints, which symbolize and effectuate this divine protection. Second is the possible loss of faith in divine salvation in the face of the brutality of war, as expressed by Agu's realization that God is, in fact, "forgetting everybody." This loss is narrated as a possibility or threat but not as a fait accompli; after all, we are told at the end of the novel that Agu likes hearing the priest's message that "God is still alive in this place," even though he remains unsure whether to believe it. Third is the quest to find and experience God's presence in the rubble caused by the war and to cling to the hope for survival and redemption. Just as the statues of Jesus and Mary are scarred but remain sacred, so child soldiers and others affected and traumatized by conflict, violence, and war in West Africa will, ultimately, not get lost and will not be dehumanized. The answer to the question of salvation, asked by Preacher's quoting of the Psalm, then perhaps lies in the endings of both novels, which underscore unfailing motherly love. Regardless of whether the mother figures are seen as symbolizing God, as I suggested above, or alternatively as symbolizing "mother Africa," the crucial point is that they reject the dehumanization and social death of their wounded children.

The provisional and fragile nature of forgiveness is narratively conveyed as both texts raise the question of the possibility of divine forgiveness and reference feelings of guilt and remorse but do not point in the direction of interpersonal forgiveness. As the Nigerian writer Wole Soyinka has noted, "Most African traditional societies have established modalities that guarantee the restoration of harmony after serious infractions."[46] Yet in the narrative contexts of the texts under discussion, these modalities are not engaged, as they appear to be replaced by an abstract Christian discourse about divine forgiveness for the sin of brutal war crimes. Both novels leave untouched how divine forgiveness relates to interpersonal forgiveness and how guilt, repentance, confession, and reconciliation are interconnected. Rather than a well-developed political theology of forgiveness, they offer a tentative exploration of the complexity of forgiveness in contexts of postcolonial conflict and trauma. In doing so, Abani and Iweala appear to suggest that when the distinction between offenders and victims is porous, the moral work of forgiveness is "not impossible but routinely unfinished."[47] By narrating the quest for forgiveness from the perspective of their offender-victim protagonists, these authors also indirectly pose a question to the societies affected by the atrocities of war crimes about their preparedness to forgive child soldiers and to rehabilitate them and restore their place in the community. What difference does Christianity, with its impetus for forgiveness of those who have sinned against us and its commemoration of God's gift of forgiveness in Jesus Christ, make in the context of post–civil war Nigeria?[48] Although Nigeria, and specifically Igboland, did witness a Christian revival during and following the civil war, mostly of a Pentecostal-Charismatic nature, this did not necessarily create an environment in which the complex spiritual, moral, and theological questions related to war could be processed.[49] Thus, with their novels, Abani and Iweala firmly put these questions on the Nigerian Christian agenda and invite pastoral and theological reflection about living with the memory and trauma of the conflict in post–civil war Nigeria.

Chapter 2

DELIVERANCE

Christianity, Sexuality, and Queer Embodiment

One of the main trends in twenty-first-century Nigerian literature is the emergence of queer writing, which has resulted in a recent "polyphony" of queer-themed poetry, stories, novels, and autobiographies.[1] Through these texts, the hitherto marginalized and largely invisible voices and experiences of Nigerian LGBTQ+ communities are written into existence and claim a space in the country's cultural canon and in society while responding to the heteronormative, if not explicitly homophobic, social, religious, and political culture of Nigeria. It is not a coincidence that this trend has cropped up at the same time that Nigerian society over the past two decades has witnessed an increasing public contestation over LGBTQ+ rights and related issues of sexual and gender diversity, as reflected in the passing of the Same-Sex Marriage (Prohibition) Act, which has since 2014 reinforced the already existing legal prohibition of same-sex practices and criminalized the public manifestation of, and advocacy for, LGBTQ+ related causes.[2] Clearly, in Nigeria, like elsewhere in Africa, the increasing public visibility of LGBTQ+ communities and the increasing sociopolitical contestations over LGBTQ+ rights are two sides of the same coin, of the politicization of homosexuality and queer identities in postcolonial African societies.[3] As far as African anti-queer social, political, and legal mobilizations are concerned, religion is often seen as a key driving factor.[4] In contemporary Nigeria specifically, both Christianity and Islam, but also indigenous religions, are found to be deeply invested in a politics that seeks to moralize and discipline sexuality in a heteronormative framework and that marginalizes LGBTQ+ people and de facto excludes them from the body of the nation.[5] However, religion appears to be a double-edged sword, as it is deployed not only by conservative clergy, politicians, and other opinion leaders to speak out against what they see as the moral vice of queer sexuality but also by activists, members, and allies of LGBTQ+ communities who engage with religious beliefs critically and creatively as a "terrain rich for re-negotiation" to affirm their sexual and gender identities and in support of their cause.[6]

In this chapter, I explore how queer Nigerian literature engages religion, specifically Christianity, as a site of contestation and renegotiation regarding queer sexualities. I begin with a section that reviews a range of recent texts for their engagement with Christianity, specifically examining how the theme of deliverance of the queer body is a common trope in many queer Nigerian writings.[7] I will demonstrate how these texts represent deliverance as a violent and traumatizing religious ritual imposed on queer bodies, and I will analyze the insights this offers into the understanding of sexuality and embodiment in the largely Pentecostalized Christian culture of Nigeria. The following sections will focus on one major text, Chinelo Okparanta's novel *Under the Udala Trees*, which offers a particularly rich example of the renegotiation of Christianity in a quest to affirm same-sex sexuality.

Christianity in Queer Nigerian Literature

In 2020, the Nigerian poet Romeo Oriogun published his first poetry collection, which, as stated on the back cover, "fearlessly interrogates how a queer man in Nigeria can heal in a society where everything is designed to prevent such restoration." Two years later, Oriogun was awarded the Nigeria Prize for Literature—a public recognition that itself complicates any monolithic narrative of "Nigerian homophobia."[8] As already indicated by the title of this collection, *Sacrament of Bodies*, several of the poems draw on religious imagery, and collectively they make a case for the sacred nature of queer embodiment. The queer body, and indeed queer sex, for Oriogun is sacramental, meaning that it has spiritual significance and may even mediate an experience of divine presence. "Give the body what it deserves / this is what it means to know God," Oriogun writes in the volume's title poem, which explicitly captures sexual desires and experiences.[9] Blurring the boundary between the erotic and the spiritual, these lines suggest that bodily and sexual pleasure are a means of knowing and experiencing God. In the same poem, the quest for survival of queer people in a society that wants them dead is described with the word "resurrection," which, in a Christian context, immediately evokes the mystery of Jesus Christ being raised from the dead thanks to divine intervention. The queer spirituality reflected here is clearly born out of an experience of existential and embodied struggle— struggle with internalized societal stigma and with imposed sociocultural and religious norms. This is perhaps reflected most explicitly in the prose poem "What We Do Not Want," in which Oriogun intimately captures and responds to these traumatizing experiences of struggle. It includes a passage that speaks directly to queerphobia in a Christian context of church and family: "We do not want the tears, no mother dragging us to church, no altar filled with the smell of burning incense, no prophet clad in a white gown, no Bible raised high like a sword, no whip coming down hard on bare backs, no boy holding his lover's name in a song of pain, no words of deliverance hanging over beautiful heads."[10]

The experiences alluded to here—of Christian parents dragging their gay children to church, and of priests, pastors, or prophets using the Bible as a weapon, performing deliverance, and even whipping these children into heteronormativity—are narratively captured in many other queer Nigerian writings, both fictional and autobiographical.[11] For instance, the novel *Walking with Shadows*, by Jude Dibia—published in 2005 and hailed as the first gay Nigerian novel in English—narrates how the gay adult protagonist, Adrian, is taken to a Pentecostal pastor by his brother. A dramatic scene describes how the pastor in question not only prays and speaks in tongues over Adrian but also whips the latter's naked upper body till Adrian loses consciousness, while the pastor screams that his victim should "banish the devil" from his heart.[12] Uzodinma Iweala's novel *Speak No Evil* tells of a father who takes his gay teenage son, Niru, from the United States, where the family lives, back to Nigeria, in order to have his son purified from his "abomination" through some "serious spiritual counseling and deliverance" by a Pentecostal pastor. The latter subjects Niru to intense prayers, asking God in a shouting voice to bind and cast out "the spirit of homosexuality and perversity" that is threatening to harm the boy's life.[13] In the graphic novel *On Ajayi Crowther Street*, by Elnathan John and Àlàbá Ònájìn, the figures of the father and the pastor merge: Reverend Akpoborie, pastor of a Pentecostal church in Lagos, subjects his own son, Godstime, and his boyfriend, Onyeka, to a deliverance ritual. While sprinkling the two teenage boys with "anointing oil," the pastor calls upon "the mighty name of

Jesus" to "command every demon of Sodom to get out of these children."[14] The experience is so traumatizing that Onyeka commits suicide soon after, leaving Godstime in a severe depression. The mental distress caused by deliverance rituals is also narrated by Akwaeke Emezi in their novel *The Death of Vivek Oji*, which centers around a gender-nonconforming young gay man whose aunt takes him to her pastor to be freed from "the demon inside him."[15] Likewise, in the novel *An Ordinary Wonder*, by Buki Papillon, a mother takes her intersex child, Oto, to the prophet of an Aladura (indigenous Pentecostal) church, called Seraphic Temple of Holy Fire. This prophet, Woli Omolaja, makes her believe that Oto's condition is caused by a demon that needs to be exorcised. He subjects Oto to two subsequent deliverance rituals, the second one being even more violent (including whipping and drowning) and traumatizing than the first, while calling upon angels "to sever this child from the bonds of evil."[16] In Chukwuebuka Ibeh's novel *Blessings*, the gay protagonist, Obiefuna, internalizes the belief that his sexuality is an evil vice he needs to be delivered from, and he subsequently joins a Christian prayer group—the Prayer Warriors—at his boarding school, "dutifully attending every session on Friday nights, staying long after everyone else had gone, kneeling before the altar."[17]

These literary accounts have in common that they all narrate a religious culture in which queer sexuality is seen not just as immoral and sinful, as traditional Christian teaching would have it, but as demonic—that is, caused by evil spirits and demons: the "demon of Sodom" or the "demon of homosexuality."[18] Partly, this reflects an indigenous worldview in which spirits, such as the water deity Mami Wata, are frequently sexualized and in which sex and sexuality are subsequently also spiritualized. Indeed, several of the aforementioned novels subtly allude to such interpretative frames, such as Papillon's *An Ordinary Wonder*, where the *babalawo* (diviner) explains Oto's intersex condition with reference to indigenous Yoruba cosmology and where Oto's gender identity is affirmed through visions of a female mermaid-type spirit, Yeyemi. However, in contemporary Nigeria this understanding is often reframed in the dualist worldview of Pentecostal Christianity, meaning that the indigenous spirits associated with gender ambiguity and sexual transgression are directly associated with the devil. As a result, this religious culture deals with queer sexuality primarily in a discursive register not of sin, repentance, and forgiveness but of deliverance. After all, queer sexuality is seen "as caused by, and/or as the cause of, demonic spirit possession," and such possession can only be broken, it is believed, "through deliverance rituals that invoke the power of

God."[19] Thus, these novels also share a common narrative emphasis on the practice of deliverance, as in each text the queer protagonist is subjected to deliverance rituals through which the perceived evil spirits are supposedly cast out of the queer body. These narratives are written empathetically, clearly conveying the physical, emotional, and spiritual violence associated with deliverance practices, as well as the long-term trauma resulting from it.

Where Oriogun in his poem writes that queer people do not want "words of deliverance hanging over beautiful heads," the fictional narratives provide insight into the lived realities of many Nigerian queer persons whose heads and bodies are nevertheless subjected to deliverance practices. The speaking of such words, in the context of Nigerian Pentecostalized Christianity (which is not restricted to Pentecostal-Charismatic churches, as Pentecostalism has influenced the religious culture of other denominations), is a form of "performing power," specifically spiritual power.[20] Supposedly "anointed" men and women of God—be they called pastors, prophets, bishops, or apostles—summon the power of God, Jesus Christ, or the Holy Spirit through intense prayer in an attempt to subjugate and exorcise demonic spirits. Thus, the ritual performance of deliverance is a spectacle that often turns out to be aggressive, forceful, and violent. As the religion scholar Nimi Wariboko observes: "In some Pentecostal circles in Nigeria, deliverance involves ministers (exorcists) flagellating the bodies of those supposedly possessed by evil spirits. The punishment of the physical body is believed to drive out the nonphysical spirit lodged inside the person. The punishment of the visible cleanses the invisible, settles the debts (sins) that gave Satan permission to enter into the body."[21] Thus, fictional accounts such as *Walking with Shadows* and *An Ordinary Wonder* do not exaggerate when they include references to physical whipping in the narratives about their queer protagonists being subjected to deliverance rituals. Beyond the physical effects, queer Nigerian literary texts also explore the emotional and spiritual impact of deliverance practices, problematizing how the discourse of deliverance centers around, and reproduces, the notion that queer bodies, desires, intimacies, and identities are, fundamentally, demonic—that is, in this religious culture queerness is seen as intrinsically evil, with queer people believed to be in the realm and under the influence of the devil rather than of God. The subsequent stigma around queerness is often internalized, causing trauma and leading to depression, self-harm, and suicide, as can be seen in the characters of Godstime and Onyeka in *On Ajayi Crowther Street* or in *An Ordinary Wonder*'s Oto, who, when looking into the eyes of the prophet forcefully delivering him, realizes that he "wasn't meant to survive this. Not intact."[22]

As much as these literary texts offer narrative insight into the impact of deliverance practices on queer bodies, they also respond to deliverance culture and its demonization of queerness, and they explore alternative possibilities within Christianity. In some cases, this is clearly reflected in the titles of these texts, such as in Azuah's *Blessed Body* or Ibeh's *Blessings*, which both make the critical claim that the queer body can be seen as manifesting divine blessing, rather than demonic possession. In other cases, the literary accounts themselves include various sorts of religious reasoning. In *On Ajayi Crowther Street*, this happens in passing when the homophobic pastor Reverend Akpoborie is contrasted, by his gay son, Godstime, with the character of Jesus, who "didn't drive people away!"[23] This single sentence invokes a model of religious ministry that does not exclude or discriminate against queer people but instead accepts and affirms them the way they are. The name Godstime itself can also be seen as suggesting that the current push for the recognition of LGBTQ+ identities and rights is a God-given moment for humankind to accept all human persons, regardless of their sexuality, as created in the image of God. Ani Kayode Somtochukwu's coming-of-age novel *And Then He Sang a Lullaby* includes a passage where the gay protagonist, August, comes out to his sister, Uzoamaka. Reminding her brother that he is the only son and that this comes with certain responsibilities, Uzoamaka says: "August, please. This thing, we can do something about it. I've heard of miracles. There's nothing God cannot do." The novel here invokes a discourse of miracle, instead of deliverance, but both operate in a similar register of divine intervention, with an underlying assumption that homosexuality is something to be healed or freed from rather than to accept and embrace as part of one's embodied existence. Following Uzoamaka's suggestion, the narrator writes: "But August did no longer want God's redemption. He felt redeemed, and sure in his newfound redemption." This sentence and the broader narrative of the novel suggest that August could reach self-acceptance by refusing any interference by the homophobic God whom his sister believed in and who had been preached by a pastor at school. Indeed, the last mention of God in this novel is that August was "angry at God."[24] Nevertheless, the language of redemption invoked in this narrative is significant for its explicitly religious undertones: Accepting one's sexuality and coming out as gay is a redemptive experience and, for August, is more redemptive than any miracle or deliverance could have been.

Refusing deliverance may enable queer redemption, yet in the case of Somtochukwu's novel, it leaves the gay protagonist angry with God, as he does not find a way to renegotiate and reconcile his faith with his sexuality. In contrast, Akwaeke Emezi's short story "Who Is Like God" features a young queer protagonist who, as the title signals, boldly claims to be "like God."[25] Kachi grows up with a fervently religious mother who one day, when she finds her son using makeup, immediately concludes that "some demon of homosexuality is making you wear eye liner" and prays to "release him in Jesus' name." Mama's fury is fueled by Kachi's counterquestion, "Why is it always some kind of devil or demon with you, ehn? Why can't it be something else? Like maybe God is speaking to me, for instance." For Mama, the suggestion that her gender-nonconforming son might reflect the image of God is blasphemous. Yet for Kachi it is a deeply affirming experience to stand in front of a mirror and "see Him in my face." Believing that God lives in him, he even wonders whether God might be feeling the pain that he is feeling—the physical pain of Mama's beating, but also the emotional pain of her rejection and the hurtful demonization of his queer body. Thus, this fictional story explores the fundamental notion of the queer body as a creation of God, reflecting God's image and manifesting God's presence. Kachi's queer body refuses deliverance because it understands itself as divine and sacred.

The above review demonstrates that queer Nigerian literature initiates a rich and insightful discourse about queerness and Christianity in Nigeria. Literary texts narrate and problematize the contested status of same-sex-desiring and gender-nonconforming bodies and identities in Nigerian Christian cultures, and they are specifically concerned with the widespread demonization of queerness and the subsequent tendency to subject queer bodies to violent deliverance practices. The novel *An Ordinary Wonder* suggests that Christianity is irredeemably queerphobic and that the spiritual affirmation of queerness is better served by drawing on the resources of indigenous religious traditions. However, several other texts begin to explore the beliefs and symbols available in Christian traditions to affirm queer embodiment. The most notable example of the latter quest is the novel *Under the Udala Trees*, to which I will now turn. Like many of the aforementioned texts, this novel features a deliverance scene where the queer protagonist is subjected to a deliverance ritual by her deeply religious mother. Paraphrasing literary scholar Ato Quayson's notion of "reading for the social"—meaning that literary texts do not simply represent but "calibrate" social reality and are driven by a quest for "social enlightenment"—I propose a method of "reading for deliverance."²⁶ This allows me to explore how this novel not only is *about* deliverance but can also be read *for* deliverance, in the sense not of a Pentecostal exorcism but of what could be called "religious enlightenment." Such a reading reveals how *Under the Udala Trees* engenders an alternative to Pentecostal deliverance, as it narrates the queer body of the protagonist, Ijeoma, into a liberating space of spiritual freedom and as it reimagines Christianity as a queer-affirming faith. Deliverance, after all, is not inherently bound to the threat of the demonic but is a term that "invokes freedom, capacity, renewal, and possibility."²⁷

Reading *Under the Udala Trees*

Under the Udala Trees, published in 2015, is the first novel by Nigerian-born writer Okparanta. Like the stories "America" and "Grace," in Okparanta's earlier collection *Happiness, Like Water*, the novel explores the theme of female same-sex sexuality. As such, it has been recognized for its transgressive narrative representation of sexuality and gender, as well as its queer contribution to African literary feminism.²⁸ In an author's note, Okparanta explicitly acknowledges that by writing this novel she sought to intervene in the contemporary Nigerian politics of sexuality and to respond to the Same-Sex Marriage (Prohibition) Bill that President Goodluck Jonathan signed into law in January 2014. She does so by writing a story of same-sex love unfolding in two parts: first, between a teenage Ijeoma and her friend Amina and, second, between Ijeoma as a young adult and her friend Ndidi. As an explicitly political intervention, *Under the Udala Trees* exemplifies how the literary writer as a social thinker can also become a social activist and advocate.²⁹

The historic setting of the novel is significant: The story begins during, and unfolds in the aftermath of, the Nigerian Civil War, also known as the Biafra War (1967–70). This war erupted after the eastern part of the country, mainly populated by the Igbo people, declared secession, following years of rising ethnic tensions and violence in postindependence Nigeria. As mentioned in the introduction, decades after the war ended, "writing Biafra" continues to be a prominent trend in Nigerian cultural and literary production, to which Okparanta gives her own original twist.³⁰ The war is prominent in the opening chapters of the novel and triggers the dramatic events that unfold in the life of Ijeoma, the Igbo girl at the center of the novel: Ijeoma's father tragically dies during a bomber plane raid; her mother,

Adaora, falls into despair and depression and leaves Ijeoma at the home of family friends, a retired grammar school teacher and his wife; Ijeoma stays there for one and a half years, working as a house girl till the war is over; during that time she meets and falls in love with Amina; when the teacher finds out, he reports it to Ijeoma's mother, who comes to fetch her daughter and begins the project of "curing" her. Several years later, Ijeoma is pressured into marrying her childhood friend Chibundu, which means a break with her female lover at that time, Ndidi. Her marriage results in the birth of a daughter but does not bring any happiness. At the end of the novel, a depressed Ijeoma decides to leave her husband in Port Harcourt and return to her mother, and Ndidi, in Aba. The epilogue, dated January 2014 (the month in which the antigay bill mentioned earlier became law), mentions how Ijeoma and Ndidi "have now shared decades together" and feel "every bit a couple" (320).

For Okparanta, using Biafra as the historical background was a way of bringing her own family history into the novel, as her own grandfather died during the war.[31] However, on a deeper level it also allows her to convey the point that the current struggle about same-sex relationships is of a similar significance to that of the civil war, another watershed moment in Nigerian postcolonial history: "Sometimes when we think about sexuality we think, 'Oh, it's just sexuality,' but for some people, that's a big war going on within them. I think that's all the novel is doing—it's telling a story of a character who has to survive two different kinds of war."[32] By juxtaposing these two battles, Okparanta makes a narrative connection between ethnicity and sexuality, suggesting that both categories can be equally divisive and the cause of conflict, violence, and human rights offenses. Notably, Ijeoma's first love, Amina, is a Hausa Muslim girl, and their relationship blossoms in the final year of the war, as a narrative expression of hope that the ethnic tensions between the Igbo and Hausa that culminated in the civil war can be overcome. For Ijeoma's mother, the romantic relationship between them is despicable: "That girl is Hausa. Even if she were to be a boy, don't you see that Igbo and Hausa would mean the mingling of seeds? Don't you see? It would be against God's statutes" (76). Ironically, Adaora cites the Bible (Leviticus 19) to make the point that both a relationship between two girls and between an Igbo and a Hausa person (and probably also between a Christian and a Muslim) is abominable. Adaora's persistent invocation of the Bible, as well as her practice of fervent prayer, which she developed after the death of her husband, can be seen against the historic background of the Civil War Revival, which occurred among the Igbo during and in the aftermath of the Biafra War, with the growing popularity of new charismatic Christian movements.[33]

Although the politics of writing same-sex and interethnic love has been a central theme in scholarly discussions of *Under the Udala Trees*, less in-depth attention has been paid to the way Okparanta engages the religious dimension of Nigerian same-sex debates.[34] In contemporary Nigeria, these debates are heavily influenced by discourses from the two major religions, Christianity and Islam. Both traditions, which play a prominent role in the Nigerian public sphere, are largely mobilized to advocate against the recognition of same-sex relationships and the rights of sexual minorities, and many of their leaders actively supported the Same-Sex Marriage (Prohibition) Bill.[35] Okparanta, who was raised as a Jehovah's Witness herself, explicitly engages these dynamics, specifically in relation to Christianity, by creating a space in the novel for questioning conservative Christian arguments against same-sex relationships, developing alternative interpretations of the Bible, and probing innovative understandings of God.[36] As she commented in an interview: "Christianity has historically been the greatest platform on which homosexuality has been condemned. I thought it might be nice to write a novel that meets the naysayers on their own platform."[37] Thus, the novel illustrates how the writer as a social thinker can also become a religious thinker and how such religious thought is crucial to the writer's quest for social advocacy.

Importantly, Okparanta not only presents a narrative critique of the way Nigerian Christianity is a constituting factor of the current antigay climate in the country but also explores the possibility of alternative imaginings of Christian faith in relation to sexuality. The epigraph of the book—a quotation from the New Testament (Hebrews 11:1)—is telling in this regard: "Faith is the assured expectation of things hoped for, the evident demonstration of realities, though not beheld."[38] If *Under the Udala Trees* is relatively "optimistic about the possibility of change" in relation to queer issues in Nigeria,[39] the basis for that optimism might be the connection between faith and hope captured here.

The following sections explore the representation of Christianity and sexuality in *Under the Udala Trees*, addressing three subthemes: the church, prayer, and the Bible. I specifically focus on the latter theme, examining the novel's decolonial queer interpretation of the Bible. In doing so, I read the novel through the lens of the work of Musa W. Dube, a postcolonial feminist biblical scholar from Botswana. Although the context of Botswana is different from that of Nigeria, my point is to demonstrate that Okparanta, like Dube, engages in a critical and liberative reading of the Bible to effect change in the politics of gender and sexuality in contemporary African contexts. In doing so, they both contribute to a progressive reimagination of Christianity in African contexts. Although some critics may link Okparanta's progressive Christian thought to the fact that she grew up (from the age of ten) in the United States and may have therefore been exposed to religious discourses and theological thought uncommon in Nigeria, this chapter demonstrates that there are progressive traditions within Nigerian and African Christianities that Okparanta shares affinity with and contributes to.[40]

Imagining the Church as a Safe Haven

The church that Ijeoma and her parents attended, in the town of Ojoto where they lived, is called Holy Sabbath Church of God. Despite what the name suggests, it is not a Sabbath-observing church worshipping on Saturdays.[41] Sabbatarianism was a trend among independent churches that emerged in Igboland and elsewhere in Nigeria from the early twentieth century.[42] However, in the novel Ijeoma explicitly states that "we went [to church] every Sunday" (11). Regardless, the narrative description of "the fervent worship" at this church resembles the broader characteristics of what the historian Ogbu Kalu describes as the "early charismatic movements" that formed the first wave of Pentecostalism in Nigeria: centered on the Bible, with a strong emphasis on preaching, intense prayer, and embodied worship.[43]

During the period that Ijeoma stays at the grammar school teacher's house, she attends church only sporadically. Yet after returning to her mother in Aba, she starts going to church again, realizing how much she had missed it. No details are given about the church that Ijeoma attends with her mother and where she and Chibundu have their wedding; the use of the title "Father" for the pastor/priest in charge suggests that it might be an Anglican or Catholic church, rather than Pentecostal-Charismatic (81).[44] This suggestion is reinforced by the short prayer, "Lord, have mercy," that Ijeoma continuously whispers in the church she attends in Port Harcourt, after her marriage, as this prayer is a standard phrase in Anglican and Catholic liturgy (228). Later in the novel, however, Ijeoma explicitly states she is not Catholic, which leaves open Anglicanism, or another denomination in the broad spectrum of Protestantism. The sparsity of details that the novel gives about denominational specifics might well be deliberate, implying that the Christian setting of the novel is not restricted to a particular denomination but represents Nigerian Christianity more generally.

Notably, the novel does not depict the church as a place where homophobia is actively preached and promoted. The biblically inspired messages against homosexuality come from Ijeoma's mother, rather than from pastors and priests. This is not necessarily a way of absolving the church from its involvement in perpetuating anti-queer rhetoric. Rather, it conveys how this rhetoric has been embraced and internalized by Christians on a grassroots level. Yet the novel possibly also suggests implicitly that the church is not necessarily an anti-queer space. Pushing this further, my interpretation diverges from that of Vincent Ogoti, according to whom the novel "unravels the myth of the church as a safe haven."[45] In fact, throughout the novel, Ijeoma seeks refuge in the church at times of personal struggle, in relation to her sexuality, pregnancy, and unhappy marriage. After her affair with Amina is discovered and she moves back to her mother in Aba, the first thing she does is visit church, where she is overwhelmed by the holiness of the place. Later, when she starts going out with Ndidi but is racked by feelings of guilt, she again goes to church, interpreting the flickering of light through the window as a sign of God. And when she is married and has fallen pregnant, she visits church daily, praying that her child will not be cursed, and again she is reassured by "sunlight . . . making its way inside the church" (229). This thread of Ijeoma seeking refuge in church narratively conveys the crucial point that she is not a "godless sinner," as popular Nigerian Christian rhetoric about queer people would have it, but is in fact a God-seeker. It also is an implicit appeal for the church to offer shelter to people like her.

Similarly significant is that the queer women's club to which Ndidi introduces Ijeoma, and where the latter "felt a sense of liberation," is hidden in a church, called Friend in Jesus Church of God (193). This can be read as suggesting that church can potentially be a place where queer people experience liberation and celebrate life. Yet this potential is far from realized: The party that Ijeoma and Ndidi attend in the church ends in tragedy, as a mob lights the building on fire and one of their friends dies, in a scene that evokes the traumatic memory of violence during the civil war.[46] Nevertheless, the name of the covert club/church can be seen as prophetic. Possibly inspired by the well-known Sunday school song "What a Friend We Have in Jesus," this name claims Jesus as a friend of the queer community. The image of Jesus as a friend has been found to "feature prominently" in the way Christians across Africa experience their faith, delineating notions of closeness and companionship.⁴⁷ African feminist theologians have explicitly claimed Jesus to be a friend of women, as he shares their struggles and brings liberation.⁴⁸ Similarly, the notion of Jesus as a friend of queer people has liberatory salience in the context of this novel. For Ijeoma, the words spoken by Jesus in the story about the woman caught in adultery (Gospel of John, chapter 8), directed at the Pharisees—"He that is without sin among you, let him first cast a stone at her"—are comforting and bring relief (202). Although these words can be seen as still rendering the woman as sinful, African feminist theologians have drawn on this story to address and overcome the stigmatization of women based on patriarchal norms of gender and sexuality.⁴⁹ The novel extends this tradition, applying it to same-sex-loving people. Where her mother calls upon Jesus as a force to conquer "demonic spirits" such as homosexuality, Ijeoma through this biblical story is reassured of Jesus's nonjudgmental attitude, unconditional love, and, indeed, friendship (92). This Jesus can be seen as presenting a model of affirmation and inclusivity that the church should follow.

The most cynical comment about the church uttered in the novel comes from Chibundu, who, unlike Ijeoma, is not a churchgoer at all. When he finds his pregnant wife in church, praying in great despair about the "abomination" she is trying to overcome, he tells her not to worry. In his view, "religion is basically a business, a very large corporation," and "the Church is the oldest and most successful business known to man" (231–32). This view echoes an economic theory of religion that various scholars have applied to Nigeria as a religious marketplace.⁵⁰ According to Chibundu, the church's moral politics, including about sexuality, are driven by its business concerns—aiming to exercise control over its followers and to recruit new ones. He concludes by saying: "It's the Church that has interpreted God's words to its own benefit" (232). Keeping Chibundu's cynical words in mind, *Under the Udala Trees* can be read as a way of reclaiming the Bible, and the figure of Jesus Christ, from the church in a quest for personal empowerment and liberation, as will be discussed in more detail below. However, by rendering the space of the church ambiguous, the novel also keeps open the possibility of change in the church, and it underlines the need for such change to occur.

Overcoming the Problem of Prayer

As much as the church is featured as a space of refuge, it is also a space of struggle, which is represented through the narrative trope of the problem of prayer. This problem manifests itself in relation to two key themes of the novel: war and sexuality. In the opening chapters, we read that Ijeoma, then eleven years old, prays several times about the war. Her first prayer, narrated in a flashback, is dated March 1967, several months before the official start of the Biafra War: "It was inside that church [Holy Sabbath Church of God], at the tail end of the harmattan, that I prayed my war prayer, because it was there and then, just before the morning service, that Chibundu had joked that soon bomber planes would be everywhere. . . . I prayed about the war, pleaded with God to make like a magician and cause all the talk of war, even the idea of it, to disappear" (11–12). Despite this prayer, the war did break out. A year later, when the bomber planes are raiding Biafra, and Ijeoma and her mother are hiding in the bunker, she prays again: "Dear God, please help Papa. Please make it so that the bomber planes don't go crashing into him." Nevertheless, shortly after, they find him dead inside the house. Ijeoma's disillusioned conclusion is: "It didn't appear that God had been bothered to answer my prayer" (13).

The Biafra War, according to several commentators, was somewhat inevitable because of historical and political conditions.[51] Perhaps that is why it could not be prevented, regardless of how many prayers were said. But what about Ijeoma's struggle with her sexuality? After finding out about her daughter's affair with Amina and taking her back home, Adaora puts her daughter on an intensive regime of prayer. Handing Ijeoma a black prayer scarf as "the mark of true penitence," she prays: "Almighty God in heaven, protect this my child from the devil that has come to take her innocent soul away. Protect her from the demons that are trying to send her to hell. Lead her not into temptation. Give her the strength to resist and do Your will. May her heart remember the lessons You have given, the lesson of our beginning, of Adam and Eve" (67, 72). When there is no immediate effect, Adaora performs a ritual of deliverance, trying to exorcise the demonic spirit holding possession over her daughter. As discussed earlier, the theme of deliverance is common in recent Nigerian queer literary texts, exemplifying how many Nigerian Christians have come to relate homosexuality and queer identities to the devil, demons, and evil spirits. *Under the Udala Trees* narrates deliverance as an intimate yet dramatic ritual performance, with Adaora invoking the power of God to cast out the supposedly demonic spirit inhabiting her daughter. It is intimate because it takes place in a domestic setting featuring only mother and child. It is dramatic, as Adaora's voice gets "progressively louder" each time she repeats the instruction to the demon to come out, with Adaora "speaking to the devil, crying for him to turn back and leave me alone" (88). The deliverance has no effect, however. All that Adaora can do in the end is pour some water over Ijeoma's head, as a ritual cure, saying that she will continue to pray for Ijeoma and that Ijeoma must continue to pray for herself, because "there's nothing that can't be conquered when we receive Jesus as our Lord and Savior" (92).

As much as Ijeoma tries to follow up on her mother's instruction to pray in order to be delivered from the demon of homosexuality, she fails. On three occasions, the novel narrates this failure, where Ijeoma is unable to speak words of prayer herself and cannot even utter the word "Amen" in response to her mother's prayer (71–72, 201). In each of these cases, the prayer that fails to come out is based on feelings of guilt, if not internalized disgust, and she petitions God for forgiveness. The failure of these prayers can be seen as a narrative suggestion that perhaps such prayers are not needed in the first place, because same-sex attraction is not a reason to feel sinful and seek repentance. One prayer that is answered, on the other hand, is born out of confusion, where Ijeoma is no longer sure whether homosexuality is a sin and finds words to articulate this as follows: "Lord, I am confused. Please give me a sign. If there is any evil in my heart, please give me a sign so that I might recognize it and, in doing so, avoid it" (197). The answer to this prayer comes, first, in the form of sunlight shining into the church where she is seated, as a sign of God's comforting presence and, second, by her mother entering the church, leading Ijeoma to the conclusion: "If this was God's sign, then Mama was the evil in my heart" (197). Reflecting the genre of the bildungsroman, the novel suggests that if Ijeoma needs to be delivered from anything to accept and grow toward her real self, it is from her homophobic mother, who hinders this process of reaching maturity. Thus, instead of prayer being an effective tool to "dominate my thoughts and desires," for Ijeoma it turns out to be a method through which she gradually comes to accept her desires (229).

The problem of prayer, as represented in the novel, fundamentally relates to the question of the nature and purpose of prayer. Is prayer about trying to avert historic events, such as war, and to overcome innate desires, such as same-sex attraction? Many Nigerian Christians would believe so, using prayer as a magic tool, even a "machine gun," in spiritual battles.[52] Yet by leaving this kind of prayer unanswered, *Under the Udala Trees* appears to implicitly critique this culture of interventionist prayer—among other reasons, because people direct "contradictory requests" to God, as Ijeoma muses (163). Instead, the novel suggests that prayer is a way of coming to terms with life and its inevitable challenges and a method of personal growth toward self-acceptance and maturity. But prayer is also suggested to be a method of channeling hope. In the epilogue, we read about nightly conversations between Ijeoma and Ndidi, in which the latter dreams of a town where "love is allowed to be love," regardless of the gender and ethnicity of the persons involved:

> "What is the name of the town?" I ask.
> ... One night, she mumbles that it is Aba. The next night it is Umuahia. With each passing night she names more towns: Ojoto and Nnewi, Onitsha and Nsukka, Port Harcourt and Lagos, Uyo and Oba, Kaduna and Sokoto. She names and names, so that eventually I have to laugh and say, "How is it that this town can be so many places at once?"
> Her voice is soft like a hum, and the words come out quiet like a prayer.... She says, "All of them are here in Nigeria. You see, this place will be all of Nigeria." (321)

Although Ndidi's words are only comparatively described as "like a prayer," the hope they reflect can be linked to the hope alluded to in the epigraph to the book—that is, a hope born out of faith.

Reading the Bible for Social Change

The Bible plays a prominent role in *Under the Udala Trees*, especially in part 2 of the novel, which narrates the Bible lessons that Ijeoma receives from her mother. After Ijeoma and Amina were caught in the act by the teacher, Ijeoma is returned to her mother, who attempts to "cleanse" her daughter's soul through daily Bible study and prayer sessions (65). Over a period of six months, they literally read through the whole Bible, her mother linking many of the passages to what she considers the demonic sin of homosexuality.

The prominence of the Bible, and Adaora's rather fundamentalist approach to it, in this novel might reflect Okparanta's own upbringing in the milieu of the Jehovah's Witnesses, an originally American Protestant group that arrived in Nigeria in the early twentieth century and is known for its emphasis on biblical inerrancy and infallibility.[53] It may also reflect the status and role of the Bible among Igbo Christians more generally, especially in the aftermath of the Civil War Revival. As the biblical scholar

Anthony Nkwoka puts it: "Christianity is a religion of the Book in Igboland. Much of Igbo Christianity may be summarized by the phrase, 'Is it in the Bible?'" The Bible was initially introduced to the Igbo by European missionaries who controlled its interpretation, but according to Nkwoka it was gradually appropriated by local communities, resulting in an "advent of Igbo reading and understanding of the Bible" in the twentieth century.[54] This was catalyzed, among other reasons, by the Biafra War, which caused waning missionary control and simultaneously led to a religious revival. The war and its tragic ending created a situation of anxiety, insecurity, and disillusionment in which many Igbo Christians resorted to the Bible for certainty, comfort, and guidance.[55] This clearly applies to Adaora, who had lost her husband during the war and who shortly after the end of the war fears that she might lose her only child to an "abomination."

By invoking the language of abomination to refer to homosexuality, and by using biblical texts to argue that Ijeoma had committed an abominable act, Adaora demonstrates her reliance on the Bible as a source of moral authority. It is striking that she never uses the cultural argument—the idea, which has become widespread in recent times, that homosexuality is against Igbo, Nigerian, or African culture. Perhaps she realizes that such a claim is somewhat problematic, given the history of woman-woman marriages among the Igbo, as among other African people (although such marriages should not be equated to modern same-sex relationships).[56] Adaora is likely to be part of "the majority of Igbo women [who], presumably under the influence of the Church, disapprove of woman-woman marriage."[57] Indeed, she repeatedly quotes the Bible to underline the abominable nature of same-sex relationships. She uses the Genesis creation story to argue that it is "man and wife. Adam *na* Eve," and "if God wanted it to be otherwise, would He not have included it that other way in the Bible?" (67, 68) Likewise, she draws this lesson from the story of Sodom and Gomorrah: "Man must not lie with man, and if man does, man will be destroyed" (74). These and other so-called clobber passages are quoted by Adaora to underline that homosexuality is "something disgusting, disgraceful, a scandal"; any objections that Ijeoma makes are silenced with the conversation stopper that "the fact that the Bible says it's bad is all the reason you need" (75).

The character of Adaora appears to be a colonized mind, rigidly adopting the Bible, introduced by European missionaries, as authoritative sacred Scripture, and forgetting about indigenous traditions of what has been described as "female Igbo gender bending," which was opposed by the same missionaries.[58] As Dube argues, what characterizes colonized minds is that they become "the mouthpiece" of colonial and imperialist agendas, which was effectively encouraged by the colonizers through the transmission of the Bible, among other strategies.[59] Although the extensive quotations from the Bible in the novel are mostly in English, a few quotations are in Igbo, from the early twentieth-century Igbo Union version, translated by the British Anglican missionary Thomas J. Dennis. This Bible translation has been famously criticized by Chinua Achebe, according to whom Dennis "in his missionary overzealousness and colonial mentality [had] done irreparable harm to the Igbo language in particular and Igbo culture in general."[60] Adaora appears to be equally zealous and reflective of a colonial mentality when she uses this Bible to condemn her own daughter for loving another girl. Her efforts are reminiscent of the "civilizing" agenda of missionaries seeking to promote "Igbo Christian family life" based on the model of the nuclear, patriarchal, and heteronormative family, and banning practices such as polygyny, divorce, and woman-woman marriage.[61]

Ijeoma, like her mother, takes the Bible seriously, and throughout the novel she is frequently seen reading and invoking it. However, she does not approach the Bible as rigidly as her mother does. Instead, she demonstrates an attitude of questioning, not so much the status of the Bible itself but its taken-for-granted interpretations. Thus, in the Bible study about the story of Sodom and Gomorrah, she takes issue with her mother's suggestion that this story is a warning against the sin of homosexuality and instead suggests that it is a lesson on hospitality and that God destroyed these two cities because its people were "selfish and inhospitable and violent" (74). In their discussion of Leviticus 18, she questions her mother's argument about abominations, wondering how it applies, for instance, to married couples who cannot have children. And in the Bible study of Judges 19, she fails to see how this is a story about homosexuality and instead concludes that it is a "horrible story" full of violence and rape (80). The biblical text most cited in the novel is the Genesis creation story about Adam and Eve. As mentioned earlier, for Adaora this story constitutes the norm of heterosexual marriage. This interpretation is common across Christian traditions that derive from the book of Genesis a heteronormative "order of creation" according to which Adam and Eve are paradigmatic of binary sexual differentiation and of male-female complementarity. Recent global Christian antigay discourses have popularized this in the statement that "it's Adam and Eve, not Adam and Steve."[62] Directly interrogating this, Ijeoma muses:

> Yes, it had been Adam and Eve. But so what if it was only the story of Adam and Eve that we got in the Bible? Why did that have to exclude the possibility of a certain Adam and Adam, or a certain Eve and Eve? Just because the story happened to focus on a certain Adam and Eve did not mean that all other possibilities were forbidden.... Infinite possibilities, and each one of them perfectly viable.... What if Adam and Eve were merely symbols of companionship? And Eve, different from him, woman instead of man, was simply a tool by which God notes that companionship was something you got from a person outside of yourself? (82–83)

These musings contain vital biblical-theological reflections. Ijeoma reinterprets the Genesis account of creation, taking Adam and Eve as a narrative model not of gender complementarity and compulsory heterosexuality in marriage but of human difference, companionship, and relationality that can be found and enjoyed in multiple, equally viable forms. She innovatively advances here, so to say, a queer interpretation avant la lettre, calling into question common interpretations that take the story as foundational to the "heterosexual contract" and instead reading it in recognition of the "multiple forms of intimate alliance."[63] Ijeoma's reading seeks to affirm sexual diversity, in a way that is similar to Dube's interpretation of the same biblical story. For Dube, the Garden of Eden, in which God, according to Genesis 2, placed Adam and Eve, is a garden with "many different flowers" that were all created good, and God as the creator "created life in wide diversities."[64]

Although the teenage Ijeoma calls into question her mother's rigid interpretations of the Bible, she remains uncertain about the alternative interpretations she puts forward. Reflecting the genre of the bildungsroman, *Under the Udala Trees* narrates Ijeoma's process of coming to terms with her sexuality and faith as an existential and spiritual struggle with considerable setbacks. While married to Chibundu and pregnant with their child, she seriously contemplates the possibility that God *is* punishing her for the nature of her love and that her baby might be cursed as a result. However, in the end, her contestation of established religious views and her exploration of alternative biblical and theological views are matters not merely of recalcitrant puberty but of maturity. Ijeoma grows into the conviction that "the Bible itself is an endorsement of change.... Maybe the rules of the Bible will always be in flux. Maybe God is still speaking and will continue to do so for always. Maybe He is still creating new covenants, only we were too deaf, too headstrong, too set in old ways to hear" (322).

Importantly, the insight that the Bible and its meaning are not fixed but are subject to change and to varying interpretations is informed by Ijeoma's memory of her father. When Ijeoma and her mother go through the Bible lessons, the former is reminded of how her father used to tell her folktales at night and used these to explain that stories are often allegorical—that is, they should be taken figuratively rather than literally because they "represent something very big, a larger idea, something so big that often we don't fully grasp the scope of its meaning" (78). Yet when Ijeoma applies this lesson from her father to the Bible stories she is reading with her mother, the latter abruptly dismisses the suggestion, saying: "The Bible is the Bible and not to be questioned. What we read in it is what we are to take out of it" (81). Nevertheless, Ijeoma does not let the thought go, as demonstrated by her creative interpretation of the story of Adam and Eve, not taking it at face value but exploring a deeper meaning. In the novel's epilogue, she meditates on Hebrews 8, the biblical text about the new covenant God made with his people, and she draws the following conclusion from it: "This, it seems to me, is the lesson of the Bible: this affirmation of the importance of reflection, and of revision, enough revisions to do away with tired, old, even faulty laws" (321). Ijeoma's indebtedness to her father in her approach to the Bible is further illustrated in the novel by the role that her father's old Bible—"the one he used to read from every Sunday at church"—plays (51). This Bible is handed to Ijeoma when her mother leaves her at the grammar school teacher's. The same Bible appears many years later in a dream, on the last night she spends under Chibundu's roof, as if to confirm her decision to leave her unhappy marriage.

The novel makes an important point about textual hermeneutics—that is, methods of interpretation. Through Ijeoma, and the memory of her father's lesson about allegorical, metaphorical, and symbolic meaning, *Under the Udala Trees* suggests that the hermeneutics of indigenous Igbo folktales provides a model for biblical hermeneutics, too. In doing so, it interrogates the tendency among many contemporary Igbo Christians to simply ask, "Is it in the Bible?"[65] Instead, it proposes a critical, dynamic, and reflective engagement with Scripture, in which its interpretation is determined not by the letter of the text but by the bigger picture of the understanding of God. And God, for Ijeoma, in the end is not the controller of a fixed, static truth that people must obey blindly but is a source of ongoing revelation; God is still speaking and creating new covenants in the present day. Thus, for her the Bible is an endorsement of change, because Godself constantly enacts change. Already as a child, Ijeoma contemplated that change might be "a thing sanctioned by God" because it is "part of His aesthetic, part of His vision for the world" (37). These words are echoed in the epilogue, where she reflects: "God is nothing but an artist, and the world is His canvas. And I reason that if the Old and New Testament are any indication, then change is in fact a major part of his aesthetic, a major part of his vision for the world" (321–22).

As discussed above, the character of Adaora and her approach to the Bible present an example of a colonized mind. She is depicted in the novel as a representative of a conservative Christianity that, in Dube's words, is "mirroring the missionary teachings that sought to uproot African people completely from their religious beliefs by teaching the strictest biblical adherence."[66] In contrast, Ijeoma can be seen as representing a decolonizing approach to the Bible. This suggestion may come as a surprise to some readers for whom the Bible is inherently linked to the history of colonial exchange, as captured in the popular saying: "When the missionaries came to Africa, they had the Bible and we had the land; They said, 'Let us pray.' We closed our eyes. When we opened them, we had the Bible and they had the land."[67] However, as the biblical scholar Gerald West has argued, the Bible may have been introduced in many parts of Africa as a "tool of imperialism," but via complex processes of appropriation by local communities it has become an "African icon" and a "people's Bible."[68]

Importantly, *Under the Udala Trees* extends this history of appropriation by demonstrating that the Bible, which in contemporary contexts is widely used to create a queerphobic climate, can also be drawn upon by same-sex-loving people to support their quest for affirmation and liberation. Thus, in the novel, Ijeoma, instead of being a mouthpiece of colonial agendas, resists the terminology of "abomination" that missionaries and colonial authorities had introduced and their underlying rigid approach to biblical interpretation. Her critical attention to the allegorical meanings of the Bible is informed by traditions of Igbo folktales, thus mobilizing an indigenous cultural hermeneutics and applying that to Scripture. Okparanta captures this while reflecting on the protagonist in her novel: "These days, for many Nigerians, Bible verses have replaced our traditional proverbs. . . . But for Ijeoma, I think the Bible stories and verses were in some ways an extension of the folktales. For her, it was a sort of juggling act: using elements of the folktale (and storytelling elements, in general) to try to understand the Bible."[69]

Dube, in her book *Postcolonial Feminist Interpretation of the Bible*, conceptualizes African decolonizing feminist readings of the Bible with the term *Semoya*. This Setswana[70] word means "of the Spirit," and it was originally used in Botswana as a term for a category of churches that in academic literature are generally referred to as African Indigenous Churches (AICs). These churches put a strong emphasis on the experience of the Holy Spirit and, related to that, on the practice of prophecy and healing. AICs emerged in the early twentieth century, often as a breakaway from the European-planted mission churches, and it has been argued that they represent an "African reformation" and an indigenous form of Pentecostal Christianity.[71] Emphasizing the independent nature of the AICs as local African appropriations of Christianity, their resistance to European-dominated missionary Christianity, and the prominent role of women as founders, leaders, preachers, prophets, and healers in these communities, Dube argues that these churches present a combination of "political protest of racial and religious discrimination, a search for cultural liberation through integrating biblical views with African religious views, and an experience of God's Spirit empowering both women and men of various races to serve creation."[72] Her particular interest—which is most relevant here—concerns the interpretative practices of women AIC members—that is, the way women interpret the Bible, reclaiming this sacred Scripture from a colonial and patriarchal missionary church and appropriating it in their quest for liberation and empowerment. Thus, Dube conceptualizes the interpretative practice of Botswanan AIC women as a *Semoya* space:

> A *Semoya* space reserves a critical and liberative reading of texts that have been instrumental in the colonization of Africa and oppression of women. It insists on hearing God afresh, in a new space—one that operates outside the oppressive structures and their symbols. The *Semoya* space insists on imagining a framework that enhances the lives of women and men and that does not embrace patriarchal and imperialist oppression. . . . To speak or to interpret the Bible from a *Semoya* space is to insist on hearing God anew—free from the often oppressive space of our current social structures.[73]

Despite the differences in context between Botswana and Nigeria, and even though *Under the Udala Trees* is not specifically about AICs, I draw on Dube's work to suggest that Ijeoma engages in an interpretative practice that is somewhat similar to Dube's *Semoya* readers. This similarity centers around at least two aspects. First is the search for cultural liberation through integrating biblical views with African religio-cultural views. In Ijeoma's case, that manifests itself in the form of an approach to biblical interpretation modeled after indigenous folktale traditions. Foregrounding the figurative and symbolic meanings of sacred storytelling, when applied to the Bible, these traditions interrogate the static approach to biblical truth that had been introduced by European missionaries and embraced by many Igbo converts. This way of engaging the Bible allows Ijeoma to see the Bible as endorsing change and to reclaim the nature of her love, which had been opposed by missionaries and their legacy. Doing so, she also reclaims indigenous histories of woman-woman marriage and gender bending among the Igbo. Second, the similarity centers around the critical and liberative reading of the biblical text. Yet whereas Dube's *Semoya* readers are concerned with oppression in terms of patriarchy and colonial imperialism, Ijeoma foregrounds sexuality, and specifically homophobia and heteronormativity, as the primary concern.

Trees play an important role in the novel's indigenous cultural hermeneutics that enables a queer reading of the Bible. The udala tree, central in the novel's title, is a sacred tree in Igbo mythology. Achebe—claimed by Okparanta as a major source of inspiration[74]—has described this tree as "sacred to ancestral spirits."[75] Okparanta's novel can be seen as implicitly linking the tree to the spirit of Ijeoma's father: The udala tree and her father's old Bible appear to her in the same dream. This is particularly significant because earlier in the novel Ijeoma meets her first love, Amina, under an udala tree. If this tree is a symbolic manifestation of her father's spirit, the suggestion is that her deceased father (different from her mother) endorses the nature of his daughter's love. The ancestral spirits, after all, are familiar with Igbo traditions of gender bending and woman-woman marriage. That her father's spirit is also familiar with the Bible is not a cause of conflict, because the Bible itself is to be interpreted through the lens of indigenous folktales—or so the novel suggests.

Following that suggestion, a connection can be made between the symbolic meaning of the udala tree in Igbo folktale and the biblical tree of knowledge of good and evil. This tree, according to Genesis 2, had been planted by God in the Garden of Eden, with the instruction that Adam and Eve were not allowed to eat from it, or they would die. Achebe, in *Arrow of God*, suggests that a similar taboo applies to the udala tree. Because of its sacred significance, "no one, young or old" was to pick from the tree's "tempting fruit."[76] According to the biblical story of Genesis 2–3, the serpent persuades Eve to ignore God's instruction and eat from the tree nevertheless, and she shares the fruit with Adam. Then both become aware of their nakedness and experience shame; when God comes into the Garden of Eden to call them to account, they hide in the bushes. *Under the Udala Trees* directly engages this biblical story in the scene where the teacher walks into Ijeoma and Amina fondling and kissing each other and shouts, "Abomination!" The novel then reads: "Amina and I began to cry, deep cries that made our shoulders heave. Our clothes lay scattered on the floor, dispersed like discarded seeds. We were naked, and we felt our nakedness as Adam and Eve must have felt in the garden, at the time of that evening breeze. Our eyes had become open, and we too sought to hide ourselves. But first we had to endure the grammar school teacher's lecturing. . . . He lectured and he lectured, and he lectured. As God must have lectured Eve" (125).

As the literary scholar Cédric Courtois has observed, in this scene "the two characters [Ijeoma and Amina] are described as the original couple: a rewriting of the Biblical text is therefore at stake."[77] In this rewriting, the biblical text and Igbo mythology merge, with the udala tree and the tree of knowledge blending together. Both trees represent the taboo of eating from a forbidden fruit. Clearly, in the novel, this fruit is the taste of same-sex intimacy and love. After all, Amina's tongue made Ijeoma's body wash over with euphoria. As in the case of Adam and Eve, so also for Ijeoma and Amina, eating the fruit results in shame, as they become painfully aware of their nakedness. They have no chance to escape the penetrating gaze of the teacher and his damning judgment, summarized in that word "abomination." Soon after, Ijeoma is forced to leave Amina, and although they later study at the same school, their relationship never becomes as it used to be. They ate the fruit and lost paradise. Or did they?

In the short story "Runs Girl," about a girl drawn into the sex industry to pay her mother's hospital bills, Okparanta concludes with a reimagination of the story of Eve in the Garden of Eden: "This new Eve would walk amongst the trees of the garden. And she would drink from the waters of the river of the garden. And again, she would eat the forbidden fruit. But she would not be cast away from the garden, because she would be given the opportunity, just once, to ask for forgiveness. And she would be forgiven."[78] Here, too, the forbidden fruit refers to a consumption of sexuality deemed morally transgressive from a Christian perspective, but which Okparanta suggests is forgivable by God. In *Under the Udala Trees*, it is Chibundu who reassures Ijeoma of God's forgiveness, saying: "If I were God, and if it turned out that you were actually committing an abomination, then I'd forgive you" (232).[79] So, even if same-sex intimacy were abominable in the eyes of God, it is forgivable, and not a reason to be cast away from paradise.

Yet the novel calls into question the view of "abomination" in the first place. Even Adaora, at the end of the novel, when Ijeoma has left her failed marriage and returns to her mother, admits: "God who created you must have known what He did. Enough is enough" (323). After this return, something like paradise is regained for Ijeoma, as the epilogue narrates how she and Ndidi live their lives as "more than friends"; despite the limitations of the context in which they find themselves, they feel themselves "every bit a couple" (320). This positive ending of the novel reaffirms the hope that Nigeria is a place "where paradise will hopefully one day be."[80] The udala tree, as a sacred indigenous tree and as a symbolic representation of the biblical tree of knowledge, is a reassurance that this paradise of queer love will come.

Conclusion

In a context where LGBTQ+ identities and rights have become highly politicized and contested, and where Christianity is by and large invested in anti-queer mobilizations, queer Nigerian literature has emerged as an important site of social, political, and religious critique and imagination. As demonstrated earlier in this chapter, deliverance is a central theme in queer Nigerian writing, with many literary texts narratively representing and problematizing the impact that this popular Nigerian Christian practice has on already stigmatized and traumatized queer people and how it reinforces the notion of queer embodiment as demonic. The innovative contribution of *Under the Udala Trees* to this ever-growing body of literature is that it not only represents and problematizes the Pentecostalized culture of deliverance of queer bodies, and the fundamental heteronormative and queerphobic orientation of Nigerian Christianity across denominations, but also creatively explores and boldly imagines alternative possibilities by drawing on Christian beliefs, texts, and practices. Reading this novel *for* deliverance, I have unpacked how it seeks to deliver Nigerian Christianity from its queerphobic tendencies and reimagine it as a liberative and queer-affirming space of freedom.

Reading Okparanta's novel in dialogue with the work of the feminist theologian Musa W. Dube, I have shown how both convey a key point in their writings: The Bible can be a resource for imagining progressive social change in matters of gender and sexuality in postcolonial African contexts. When read in a critical and liberating way, the Bible, in Dube's earlier-quoted words, can allow for "hearing God anew," opening up a space of women's empowerment and of transformation. Similarly, the words that Okparanta puts in Ijeoma's mouth—that "the Bible itself is an endorsement of change"— reflect the author's personal quest for a reading of the Bible that engenders hope and inspires change: "I wanted a novel that explored possibilities, a novel that spoke against the black and white interpretations of the Bible."[81]

Dube's quest for a postcolonial African feminist interpretation of the Bible is particularly concerned with the major issues of colonialism, imperialism, and patriarchy, and the ways these realities affect women's lives. However, as she acknowledges herself, "the struggle continues," with sexual minorities being another oppressed group searching for justice and liberation.[82] Indeed, in addition to the "decolonizing and anti-patriarchy liberation movements" that emerged across the African continent in the late twentieth and early twenty-first centuries, recent years have also witnessed the emergence of queer liberation movements that seek to overcome the problems of heteronormativity, homophobia, and anti-queer violence. Okparanta's novel is a literary expression of this development. By using the Biafra War as the context of the narrative, she underlines the criticality of the issues at stake, as if the current struggle for queer liberation is another watershed moment in the history of postcolonial Nigeria, and Africa more generally.

Like colonialism and patriarchy, heterosexism, too, is often based on hegemonic interpretations of biblical texts Christian beliefs. Yet in a similar spirit as Dube's postcolonial feminist approach, Okparanta in her novel pushes for a queer interpretation of the Bible in which sacred Scripture not only is part of the problem but also can be creatively used as part of the solution. Queer readers such as Ijeoma can be similarly inspired, affirmed, and empowered by the Bible as Dube's *Semoya* readers are. Innovatively, Okparanta suggests that the key for such a queer liberating reading of the Bible is in an indigenous cultural hermeneutics that recognizes the figurative and symbolic dimension of folktales and sacred myths. Such a hermeneutics allows for a creative reimagining of social order with the help of biblical and Christian traditions, thus opening up infinite possibilities of love and human existence. Thus, *Under the Udala Trees* makes an important contribution not just to Nigerian queer literature but also to the development of a Nigerian queer Christian theology as it seeks to carve out a queer-affirming space within Nigerian Christianity.

Chapter 3

APPARITION

Catholicism, Marian Devotion, and Gender

Since missionary activity started in the late nineteenth century, Catholicism has firmly established itself in Nigeria.[1] Estimations of the number of Catholics in the year 2020 range from twenty-five million to over thirty-two million, which equals 12 to about 15 percent of the total population.[2] This makes Nigeria the country with the second-largest Catholic population on the African continent, reportedly with the highest level of Mass attendance in the world.[3] The Catholic Church has a strong presence in society, through schools, clinics, and other social services, and also holds considerable political influence, with the Church publicly positioning itself as the conscience of the nation—for instance, by promoting democracy, defending human rights, and addressing corruption.[4] The southeastern region, also known as Igboland, is considered to be a particular Catholic stronghold. Yet among the Igbo, as among other African people, the introduction, acceptance, and expansion of Catholicism was not straightforward, because of the tension, which was at the heart of the missionary project, between Christianity and indigenous religion and culture. As the Nigerian theologian Simon Aihiokhai puts it in his historical discussion of Catholicism in Nigeria: "The bias of the missionaries and the colonial agents emerges in the accounts describing the religious heritage of the people. The indigenous religions were simply referred to as fetishism."[5] Likewise, David Asonye Ihenacho, in his two-part study of Igbo Catholicism, points out: "For the Igbo people, the real area of concern was the continued dichotomy between

Catholicism and Igbo culture. There was almost a consensus among the rank-and-file Igbo Catholics that there was still an outstanding major work for the Church with regard to the Igbo culture. All such perceptions and criticisms gradually became a major pressure on the Nigerian theological experts who began to address the issue of inculturation in Nigerian Catholicism with some urgency."[6] According to Ihenacho, two events have been crucial in the development of a locally rooted form of Catholicism in Igboland in the postcolonial era. First was the Nigerian Civil War (1967–70), as the aftermath of the war came with a revival in Igbo Christianity, as well as with a sudden transition of the Church into the hands of indigenous clergy, after the Nigerian authorities, until the mid-1970s, banned expatriate priests (in response to the Church's perceived support of Biafra). Second was the first papal visit to Nigeria, in 1982, during which Pope John Paul II called for "a new era of evangelization," which instilled a sense of optimism and self-confidence in the Church.[7]

The complex and delicate process of the Catholic Church's reinventing itself and becoming locally rooted in Nigeria, and specifically in Igboland, is at the heart of Chimamanda Ngozi Adichie's debut novel, *Purple Hibiscus*, first published in 2003, which is the focus of this chapter. As discussed in the subsequent sections, by featuring and contrasting two different forms of Catholicism, Adichie explores the aforementioned transition in the Church and the quest for the inculturation of the Catholic faith in Igboland in the late twentieth century. In doing so, she demonstrates a particular concern with gender issues in the Church and in society, similar, for instance, to the Nigerian theologian Rose Uchem, who, in her book *Overcoming Women's Subordination*, seeks to promote an "inclusive theology" for Igbo women in the Catholic Church. Adichie addresses this concern critically and creatively by engaging with one of the most distinct symbols of Catholicism, the Virgin Mary. Indeed, the novel narrates an apparition of Mary in a local Nigerian landscape, as a literary expression of how Catholicism has become locally rooted, not just as a faith but as a lived and experiential spirituality. There are other recent examples of Nigerian and West African literary representations of Mary. In Chris Abani's *Song for Night* (discussed in chapter 1), a statue of Mary is saved from the rubble of a church bombed during the war, representing the hope for divine presence and redemption amid the atrocity. Another novel by Abani, *The Virgin of Flames*, and Francesca Ekwuyasi's novel *Butter Honey Pig Bread* both feature the figure of Mary in the context of narratives that cross boundaries of gender and sexuality. And the novel *In the Company of Men*, by the Ivorian writer Veronique Tadjo, features a desperate mother who has seen her children die of Ebola, and who prays to Mary for comfort and strength.

These various texts exemplify the influence of Catholic tradition and imagery in contemporary African literary writing. Adichie's engagement with the figure of the Virgin Mary, and with Marian devotion as a Catholic religious practice, is most elaborate, and it is embedded most explicitly in a broader project of a literary representation of Catholicism as an "African lived Christianity" in a Nigerian context.[8] In the following sections, I will first briefly summarize the novel's plot, review existing scholarly interpretations, and outline my own approach to the novel as a key text for the study of Nigerian, African, and indeed world Christianity. My analysis will then unfold along three relevant themes: the question of inculturation, which centers around the relationship between Catholicism and indigenous religion; the theme of Marian devotion and apparition, and how this intersects with gender; and, finally, the theme of masculinity.

Reading *Purple Hibiscus*

Set in the late 1980s, when Nigeria was under military rule and faced political unrest, *Purple Hibiscus* tells the story of a young girl, Kambili, growing up with her brother, Jaja, in the house of their father, Eugene Achike, in Enugu, a city in the southeastern region of Nigeria. As a self-made, successful businessman and a devout Catholic, Eugene embodies a religious version of the Nigerian "Big Man," who at home is a despotic patriarch terrifying his children and his wife, Beatrice. Eugene stands in contrast to his sister, Aunty Ifeoma, who is a widowed university lecturer living in Nsukka, just thirty miles north. She is struggling to make ends meet but parents her three children—Amaka, Obiora, and Chima—and practices her Catholic faith with a sense of warmth and joy that appears unreal to Kambili and Jaja, when they are finally allowed to visit their aunt and cousins. A major point of departure between Eugene and Ifeoma is their relationship to their father, Papa-Nnukwu, who lives in the family's rural hometown and adheres to indigenous Igbo belief and ritual. While Eugene dismisses his father as "worshiper of idols," Ifeoma refers to him respectfully as a "traditionalist" (70, 166).

Purple Hibiscus is a widely acclaimed novel, which won the 2005 Commonwealth Writers Prize in the categories "Best First Book (Africa)" and "Best First Book (Overall)," among other honors. It has been recognized by literary scholars for its contribution to the field of religion and African literature, in particular addressing the question of the status of Catholicism, as an originally missionary religion from Europe, in a postcolonial African context. For instance, Susan VanZanten discusses the novel as a key text of contemporary world Christianity, inviting readers to acknowledge that Christianity is no longer an exclusively Western religion (if it had ever been) and introducing them to the realities of Christian faith in sub-Saharan Africa, where the church has witnessed phenomenal growth in the twentieth century and into the twenty-first. According to VanZanten, Adichie seeks "to interrogate different expressions of Christianity and to affirm a vigorously local African Christianity."[9] Making a comparison to earlier African novelists writing about Christianity, such as Ngũgĩ wa Thiong'o and Mongo Beti, of which Adichie is a "literary grandchild," Anthony Chennells observes that Adichie "belongs to a generation for whom Christianity in its many manifestations is as much a part of African cultures as traditional religions are or perhaps were," with *Purple Hibiscus* representing the quest for inculturation of the church in contemporary Nigeria.[10] Another literary scholar, Cheryl Stobie, reads the novel along somewhat similar lines, pointing out that Adichie, through the various characters, "raises questions about the possibility of change within the family, the church and the nation," and arguing that the novel reflects the author's reformist agenda that endorses and promotes the changes in the Catholic Church initiated in the aftermath of the Second Vatican Council (1962–65).[11] Borrowing the concept of "cultural hermeneutics" from the theologian Mercy Amba Oduyoye, Cynthia Wallace considers *Purple Hibiscus* to present a "paradoxical blend of critique and celebration of both traditional African cultures and the Christian tradition within a postcolonial context."[12] The theologian Musa W. Dube offers a postcolonial feminist interpretation of the novel, suggesting that two of its main characters, Papa Eugene and Aunty Ifeoma, embody "different types of Christianities," described by Dube as "colonized" and "decolonizing" minds, respectively.[13]

Although at least one critic has offered a divergent reading of the novel, emphasizing its critique of Christianity and its postcolonial "Gothic-like reclamation" of Igbo heritage, including indigenous religion,[14] I sympathize with the readings that foreground Adichie's complex narrative exploration and negotiation of the possibilities of Christianity, specifically Catholicism, in contemporary Nigeria. Those readings acknowledge that the structure of the novel—its three parts being titled "Palm Sunday," "Before Palm Sunday," and "After Palm Sunday," respectively—already indicates that Christian faith plays a prominent role. In the Christian liturgical calendar, Palm Sunday (the Sunday before Easter) commemorates the biblical event where Jesus enters Jerusalem, riding a donkey and being hailed by the crowds as "Son of David"—the same crowd that, days later, calls for him to be crucified. Whatever the meaning of this framing is (see below), it does add a layer of theological significance to the narrative. Those readings also stay closest to Adichie's own allusion to the ways the novel reflects her personal quest for religious identity. For instance, in an interview with Ike Anya, she states:

> I am fascinated by the power of religion. I grew up Catholic, still am although I am what may be called a Liberal Catholic, which is that I believe in Lourdes but also think that contraception is a good thing. Religion is such a huge force, so easily corruptible and yet so capable of doing incredible good. The streak of intolerance I see masquerading itself as faith and the way we create an image of God that suits us, are things I am interested in questioning. I am also interested in colonized religion, how people like me can profess and preach a respect of their indigenous culture and yet cling so tenaciously to a religion that considers most of that indigenous culture evil.[15]

What is obvious from this quotation is Adichie's self-identification as a "liberal Catholic," her acknowledgment that Catholicism in Nigeria is a colonial religion, and her own quest to practice the faith in a way that allows her to maintain respect for indigenous Igbo traditions. The latter quest is central in the novel and is specifically embodied by Kambili, who, faced with the different forms of Catholicism represented by her father and aunt, must carve out her own path toward maturity and faith. Thus, the question of Christian faith and Igbo identity are at the heart of *Purple Hibiscus* as a bildungsroman.

The broader question of Christianity and African cultural traditions is central in the book *Theology Brewed in an African Pot*, by the Nigerian theologian Agbonkhianmeghe Orobator. This chapter reads both texts in dialogue to elucidate themes relating to Catholicism and its possibilities in postcolonial Africa, with specific reference to the context of Nigeria. Although Orobator does not share the same ethnic background as Adichie—she is Igbo, from the southeastern region, while he is Edo, from southern Nigeria—they share their Catholic identity and, as we will see, a reformist agenda. Both are prolific and acclaimed authors with an international profile: Adichie in the literary scene, and Orobator in the circles of African and Catholic theology. *Theology Brewed in an African Pot* proves a rich text to be put in conversation with *Purple Hibiscus*, not only because it allows for an exploration of the general theme of inculturation and Catholicism but also because of the specific interest that both texts share in the figure of the Virgin Mary. Indeed, Orobator's book is one of only a few African theological texts that includes a substantial discussion of Mary. Moreover, it is noteworthy that Orobator himself in this book demonstrates a considerable interest in literature, using excerpts from Chinua Achebe's novel *Things Fall Apart* as a framework for his writing, describing it as a "literary masterpiece" unmatched in its "power, fascination, and brilliance."[16] Adichie, for her part, has also repeatedly stated that she is highly indebted to Achebe, whom she describes as "the writer whose work is most important to me."[17] She explicitly cross-references Achebe's debut novel in the opening sentence of *Purple Hibiscus*: "Things started to fall apart at home when my brother, Jaja, did not go to communion and Papa flung his heavy missal across the room and broke the figurines on the étagère" (3).

Orobator uses *Things Fall Apart* as an "accessible methodology for giving theological reflection a distinctively African flavor," reading the novel as a "literary account of the conflict ridden encounter between missionary Christianity and African religious and cultural worldviews."[18] In this chapter, I explore how *Purple Hibiscus* offers insight into the phase after this initial encounter, in which the conflict and tension have not disappeared but are negotiated through a process of inculturation, with Catholicism becoming part of sociocultural life in contemporary Nigeria. In the second half of the chapter, I will specifically focus on the novel's representation of the Virgin Mary, and related to that, I will analyze gendered themes.

From Colonial to Inculturated Catholicism

Purple Hibiscus sketches the context of a postcolonial Nigerian society in which Christianity has settled and become part of sociocultural life. This is a novel not about the arrival of a new religion brought by foreign missionaries—although a European missionary priest and white religious sisters are still present in its pages—but about how this originally European religion takes shape in Igboland, Nigeria, in the late twentieth century, a hundred years after the first Catholic missionaries arrived there.[19] The novel is set in the 1980s, in the second decade after the monstrosity of the Nigerian Civil War (1967–70), which left Igboland and its people devastated and malnourished. Although *Purple Hibiscus* only includes a few references to memories of this tragic chapter in Nigerian postcolonial history (Eugene was studying in England during the war), it has been suggested that through its main protagonists, Kambili and Jaja, Adichie "pays homage to the silent children of Biafra" and that the novel reflects a deliberate effort to reclaim Igbo cultural identity in the postwar era.[20] As part of that effort, Adichie explores in the novel whether and how Christianity can be part of the quest for Igbo identity.

The religious setting of the novel is dominated by Catholicism, yet some mention is made of the "mushrooming Pentecostal churches" and their "fake pastors" (5, 29, 208). These references reflect the disdain with which the Catholic Church treated Pentecostal-Charismatic churches when they began to emerge in the last few decades of the twentieth century.[21] The novel's Catholic religious universe is described with numerous allusions to a domestic devotion centered around praying the Rosary, weekly Mass attendance, and a material religious culture defined by crucifixes, medals of the Virgin Mary, rosary beads, missals, palm fronds, ashes, holy water, wafers, flowers on church altars, and Sunday dresses. This universe characterizes both Eugene's and Ifeoma's families. Yet the forms of Catholicism that the two embody and that are practiced in their respective households are very different.

Papa Eugene is depicted as the product of missionary Christianity. He himself testifies to that, telling his children: "My father spent time worshiping gods of wood and stone. I would be nothing today but for the priests and sisters at the mission" (47). Serving as a houseboy and gardener for missionary priests while attending the mission school, Eugene later studied in England and, upon his return to Nigeria, began to gradually build his business empire. Hardly ever speaking Igbo himself, he instructs his children "to sound civilised in public" and speak English, and he even expects the villagers in his hometown to speak English around him (13). The parish church in Enugu that the Achike family attends—always prominently seated in the front pew, Eugene being the first to receive Communion every Sunday—is led by a British missionary priest, Father Benedict, who insists that the most important parts of Mass, such as the Kyrie and Credo, are spoken in Latin and that "native songs" in Igbo are only allowed during the Offertory, with clapping being kept to a minimum in order not to compromise the solemnity of Mass (4). Once, when a young visiting priest halfway through his sermon starts singing an Igbo song, Eugene indicates that his children should keep their lips sealed; he later disparagingly compares the priest to "a Godless leader of one of these Pentecostal churches" (29).

Because Eugene is a devout worshipper and the main donor of the richly decorated parish church, the incumbent priest publicly praises him and presents him as an exemplar to the faithful in his sermons. "Father Benedict," Kambili recalls, "usually refers to the pope, Papa, and Jesus—in that order. He used Papa to illustrate the gospels" (4). The strict discipline of monastic life that Eugene observed from the missionary priests who educated him is applied by him to his family. Not only does he provide detailed daily schedules for his children, outlining their daily tasks and duties, but he also leads them in an intense domestic devotion of prayer and Bible reading—saying the grace at the start of a meal could take over twenty minutes—and he enforces a harsh regime of punishment for any perceived offense or underperformance. Praised by the priest, held in high esteem by many people in the community who benefit from his generosity, and even receiving an international human rights award for publishing a prodemocracy newspaper critical of the government, Eugene has another side that Kambili, Jaja, and their mother are painfully aware of. To them, he is an intimidating presence in the home whose will is law and who exercises an "overwhelming control and tyranny."[22] People from his *umunna* (relatives) whisper that a man of his status should have more than two children and that his wife's womb may have been tied up by witchcraft. But in fact, Beatrice suffers several miscarriages because of the battering she receives from her husband, with whom she stays, nevertheless, maintaining that "a husband crowns a woman's life," despite her own experience (75). The depiction of Beatrice's character in the novel illustrates Oduyoye's critical observation that Christianity in West Africa "reinforces the cultural conditioning of compliance and submission, and leads to the depersonalization of women."[23] Catholic religion, Igbo tradition, and Nigerian Big Man culture appear to strengthen the patriarchal power that provides Eugene with "a quasi-divine status."[24]

Aunty Ifeoma is a confident, independent woman who stands in contrast to the quiet and docile Beatrice. As a widow, she is not bothered about remarrying. When her father offers to ask Chukwu, the Igbo supreme being, to send a "good man to take care of you and the children," she counters that his time would be better spent praying for her promotion at university (83). She encourages her house-battered sister-in-law to leave her abusive husband, telling her that "sometimes life begins when marriage ends" (75). Not intimidated by her brother's status and wealth, she also stands up to Eugene and refuses to "lick his buttocks" (95). As a university lecturer, she encourages critical thinking, as reflected in her children.

Like Eugene's family, Ifeoma's household is organized around Catholic devotion, praying the Rosary together as a family every night. But when Kambili and Jaja visit them for the first time in Nsukka, they are shocked, because after the last Hail Mary their aunt and cousins collectively burst out into "uplifting Igbo songs"—with Kambili thinking, "It was not right. You did not break into song in the middle of the rosary" (125). Another shock comes the next morning, when the family gathers for short morning prayers, again interspersed with songs. Kambili is left bewildered to hear her aunt pray "that we might find peace and laughter today" (126–27). The narrative depiction of family devotion at Aunty Ifeoma's—warm, joyful, communal—is in stark contrast to domestic devotion in Eugene's home, which is strict, sterile, and fearful. The church on the university campus that they attend is led by the young and popular chaplain Father Amadi (who turns out to be the same priest who once said Mass at St. Agnes and was despised by Eugene for singing Igbo songs and for whom Kambili later in the novel develops feelings). A missionary priest himself, Amadi stands for a social gospel according to which Christ can be seen in the faces of boys from the impoverished neighborhood—a comment that puzzles Kambili, as she cannot reconcile it with "the blond Christ hanging on the burnished cross in St. Agnes" (178). When Kambili attends Mass at the chaplaincy, she realizes that her father would be scandalized by the appearance of women who are improperly dressed. The Catholicism embodied by Father Amadi, and by Ifeoma and her family, allows for questions, is people-centered and open to the world, and is not alien to but integrated with Igbo culture. It is a form of Catholicism that engages the renewal in the church brought about by Vatican II.

As Orobator points out, the theology of Vatican II centers around the idea that the church is not first and foremost an institution but a people.[25] In the spirit of this theology, Pope Paul VI, who had presided over the council, on a visit to Uganda in 1969, famously stated that African Christians "may, and must, have an African Christianity."[26] Pope John Paul II echoed this, and developed it in much greater detail, during his visit to Cameroon in 1995, where he presented the document *Ecclesia in Africa*, which explicitly endorsed the notion of inculturation. The term "inculturation," which captures a new way of thinking about the relationship between the Christian faith and the cultural context in which it takes shape, became increasingly popular in the aftermath of Vatican II, not least in African Catholic circles.[27] Orobator, too, embraces it in *Theology Brewed in an African Pot*. Here, he critiques European missionaries and their early converts in Africa, who treated African indigenous religion and culture as, at best, "merely preparatory" and, at worst, "simply diabolical"; instead, he advocates for Christianity and indigenous traditions to engage in "a process of mutual listening, appreciation, and transformation."[28]

In *Purple Hibiscus*, Eugene represents the attitude of diabolizing indigenous religion, which he disdainfully refers to as "worshiping gods of wood and stone" (47). He is the kind of convert who completely broke contact with his own father, referring to him as a "heathen" and "pagan" (62, 81). Instead, he speaks warmly about his deceased father-in-law, who had been one of the first Christian converts in the area and had served as an interpreter and catechist to European missionaries. Eugene only allows his children to see their paternal grandfather once a year, for fifteen minutes, instructing them not to touch any food or drink because it may have been offered to the ancestors. He does not allow his son, Jaja, to participate in the *ima mmuo* (male initiation ceremony) because he "would end up in hellfire" (87). He refuses to let his children join their aunt to see the *mmuo* (masquerades) because it is "devilish folklore"—a view reinforced by Father Benedict, who sees these rituals as "the gateway to Hell" (85, 106). Eugene is the product and embodiment of the "violent conquest spearheaded by colonial Europe" that in Orobator's words defined the first encounter of missionary Christianity in Africa but has now become "outdated."[29] Adichie suggests, through the character of Eugene, that this cultural and epistemic violence has, however, had a long-standing impact.

Like Orobator, Adichie also suggests that there is an alternative approach, which in the novel is represented by Ifeoma. The latter has maintained a close relationship with her father, respecting his indigenous religious ritual and suggesting that his prayers directed to the Igbo deity Chineke are "as good" and "the same" as Catholics praying the Rosary (166). This appraisal is critical, as it relates to the theological question at the heart of the debate about inculturation: Is the divine as worshipped in indigenous religions the same as the God of Christianity? Addressing this question, Orobator states that indigenous rituals and beliefs can be seen as "signs of God's presence and action in the African religious universe."[30] Seemingly sharing this view, Ifeoma has no interest in converting her father to the Catholic faith; she also has no problem with her son, Obiora, partaking in the *ima mmuo* or with taking her children, and secretly Kambili and Jaja, to see the *mmuo*. Likewise, Father Amadi is respectful toward Papa-Nnukwu, and he challenges Kambili when she is worried about having committed a sin by sleeping under the same roof as her grandfather at Aunty Ifeoma's.

His simple question, "Why is it a sin?," encourages her to think critically about the views her father has imposed on her (175).

Kambili remembers that Aunty Ifeoma had once said, in a "mild, forgiving way," that "Papa [Eugene] is too much of a colonial product" (13). Papa-Nnukwu is less mild and forgiving, blaming the missionaries for the soured relationship with his alienated son. Their teaching of the Trinity, specifically the idea that "the father and the son are equal," would have allowed his son to disregard him (84).[31] Yet when Papa-Nnukwu suggests that "I should not have let him follow those missionaries," his daughter, Ifeoma, corrects him, retorting: "It was not the missionaries. Did I not go to the missionary school, too?" (83). Although Papa-Nnukwu maintains that it was the missionaries that misled his son, the narrative itself is ambivalent about the impact and legacy of Christian mission. Not only is Aunty Ifeoma a very different product of missionary Christianity compared to her brother, but the progressive Father Amadi is a member of a missionary congregation himself. Clearly, *Purple Hibiscus*, through its presentation of a variety of characters and the different ways they negotiate the relationship between Christianity and Igbo culture and religion, avoids a one-sided representation of Christianity but narrates the possibility of Catholicism transitioning from a colonial to an inculturated religion. The novel does suggest, however, that this process has not yet been completed, as appears from the conversation about confirmation (the ritual of initiation into the church). Amaka fervently opposes the suggestion made by Father Amadi and her mother (whose mind, apparently, is not completely decolonized) that she must choose an English name to get confirmed, and in the end she decides not to get confirmed at all. In her words, "When the missionaries first came, they didn't think Igbo names were good enough. . . . What the church is saying is that only an English name will make your confirmation valid" (272). Here and at other points in the novel, Amaka is the most radical of all characters in the novel in critiquing the church's ongoing colonizing practices.

Where African women theologians have warned that inculturation runs the risk of indigenous and Christian patriarchies reinforcing each other,[32] *Purple Hibiscus*, in the character of Ifeoma, suggests that this is not necessarily the case. In Dube's words, Ifeoma's household presents a "decolonizing feminist space of liberation," even if this decolonization is partial and a work in progress, as it always is. It is in that space where Jaja and Kambili are exposed "to another view of parenting; another view of Catholicism, another view of African Indigenous belief system, another view of life."[33]

Somewhat surprisingly, however, Dube—probably reflecting a Protestant blind spot or the unease of feminist theologians with traditional Mariology—leaves unmentioned the figure of the Virgin Mary, which is central in the novel's decolonizing and feminist account of Catholicism.

From a Blond Mary to a "Political Virgin"

Since Catholicism and Pentecostalism have become fierce rivals in the Nigerian Christian landscape, one of the major issues of contestation is the status and role of Mary, with Pentecostals frequently accusing Catholics "of worshipping images and idolizing Mary."[34] Hence, Orobator asks how one should respond to "a Pentecostal Christian who is convinced that Catholics prefer Mary to Jesus."[35] *Purple Hibiscus* engages this debate and provides an answer to that question via Father Amadi, who says that Mary "is here, she is within us, leading us to her Son" (138). This answer corresponds with Orobator's suggestion that the role of Mary is to "point to Jesus, our mediator and savior."[36] These views reflect an attempt to acknowledge but at the same time restrict the centrality of Mary in the Catholic faith, by putting her in the shadow of Jesus Christ. However, in popular Catholic devotion Mary frequently takes center stage, as is also reflected in *Purple Hibiscus*. Marian devotion is prominently present in the novel, suggesting that it is an important part of Catholicism as a lived religion in Nigeria. Few critics have paid attention to this dimension of the narrative; only Cheryl Stobie and Brenda Cooper discuss it in some detail, focusing on the apparition of Mary narrated at the end of the novel.[37] However, references to Mary abound throughout the novel, illustrating Orobator's observation that "devotion to Mary has caught on like a bushfire in the harmattan across the Catholic landscape in Africa."[38] Yet this phenomenon has received notably little attention in the study of Catholicism in Africa.[39]

Who is the Mary centered in this religious devotion, and how is she part of the agenda of inculturation propagated by the novel? The devotional life of the Achike family is characterized by a culture of intense prayer, at least partly centering around Mary. For instance, Eugene's saying the grace before a meal involves a twenty-minute-long prayer, followed by a litany of "the Blessed Virgin in several different titles," to which the children are to respond by saying, "Pray for us" (11). The children's daily morning and evening prayer consist of the Rosary, including the Hail Mary. When the family goes on a journey by car, they pray the Rosary, too, with several decades of Hail Marys. While driving, they "all stayed silent and listened to the 'Ave Maria' on the cassette player" (31). Mama Beatrice is a prominent member of the parish women's prayer group called "Our Lady of the Miraculous Medal" (21). It is one of the "countless Marian devotional groups" that have emerged in Catholic parishes across Africa.[40] The name of this particular group refers to the apparition of Mary to the French nun Catherine Labouré in 1830, with Mary instructing her to make a medallion that would bring healing to those who wear it. The shrine in honor of this apparition, in Paris, has become an enormously popular site of pilgrimage, and the medal with a depiction of Mary has spread across the world and is said to have become "a model for later apparitions, such as those at Lourdes."[41] In Nigeria, this devotion is actively propagated by a specifically dedicated association and by a national shrine, run by the Congregation of the Mission (Vincentian Fathers), who have made the promotion of the Miraculous Medal a major part of their apostolate.[42] The popularity of the cult is no surprise, given the strong links between religion and healing in Nigerian and other African indigenous religious cultures, which have also defined the practice of Christianity on the continent.[43]

Mary, as depicted on the Miraculous Medal to which Mama Beatrice and her sisters in the prayer group are devoted, is white, illustrating the European origins of this Marian cult. *Purple Hibiscus* explicitly alludes to the whiteness of Mary at the beginning of the novel. Describing Mass at their parish church, Kambili depicts her father kneeling to receive Communion "at the marble altar, with the blond life-size Virgin Mary mounted nearby" (4). This statue illustrates the reverence of whiteness that was typical for St. Agnes. Eugene's act of kneeling for it symbolizes his devotion to a white, colonial Christianity. Even his self-invented Marian title, "Our Lady, Shield of the Nigerian People," reflects not so much an attempt to contextualize Mary in Nigerian society and culture but the belief that Nigeria's problems can only be solved through intervention by a white, European, colonial symbol of spiritual power (11). Eugene tells his children that if only people would pray to Mary using that title on a daily basis, "Nigeria would not totter like a Big Man with the spindly legs of a child" (11). Yet more favorably, when Eugene, after the arrest and subsequent release of his newspaper editor, calls upon Our Lady, Shield of the Nigerian People, in a prayer asking God "to bring about the downfall of the Godless men ruling our country," it appears that even the white Virgin Mary can allow for a political critique of authoritarianism and repression, being invoked in support of freedom and human rights (43).

Because of this normative image of a white, colonial Mary, Kambili is surprised, if not shocked, when Aunty Ifeoma beseeches the Blessed Virgin to pray for Papa-Nnukwu, who has fallen ill. "How can Our Lady intercede on behalf of a heathen?," she utters in disbelief (166). As much as Our Lady of the Miraculous Medal may be associated with healing power, in Kambili's religious universe, which has been defined by her father, those powers cannot extend to "pagans" such as her grandfather. This view is certainly not unique, as participants in Marian devotion in other parts of Africa, too, have been observed drawing a close connection between healing and redemption, with "the faith of the patient in God [being] generally given as the most important factor in the healing process."[44] If Kambili's father ever prayed for Papa-Nnukwu, it was for him "to be saved from hell" (61). In other words, Eugene considered eternal redemption far more important than physical healing. Yet Ifeoma was not concerned with her father's conversion, and she tells her brother "to stop doing God's job" and to "let God do the judging" (95–96). She also teaches Kambili that "sometimes what was different was just as good as what was familiar" and that "when Papa-Nnukwu did his itu-nzu, his declaration of innocence, in the morning, it was the same as our saying the rosary" (166). Ifeoma appears to have an inclusive understanding of God's grace and therefore also of the intercessory and healing power of Mary. When Papa-Nnukwu recovers, she sees it as a miracle, proving that "Our Lady is faithful" (166).

Clearly, Ifeoma's practice of Catholicism also centers on Mary, and so does the everyday religious life of her family. When her car fails to start because it has run out of fuel, she sighs, "Blessed Mother, please not now" (132). Ifeoma and her family are excited to go on a pilgrimage to a Marian apparition site in Aokpe (see below). When she first proposes to Eugene that his children come to stay with her family, so they can join for the pilgrimage, his response is reluctant, pointing out that the authenticity of the apparitions of Mary in Aokpe have not yet been verified by the Church. To this Ifeoma replies: "You know we will all be dead before the church officially speaks about Aokpe. . . . Even if the church says it is not authentic, what matters is why we go, and it is from faith" (99). Although Eugene is pleased by his sister's comment about being motivated by faith, he hides behind the authority of the Church and only agrees for his children to join their aunt after Father Benedict has given permission. The latter only does so reluctantly, on the condition that "you must make it clear that what is happening there has not been verified by the church" (107). Ifeoma, on the other hand, embodies a form of popular Catholicism that is not too bothered about official Church recognition.⁴⁵

Being familiar with the blond Mary at their home parish church, at Aunty Ifeoma's house Kambili is first confronted with the possibility of a Black Mary when faced with a painting made by her cousin, Amaka: "The watercolor painting of a woman with a child was much like a copy of the Virgin and Child oil painting that hung in Papa's bedroom, except the woman and child in Amaka's painting were dark-skinned" (118). Amaka, who is her age-mate, lives in a very different universe than the shy introvert Kambili; Amaka speaks with confidence, wears makeup, and listens to local musicians because of their cultural and political consciousness. Discussing the Marian apparition in Aokpe with the young priest, Father Amadi, who is a family friend and a popular university chaplain, Amaka rebuffs his suggestion that people are "making this whole apparition thing up." She argues that "it's about time Our Lady came to Africa. Don't you wonder how come she always appears in Europe? She was from the Middle East, after all" (137–38). The statement elicits from her brother, Obiora, the question whether Mary has become a "Political Virgin," and the whole discussion leaves Kambili baffled.

Unlike Adichie, Orobator does not explicitly problematize the question of Mary's skin color. Yet he does raise it implicitly, in a way that is reminiscent of Amaka's urge for Mary to appear in Africa. Presenting an "imaginative reconstruction of the Annunciation," Orobator rewrites the story from the Gospel of Luke, in which God's angel appears to Mary to tell her that she will give birth to Jesus. Inspired by the feminist theological criticism of traditions in which Mary is seen as "the domesticated and docile servant of the church," Orobator's reconstruction of the story is driven by the quest to reimagine her instead "as the icon of the dignity of women and an inspiration for resisting oppressive societal, religious, and ecclesial structures and attitudes founded on a warped image of the Blessed Virgin Mary," particularly in Africa. Hence, in his creative retelling of the annunciation, Mary is a young African woman who actually responds to the angel, raising critical issues with him about the status of women in Africa and about the socioeconomic and political challenges facing African societies. He further invokes African indigenous notions of the queen mother—the woman who gave birth to the king and as such should be respected and honored—to propose that "from the perspective of our African tradition it would be quite fitting to accord Mary all the honor and glory as the queen mother of God." While this notion of the queen mother may put Mary on a pedestal, distanced from ordinary women, Orobator also suggests that women in Africa can easily identify with Mary as "Our Lady of Sorrows," because "we are surrounded by so many examples of Our Lady of Sorrows in Africa. Not just any kind of sorrows but sorrows that are associated with womanhood and motherhood."[46] The latter suggestion echoes writings of other African theologians who have suggested that the figure of Mary can support the quest for women's empowerment in the light of concrete experiences of disease, poverty, and suffering.[47] Thus, where traditional images often associate the Virgin Mary with virtues such as meekness, humility, and purity, these progressive and pro-feminist contextual theological interpretations reclaim her as modeling "a spirituality of resistance" that, according to Oduyoye, inspires African women to "express themselves counterculturally over what demeans their humanity."[48]

The climax of the theme of Marian devotion in *Purple Hibiscus* comes at the end of the novel, when Aunty Ifeoma takes Amaka and Kambili, with Father Amadi, on a pilgrimage to Aokpe, the village that had turned into a popular shrine after "a local girl started to see the vision of the Beautiful Woman" (274). This part of Adichie's story captures an actual phenomenon: Aokpe, in Benue state, southeast Nigeria, has become an international center of pilgrimage after a series of visitations of Mary to a girl from the village, Christiana Agbo, starting in 1992 when she was twelve years old and said to have concluded in 2004.[49] Mary is believed to have appeared as "a beautiful Lady," making herself known under the title "Mediatrix of All Graces,"[50] which is one of the commonly used (albeit contested) Marian titles in the Catholic tradition.[51] A dedicated chapel was established on the site and was officially consecrated by the bishop of Otukpo, Michael Apochi, in 2019, which has been interpreted as illustrating the Church's effort at the "domestication of the miracle."[52] But in the mid-1990s, soon after the first apparition, the site had already begun to attract a large number of people, and it has continued to do so ever since.

Purple Hibiscus captures the early popularity of the shrine and the excitement of the faithful about the apparitions, despite the lack of formal Church approval. Kambili narrates her impressions as follows: "Hundreds of cars.... Women crashed to their knees. Men shouted prayers. Rosaries rustled. People pointed and shouted, 'See, there, on the tree, that's Our Lady!' Others pointed at the glowing sun. 'There she is!'" (274). The chaos on the site contrasts with the appearance of the girl at the heart of the apparition story, who is described as "slight and solemn, dressed in white" (274). While the girl passes through the crowd, trees start to quiver, flowers rain down from their branches, and the sun turns white. The event is narrated in the imagery of biblical revelation scenes, where the natural elements support and mediate the manifestation of the spiritual, and it culminates in Kambili receiving her own vision: "And then I saw her, the Blessed Virgin: an image in the pale sun, a red glow on the back of my hand, a smile on the face of the rosary-bedecked man whose arm rubbed against mine. She was everywhere" (274–75). As the Nigerian theologian Stan Chu Ilo has pointed out, both biblical and African indigenous traditions "appeal to the natural world as sites for divine encounter and channels for the miraculous and sublime."[53] Adichie draws on both these traditions to narrate the miraculous appearance of the Virgin Mary in the Nigerian landscape.

Moving beyond whether Mary is white or Black, European or African, this apparition narrative imagines Mary not as embodied but as omnipresent and multicolored—she is simultaneously visible in the pale sun, in a red glow, and in the smile on the face of a bystander. The catalyst for Kambili's vision is the young local girl—seemingly referring to the aforementioned Agbo—who is Black but dressed in white. Stobie comments that the girl "acts as a visual replacement of the earlier reference to the statue of 'the blond life-size Virgin Mary' in Kambili's home church, where whiteness was revered."[54] Yet such an interpretation conflates the girl with Mary, while in the story, the girl triggers Kambili's vision of Mary but does not form the vision itself. The more obvious visual replacement of the blond Mary statue in the novel is Amaka's painting of the dark-skinned Virgin and Child. Regardless, the narrative of the apparition of Mary to Kambili does deliver on Amaka's earlier suggestion that "it's about time Our Lady came to Africa" (137). As VanZanten puts it, the apparition scene "places the Virgin Mary as decisively in the African world as in the European world of Lourdes or Fátima. This Mary is not the blue-eyed blond of St. Agnes but instead is associated with the African landscape and people."[55] Moreover, the narrative suggestion that Mary is omnipresent—literally "everywhere"—can be seen as a criticism of attempts to restrict her to the confines of the Church and its institutional authority and sacramentality.

To what extent is the Mary who appears to Kambili a "Political Virgin"? Later in the novel, when Aunty Ifeoma and her children have migrated to the United States, Amaka writes to Kambili about coverage of the Aokpe apparitions in an American magazine: "The writer had sounded pessimistic that the Blessed Virgin Mary could be appearing at all, especially in Nigeria: all that corruption and all that heat" (300). The suggestion here is that Mary appearing in Nigeria is politically significant indeed, as it counters racist and colonialist stereotypes that continue to represent the African continent as "the heart of darkness," to use the infamous title of Joseph Conrad's novel published at the turn of the twentieth century. As such, *Purple Hibiscus* seeks to affirm African identity and pride, reclaiming Africa as a continent where divine revelation and spiritual enlightenment can and do happen. The positive framing of this part of the narrative also rejects any Eurocentric interpretation of the apparition as an example of "African superstition."

Within the Catholic Church, the official recognition of Marian apparitions is a complex process. According to the religious studies scholar Gerrie ter Haar, "It seems almost impossible for an African miracle to conform to the required standards," because these standards are based on Western logic and because the Church hierarchy tends to be suspicious of miraculous events happening in non-Western, and maybe specifically African, cultures.[56] *Purple Hibiscus* subtly addresses these power relations within the Church by narrating the tangible reluctance of the British missionary priest Father Benedict to acknowledge the apparition in Aokpe. Yet the novel also alludes to ways these power relations are changing, such as in the storyline about Father Amadi, who, at the end of the novel, leaves for Germany, soliciting Obiora's sarcastic comment: "From darkest Africa now come missionaries who will reconvert the West" (279).[57]

Most importantly, the story of Kambili receiving the vision of Mary, in an outdoor setting not controlled by the Church, and mediated through the natural elements, affirms female religious agency outside the contours of patriarchy and church authority. This is further confirmed by the fact that it is neither Kambili's father nor a priest—Father Amadi, who joined them on the pilgrimage—who validates Kambili's experience but Aunty Ifeoma, by saying: "Kambili is right.... Something from God was happening there" (275). As mentioned earlier, Orobator has proposed a view in which Mary serves as an icon of women's dignity and an inspiration for resisting patriarchy and other forms of oppression. *Purple Hibiscus* can be read as a narrative illustration of this view. The novel being a bildungsroman with a feminist orientation, the Marian apparition is a decisive event in the narrative transition of Kambili from a docile young girl who is obedient to her tyrannical father to her reaching maturity, supporting her widowed mother and her imprisoned brother, and even changing churches, leaving St. Agnes, with its blond Mary statue and the memories to her father, for another parish. Kambili's encounter with Mary instills a "spirituality of resistance," which, according to Oduyoye, is typical of African Christian women claiming their full humanity in the footsteps of Mary.[58]

According to Orobator, "The most important condition [for inculturation] is freedom."⁵⁹ The vision of Mary can be seen as putting Kambili in a space of freedom, as she comes to embrace her faith not in contrast to but as part of her Igbo and African identity. However, that transition to maturity and freedom comes out of another tragic incident. The chapter following the account of the apparition talks about the end of Eugene or, in Stobie's words, the "dethroning [of] the infallible father."⁶⁰ While Kambili and Jaja were staying at their aunt's in Nsukka, and the Virgin Mary appeared to Kambili, their mother, Beatrice, decided that the patriarchal tyranny of her husband over her and her family had reached its zenith. The battered wife saw no other solution but to poison her husband, and by the time Kambili and Jaja returned home, their seemingly immortal father had died. An autopsy brings the cause of death to light, and when police arrive at their house, Jaja admits guilt in his mother's place and ends up in jail.

In line with Orobator's suggestion that Mary can best be imagined as "Our Lady of Sorrows," because women in Africa carry so many burdens, *Purple Hibiscus* specifically highlights the burden of domestic violence and patriarchal oppression. Although Beatrice is a member of "Our Lady of the Miraculous Medal," she does not seem to receive any healing through her desperate act of mariticide. The novel's concluding chapter depicts her as a woman racked by guilt, having turned into "a painfully bony body, of skin speckled with blackheads the size of watermelon seeds" (296). The sorrows associated with womanhood and motherhood have become too much for her, although there still is hope, because the novel concludes with the image of Kambili embracing her mother, who then "leans towards me and smiles" (307).

Redemptive Masculinity

The discussion of gender has so far focused on female identity and agency in the novel. Yet it is worth attending to the complementary theme of masculinity. As far as critics have paid attention to masculinity in the novel, they have mostly focused on the character of Eugene as an embodiment of Nigerian "Big Man" masculinity. Some attention has been given, too, to the character of Father Amadi, with his role as a liberating force in Kambili's awakening being acknowledged, while the ambivalent and potentially troubling aspects of the blossoming relationship between them—with Kambili clearly developing feelings for the young priest, which the latter encourages by saying, "Do you love Jesus? . . . Then show me. Try and catch me, show me you love Jesus" (176)—have also been problematized. As Cynthia Wallace puts it, "In light of the recent history of sex abuse scandals, as well, Father Amadi's attentions, at the very least, highlight the risky nature of a close relationship between a young priest and a young woman in need of sexual healing, however redemptive that relationship may be."[61]

Yet the often overlooked character of Jaja is at least as important. He can be seen as modeling what in scholarship about African masculinities has been called "redemptive masculinity," a term coined by Ezra Chitando and Sophie Chirongoma to "characterize and identify masculinities that are life-giving in a world reeling from the effects of violence and the AIDS pandemic."[62] Perhaps Jaja is modeled after Adichie's own brother, about whom she writes: "The best feminist I know is my brother Kene, who is also a kind, good-looking and very masculine young man. My own definition of a feminist is a man or a woman who says, 'Yes, there's a problem with gender as it is today and we must fix it, we must do better.'"[63]

The ending of the novel, with Jaja sacrificing his freedom and taking his mother's place after she murders her violent husband, puts into perspective the Palm Sunday structure of the novel, alluded to earlier in this chapter. Palm Sunday refers to the biblical narrative of Jesus entering Jerusalem and being hailed as the new king of David, days before he is put to death—a death that Christians believe to be self-sacrificial—so the apparent suggestion is that Jaja is a Jesus-like figure. Dube, in particular, has developed this suggestion in her postcolonial theological reading of *Purple Hibiscus*, building on the notion that Jesus's entry into Jerusalem was a "subversive political act" against the Roman Empire and the religious leaders who collaborated with it. Applying this to the novel, she writes: "Jaja was thus making a triumphant entry as a subject that challenges oppression as represented by Papa Eugene and his accommodating church leaders, who pretended they did not see his violence upon his family, given the massive material support he gave to the church and its institutions."[64]

Indeed, Jaja's courage to stand up to his father is narrated in the opening pages of the novel, which tell of Jaja's refusal to receive Communion during Mass, his reasons being that "the wafer gives me bad breath" and "the priest keeps touching my mouth and it nauseates me." Upon his father's correction that the host shared during Communion is not, blasphemously, a "wafer" but "the body of our Lord," and that one cannot stop receiving it without risking death, Jaja's resolute answer is: "Then I will die" (6). This is the moment that things start falling apart in the Achike household, as Eugene's patriarchal authority is no longer uncontested. Throughout the novel, Kambili observes how her brother gradually becomes more resistant to the tyranny with which Eugene controls his family. During their stay in Nsukka, he adjusts much more easily than Kambili. The latter sees her brother's shoulders broaden within a week, symbolizing his transformation. Once back home, Jaja seeks to protect his sister and mother from Eugene's aggression. At the end of the novel, when he is in jail, he feels guilty for not having done enough, yet Kambili refers to him as "my hero, the brother who always tried to protect me the best he could" (305).

The Palm Sunday theme that presents Jaja as a Jesus figure, bringing liberation through sacrifice, is also reflected in the title of the novel. Hibiscus flowers, such as the ones in the garden of the Achike family, are usually red. Red, in this novel, is the liturgical color of Pentecost—the festival of the Holy Spirit—but also the color of blood, such as when Kambili and Jaja find blood stains on the floor, after their mother has been beaten by her husband and has had another miscarriage. Aunty Ifeoma, however, has a rare type of hibiscus, with purple flowers. Purple is the liturgical color of Lent, the season before Easter, symbolizing introspection and anticipation; the purple hibiscus flowers are "fragrant with the undertones of freedom . . . , a freedom to be, to do" (16). When Jaja visits Aunty Ifeoma, he is fascinated by the purple hibiscus; he helps water them and takes some stalks back home where he plants them in their garden. They bloom the day before Palm Sunday, when Jaja stands up to his father by refusing to receive Communion—a refusal that is the beginning of the journey to freedom.

In addition to the Palm Sunday theme that presents Jaja as a Jesus figure, the novel brings in yet another complementary messianic perspective. Aunty Ifeoma suggests that his name refers to Jaja of Opobo, the king of the Opobo people who resisted the British colonizers and subsequently ended up in exile. The story of this king demonstrates that "being defiant can be a good thing sometimes"—a lesson that Jaja takes on board (144). Thus, *Purple Hibiscus* frames Jaja's standing up to his father in a twofold way, invoking both an indigenous historical and a biblical Christian narrative of opposition against oppression and tyranny in the forms of patriarchy, colonialism, and Christian supremacy. Accordingly, Jaja's character is crafted as a redemptive masculinity, including the "spiritual dimension" that this concept deliberately evokes.[65] Carefully contrasted to his anti–role model father, Jaja is narratively constructed not only as the antonym of Eugene's toxic masculinity but also as the redeemer of its victims. He stands up against the toxic masculinity embodied by his father, and he seeks to protect his mother and sister against the violent impact that religiously, culturally, and socially condoned patriarchy has on their bodies.

Yet Jaja's character can also be seen as illustrating a potentially problematic aspect of redemptive masculinity—that it easily reinforces a notion of male saviors.[66] As protective and redemptive as Jaja's masculinity might be, it does curtail and negate female agency, especially that of his mother and sister. If *Purple Hibiscus* is about "dethroning the infallible father," as Stobie has it, the narrative depiction of Jaja as a messianic, Jesus-like figure suggests that this dethroning is not so much a feminist act as a form of patricide. Although it is Beatrice who poisons her husband, the responsibility for this act is taken by Jaja. In a sense, Beatrice's most decisive, albeit tragic, act of agency is taken away from her immediately. And if the novel is a bildungsroman about the young Kambili growing toward maturity, it is notable that her agency is not only violated by her father but also overshadowed by her protective brother and his act of sacrifice. Kambili, in the final pages of the novel, is featured as paying respect to both these men in her life: to her father, by offering weekly Mass even after his death, and to her brother, by paying him regular visits in prison.

In the light of this, one might ask to what extent the novel can be considered a feminist text. One possible response is that the development of Jaja's character as a young man protective of his battered mother and sister is narratively linked to the influence that Aunty Ifeoma has on him. It is in her home that Jaja's shoulders start broadening, as an indication of his growth toward maturity and of his awakening sense of redemptive masculinity. If Ijeoma's house is a "decolonizing feminist space of liberation," as Dube argues, its effect on Jaja appears to be more immediate and profound than on his sister. Perhaps the takeaway is that raising a new generation of caring, protective, and responsible young men is, indeed, a feminist concern.

Through the character of Jaja, *Purple Hibiscus* demonstrates the tendency in "reformist feminism," in the words of the literary scholar Gloria Ada Fwangyil, to use "positive male characters to challenge men with oppressive tendencies towards women to change and regard women as complementary partners in progress."[67] In doing so, the novel demonstrates how religious and cultural resources can be mobilized and drawn upon to reimagine and transform masculinity in Nigerian and broader African contexts. However, the novel also reveals the limitations of this reformist approach, as it alludes to the risk of female agency being restricted and overshadowed by the agency of the male redeemer who intervenes on behalf of, and out of concern for, the women he seeks to protect.

Conclusion

Purple Hibiscus is an important novel for the project in this book, of reading Nigerian Christianities. Published in the early 2000s, *Purple Hibiscus* is one of the first major twenty-first-century novels exemplifying the renewed interest in, and transformed engagement with, Christianity by a new generation of Nigerian and African writers. The novel is also important for its narrative insight into Catholicism as a lived religion in a contemporary Nigerian context. Scholarship on Christianity in Africa in general, and in Nigeria in particular, in recent years has overwhelmingly focused on Pentecostal-Charismatic movements, creating the impression that these are the only forms of Christianity that are vibrant and growing. Yet in the period from 1980 to 2012, the Catholic population on the African continent reportedly grew by a staggering 238 percent, and as mentioned earlier, in Nigeria alone the estimated number of Catholics in 2020 ranged between twenty-five and thirty-two million.[68] The novel narrates the transition that Catholicism has made in Nigeria and on the continent more generally—from an originally European missionary religion that in several respects was hostile to indigenous cultures and religions to a faith that has become rooted in local contexts and has gone through a process of inculturation to engage with, and adapt to, local contexts. At the same time, the novel suggests that this process has not been completed and that the question of the relationship between Christianity and indigenous traditions remains a pertinent one. Moreover, its references to the mushrooming Pentecostal churches allude to one of the major challenges that Catholicism faces in contemporary Nigeria: a highly competitive religious market, with Pentecostal churches finding particular appeal among the youth. One recent response of the Church has been to allow for a Pentecostalization of Catholicism itself—for instance, incorporating elements of Charismatic worship.[69] Yet *Purple Hibiscus* reflects a strategy of "Africanization," rather than of Pentecostalization, in line with the program of inculturation that was embraced by the Church hierarchy in the late twentieth century and that remains influential to date, such as among progressive theologians like Orobator.

The novel is particularly original in its contribution to inculturating the Virgin Mary, as it contextualizes Marian devotion and presents a creative narrative reimagining of Mary in the Nigerian landscape. Its account of a Marian apparition also highlights that Catholicism in the Nigerian context is an embodied and experiential spirituality, allowing for "extraordinary" religious experiences. The allusion to Mary as a "Political Virgin" demonstrates

Adichie's awareness of the different theological and political possibilities in Catholicism, even if these are not explored fully. With regard to gender politics, too, the novel plays with different possibilities. It obviously critiques a form of religion that is both colonial and patriarchal, yet it is somewhat ambivalent about the alternative it puts forward. The novel foregrounds female agency but simultaneously allows it to be overshadowed by a narrative of redemptive masculinity. Perhaps this is inherent to the Marian theme running through the novel and deployed for its pro-feminist purposes: As much as Mary, in biblical and Christian traditions, does have agency, she remains in the shadow of her son, Jesus Christ. Stobie has well captured the novel's ambiguous gender politics when she writes: "Adichie's stance is not a radical one, but is far-reaching nonetheless, as she focuses on an end point of goodness and justice, but shows that employing the means of absolutism in the pursuit of these ends is profoundly destructive."[70] The significance of Adichie's *Purple Hibiscus* with regard to the representation of Catholic Christianity in the Nigerian context is exactly in its narrative problematization of Catholicism's shadowed pasts and ongoing legacies, and in its opening up of different possibilities while pointing in a direction that is ethically and spiritually transformative.

Chapter 4

PROPHECY

Christianity, Environmental Degradation, and Ecology

In recent decades, environmental concerns have become increasingly prominent in the discourses of both African literature and African religions. In the Nigerian context, the interest in environmental and ecological issues has been sparked in particular by the recent history of environmental degradation resulting from oil extraction in the Niger Delta since the 1950s. Subsequently, this region has become "an important site from which to consider the effects of globalization and resource extraction in Africa" and, as such, has also produced a significant body of Niger Delta literature.[1] The most notable figure here is Ken Saro-Wiwa, who has been declared "a prophet, a Moses to his people."[2] The legendary poet-cum-activist was murdered in 1995 by the Nigerian military regime because of his quest for justice for his community, the Ogoni people, whose natural lifeworld has been greatly degraded due to oil pollution. In his writing, Saro-Wiwa intimately and indeed prophetically captured "the call of the ravaged land" and "the piteous wail of sludged streams," as he drew attention to decaying crops and diminishing fish stock due to what he called "th'ecological war."[3] Capturing the fluid boundaries between literary and religious writing, Agbonkhianmeghe Orobator—a Nigerian theologian himself—aptly writes that "Saro-Wiwa was no theologian. But his vision of a nation that treats its weakest and most vulnerable members with justice and equity squares well with the theologians' vision of the Kingdom of God."[4]

Standing on Saro-Wiwa's shoulders, many contemporary Nigerian writers address environmental concerns and engage the quest for ecological justice. This interest has been reinforced in the light of the environmental effects of climate change and global warming on Nigerian landscapes and communities. Thus, as much as it has been argued that "Nigerian literature is famously rich in evocations of environment, both physical and non-physical," the engagement of literary writers with environmental issues has intensified in recent decades and in some cases has been driven by explicitly eco-activist agendas.[5] In doing so, these writers also frequently engage with the spiritual and religious dimensions of the ecology of the Niger Delta and of its communities facing the consequences of environmental degradation.[6] Likewise, Nigerian theologians and scholars of religion have started to engage with environmental issues and articulate proposals for ecotheology and ecospirituality as a "prophetic voice crying for the protection and preservation of the life of human beings, their environment and the entire cosmos."[7]

In the above paragraph I invoke the word "prophetic" in relation to modes of writing—be they creative or scholarly—that combine sociopolitical and religious critique in relation to environmental issues with a constructive and at times activist edge toward sociopolitical and religious transformation motivated by a quest for environmental justice. In African-initiated and Pentecostal-Charismatic churches, the prophetic is central, too, but in a different sense. Here, it refers to visionary experiences and revelatory messages through which the word of God is applied to concrete situations in the present and the future.[8] Many Nigerian Pentecostal pastors have published books with prophetic messages addressing issues affecting the nation, although a cursory review suggests that environmental concerns are not central here. By centering the word "prophecy" in the title of the present chapter and acknowledging its loose twofold meaning, I deliberately use a term that is common in popular Nigerian Christian discursive and ritual registers but that also resonates with the Nigerian literary engagement with environmental issues. Thus, without claiming analytical precision, "prophecy" as a heuristic device allows me to explore the ways ecology and Christianity intersect in the literary texts under discussion. The choice of the term prophecy is directly motivated by the novel that is the main focus of this chapter, Chigozie Obioma's *The Fishermen*, which centers around a prophecy that turns out to be a curse. Reading *The Fishermen* as an ecological novel, I argue that by adopting a river as a central character, Obioma problematizes the desacralization of the natural environment due to Christianization and colonial modernity yet also alludes to the possibility of resacralizing the environment within an indigenized Nigerian Christianity. Before attending to *The Fishermen*, however, I will focus first on Nnedi Okorafor's novel *Lagoon*, which offers a more straightforward ecological critique of Christianity, especially in its contemporary Pentecostal form.

Lagoon's Ecological Critique of Christianity

In her 2014 novel *Lagoon*, Okorafor presents a fantastical story about aliens arriving in Lagos—sent by some higher power?—to warn against ecological disaster and prevent mass extinction. The prologue is about a swordfish, angry about the "black ooze that left poison rainbows on the water's surface," attacking an oil pipeline in order to restore the "lost paradise" of clear waters, colorful coral reefs, and rich sea life (3, 5). Thus associated with the genre of petrofiction, the novel contains a commentary on the negative environmental, economic, and social effects of Nigeria's oil industry.[9] For instance, when Ayodele, the alien's ambassador, delivers a message to the people of Lagos, she says: "We come to bring you together and refuel your future. . . . Your land is full of a fuel that is tearing you apart" (113). Okorafor has described her work with the terms "Africanfuturist" and "Africanjujuist," meaning that her writing is "rooted in African culture, history, mythology and point-of-view" and "respectfully acknowledges the seamless blend of true existing African spiritualities and cosmologies with the imaginative."[10] Thus the storyline about aliens "from beyond earth" merges with references to spiritual entities from West African traditions, such as the water goddess Mami Wata and the storytelling spider artist Udide Okwanka (111). Lagos, as well as the ocean waters in which its lagoon is located, are narratively depicted as inhabited by a variety of living beings who together embody "agitated ecologies," as they suffer from the impacts of the capitalist exploitation of the earth and its resources.[11] Yet it is recognized that spirits are still alive "deep in the polluted soil" of the city (226). The variety of living beings featured in the novel automatically decenters humans as only one among many species, as if *Lagoon* alludes to the end of the Anthropocene.

Ayodele has picked three human protagonists—a marine biologist, a rap musician, and a soldier—to support her mission to deliver a message to the people of Lagos and to meet with the president of Nigeria in an attempt to avert further catastrophe. A main role is given to Adaora, the marine biologist who is the first to meet Ayodele on one of Lagos's beaches and offers to let Ayodele stay at her house. Adaora, at that time, has just fallen out with her husband Chris, who, after his born-again conversion, has become a zealous Christian and a jealous, paranoid husband. When she returns to the house with Ayodele, Chris accuses her of witchcraft and believes she has brought along a "marine witch" (31). Swearing to Jesus Christ that his wife and her visitor should be sent back to hell, Chris calls upon his pastor, Father Oke, to intervene. This leads to an escalating confrontation between the Pentecostal pastor and the shape-shifting alien, as the former mobilizes his flock to capture the latter in what is referred to as a "crusade" (152).

Depicted unsympathetically as a smooth-talking, money-hungry, gay-bashing, and woman-slapping pastor, immaculately dressed and driving a shiny Mercedes, Father Oke represents the consumer-materialist and morally corrupt religious culture with which Nigerian Pentecostalism is frequently associated in recent literary texts as well as in popular tales.[12] As much as Father Oke preaches a message of spiritual change, he is unwilling or unable to recognize Ayodele as a prophetic messenger from outer space calling for much-needed ecological change. In a way, Father Oke is represented as an anti-prophet, defending the status quo of what has been described as "Pentecostal-capitalism."[13] Through his character, Okorafor critiques popular Nigerian Christianity for its investment in a capitalist-consumerist and environmentally exploitative system and for blocking the real change needed to save the earth. This critique echoes the arguments of theological scholars that African Pentecostalism in general, and especially the neo-Pentecostal prosperity gospel, "tends to focus more on the individual quest for welfare much to the neglect of societal needs and the care of the earth," although some of these theologians have also drawn attention to the potential within this religious tradition for "a radical neo-Pentecostal environmentalism."[14]

It has been argued that *Lagoon*, as an Africanfuturistic novel, creates "a space where Africa becomes a site for imagining new environmental futures, no longer at the periphery of geopolitics, but at a critical point for enacting change and contributing to real dialogue around environmental justice."[15] Clearly, Okorafor acknowledges the significant contribution that indigenous religions and their embedded spiritual ecologies can make to the imagining of such environmental futures. Yet she does not leave any room for Christianity to contribute to such an imagination and for enacting the change toward environmental justice. In fact, part of her issue with

Christianity is its antithetical rejection of indigenous traditions, encouraging Nigerians to develop a "nasty form of hatred of one's self," specifically their spiritual heritage.[16] At the end of *Lagoon*, the Pentecostal pastor, as the main Christian character, literally disappears with a Mami Wata–type figure, and the reader is told that "no one ever saw Father Oke again" (235). Thus, the novel leaves us wondering: Does the environmental future of Nigeria depend on the disappearance of Christianity? Or can the quest for environmental justice also be imagined and engaged from within Christian traditions?

The Ecology of Christianity in *The Fishermen*

The Fishermen, Obioma's debut, received wide acclaim, as indicated, for instance, by its being shortlisted for the Man Booker Prize in the year of its publication, 2015. Born in 1986 in an Igbo family living in the Yoruba-speaking town of Akure, in Ondo state, southwestern Nigeria, Obioma wove some autobiographical elements into the novel, while also drawing creatively on both Igbo and Yoruba sociocultural and religious lifeworlds. The story is set in his hometown and focuses on a middle-class family of Igbo descent with six children. According to Obioma, "The family lives here, in a house like the one I grew up in, and fishes at a nearby river, like the one I myself once fished!"[17] The fourth son in the Agwu family, Benjamin (Ben), is the protagonist and is nine years old at the time that the novel is set, in 1996 and early 1997, meaning that he is of a similar age as the author. The story is told in retrospect, through the voice of an adult Ben who is looking back on the days of his childhood. It makes the novel read as a fictional memoir as much as a bildungsroman, as it narrates Ben's moral and psychological development from an innocent child to a young adult who was convicted of murder.

Obioma has acknowledged that *The Fishermen* was inspired by his own upbringing in a family of twelve children. In an interview, he has recounted how two of his older brothers had a strong rivalry when they were young yet later came to grow closer; this memory made him consider: "What was the worst that could have happened at that time" if their rivalry had continued?[18] Thus, *The Fishermen* focuses on the four eldest sons of the Agwu family—Ikenna, Boja, Obembe, and Benjamin—and narrates how their initially close relationship unravels and ends in tragedy because of a prophecy by the town's madman, Abulu, that Ikenna "shall die by the hands of a fisherman" (108). At the initiative of Ikenna, the four brothers had been going fishing for weeks, despite the river being a forbidden place, and as the eldest brother, he had also initiated his younger siblings, telling them: "Follow us, and we will make you fishermen" (22). Thus, the words of Abulu, uttered near the river, are taken by Ikenna as "a vision that one of you will kill me" (108). The prophecy turns out to be a self-fulfilling one, as Ikenna internalizes it and is paralyzed by fear, which robs him of "his peace, his well-being, his relationships, his health, and even his faith" (128). Alienating himself from his brothers, his erratic behavior drives his immediate sibling, Boja, to despair, to the point where the latter indeed kills Ikenna and then commits suicide, after which Obembe and Benjamin set out to take revenge on Abulu.

Obioma has explained that he intended the novel to be a commentary on the sociopolitical situation of Nigeria, with the four brothers symbolizing the country's "major tribes with nothing in common," forced to live together and form "a nation" because of an "insane idea created by a madman," the British colonizers.[19] Most literary critics have subsequently read the novel as an allegory of Nigeria as "a dwindling nation," narrating the country's "coming of age," and portraying the "expectations and disappointments" of the Nigerian populace in the 1990s.[20] Indeed, there is much in the novel that inspires such readings: Throughout the narrative are references to the political turmoil and economic upheaval that defined the last decade of the twentieth century in the country, especially in the aftermath of the 1993 democratic elections, the results of which were annulled by the military dictatorship of President Ibrahim Babangida, eventually resulting in another military ruler, Sani Abacha, coming into power.

However, for the purpose of this chapter I am more interested in a dimension of *The Fishermen* that has received far less attention, which is the novel's ecological thrust. The literary scholar Kate Harlin has drawn attention to this aspect in what she describes as her "petrocultural reading" of the novel, yet my ecological reading is less concerned with petroculture because, as Harlin admits herself, the novel's engagement with oil is not particularly obvious and is at best indirect.[21] Although Ondo state, of which Akure is the capital, produces oil and falls under the Niger Delta Development Commission, *The Fishermen* does not engage typical themes of the Niger Delta novel, such as oil pollution, resistance against oil exploitation, and the battle for control of oil revenues. Nevertheless, I consider it an ecological novel, and I will demonstrate this by foregrounding the much more direct environmental aspect of the plot, which centers around the river, Omi-Ala. In doing so, I acknowledge Obioma's own suggestion that this river can be read as a character, while drawing theoretically on the notion that, in African environmental literature, nonhuman elements in the ecosystem, such as rivers, hold agency.[22]

To begin, I will examine the representation of, and engagement with, Christianity in the novel, which will lead into a reading of the novel through the lens of "ecology of religion" as developed by the religious studies scholar Jacob Olupona to understand the "intricate relationship between ritual and environment in African cosmology and religion."[23] Building on that, I will focus in more depth on the river, discussing what it does as a character in the novel and how it relates to the complex ecological and religious worldview espoused in *The Fishermen*. My argument is that as much as the river witnesses the prophecy of Abulu unfold and turn into tragedy, the river itself is also a prophetic presence in the novel through which Obioma underlines the importance of a notion of the natural environment as sacred. This notion may critique Western-influenced forms of Christianity that have desacralized the environment, but it is certainly not incompatible with Christianity, as Obioma illustrates with reference to the indigenous Celestial Church.

Narratives of Christianity

The Fishermen loosely draws on biblical narratives to develop its plot. The title is a direct reference to the story in the Gospels about Jesus calling his disciples from among some fishermen and telling them that he will make them fishers of men.[24] Like Jesus in the Gospel stories, in the novel Father redefines the purpose of fishing, advising his sons, after their illicit fishing endeavors have been discovered, that they rather should be "fishers of good dreams" and "fishermen of the mind" (51). Another obvious biblical narrative drawn upon is the mythical tale about the first fratricide, narrated in the book of Genesis and alluded to directly in the novel with the mention of "the Cain and Abel syndrome" (201).[25] Later in this chapter, I will also identify ways *The Fishermen* can be read in parallel with the Genesis creation story, as well as with a Christian hymn. However, Obioma does not so much seek to simply revise and retell these texts in a Nigerian context but instead combines them with "a multiplicity of additional stories, symbols, and myths from diverse cultural backgrounds," resulting in "a kaleidoscopic network of intertexts and references, explicitly and implicitly worked into and alongside each other."[26] In a way, this demonstrates how the Bible has been appropriated and become part of a cultural archive that writers such as Obioma draw on in narrating and making sense of postcolonial African experiences. Obioma's work is reminiscent in this regard of the acclaimed Kenyan novelist Ngũgĩ wa Thiong'o, whose work is characterized by a similar engagement with biblical myth and Christian symbolism alongside indigenous traditions.[27]

With regard to the novel's representation of Christianity, *The Fishermen* illustrates the literary scholar Simon Gikandi's point about how Christianity is represented as "a crucial part of the social and cultural fabric of postcolonial society" in contemporary African literature.[28] In a way, the novel reflects Obioma's own journey with Christianity: He grew up in a devout evangelical Christian family and still identifies as Christian but seeks ways to integrate Christian faith and African traditions more constructively.[29] Throughout *The Fishermen*, we find indications of a Christianized culture, with Christianity being very much part of the everyday life of the Agwu family and of the town of Akure. Thus, we repeatedly read about the family going to church and about their pastor coming to visit them in difficult times. The boys pray even when playing football, to prevent the ball going astray. One of the brothers, Boja, is said to have become a born-again Christian during the "Great Gospel Crusade" of German evangelist Reinhard Bonnke in Akure in 1994 and to have subsequently baptized his siblings, threatening that otherwise they would "go to hell" (197, 303). Alongside Bonnke, other prominent revivalist preachers are mentioned, such as the American evangelist Benny Hinn and the Nigerian founder of Deeper Christian Life Ministry, William Folorunsho Kumuyi, each associated with significant spiritual power. By mentioning these figures, who were at the height of their popularity in Nigeria in the 1990s, the novel positions itself in an important chapter of Nigerian Christian history.

Additionally, mention is made of "the most popular Christian soap in Akure at the time, *The Ultimate Power*" (26). This refers to the TV series originally broadcast in Yoruba under the title *Agbara Nla*, and later rendered in an English-language version for distribution across and beyond Nigeria. Produced by Mount Zion Faith Ministries International, the series has been called "the first Christian video picture produced in Nigeria" and a "major hit" of the 1990s.[30] Furthermore, the novel references a tradition in Akure in which everyone, "even atheists," rings in the New Year at a church service. This tradition emerged because that night was believed to be "rife with superstition, with fears of the vicious, malicious spirit of the 'ber' months that fought tooth-and-nail to prevent people from passing into the New Year" (281). The "ber months" (also known as ember months) refers to the period from September to December, which, in Nigerian popular belief, has come to be associated with disaster and mishaps, often explained with reference to malevolent, or demonic, spiritual forces.³¹ It is one of the manifestations of what the scholar of religion Nimi Wariboko has called "the spell of the invisible," which characterizes Nigeria's highly Pentecostalized public culture.³²

The Fishermen offers narrative representations of various forms of Christianity in Akure at the time-present of the text. First, there is mention of the Catholic Cathedral, a building seemingly central in the urban space of the town, but rather marginal in the story. It is only mentioned twice, in relation to the "colourful statue of the Madonna" in front of it, which was once desecrated by Abulu, who held the statue for "a beautiful woman who, unlike the other women he leered at, did not make any move to resist him" (115, 276). After this act of desecration, the statue was replaced by the church authorities, safely erected behind a fence. If the cathedral is seen as a representative of European missionary Christianity, it is striking that it plays only a marginal role in the narrative. Perhaps it reflects Obioma's view, expressed in an interview, that "the epistemological supremacy of Western worldviews, sourced from Judeo-Christian theology, . . . has failed us and that the path forward is to redeem some of those aspects of our cultures to advance our society."³³

Second, in the light of the latter comment, the novel's interest in African-initiated or indigenous Christianity is noteworthy. Reference is made to two churches in this category, often referred to in Nigeria as Aladura churches: Christ Apostolic Church, only mentioned once as the church where the poor and elderly parents of Kayode, a neighborhood friend, are "the spiritual heads" (19), and the Celestial Church, which plays a more prominent role in the story and whose indigenized form of Christianity is explicitly thematized, as discussed below. Third, there is the church that the Agwu family attends, called the Assemblies of God, which is a Pentecostal church of North American origin.³⁴ Obioma has commented that this church resembles the church his own family attended when growing up in Akure, describing it as "a traditional Bible church, with Sunday School for the children."³⁵ For the discussion in this chapter, the latter two churches—the Celestial Church of Christ and the Assemblies of God—are most relevant, and their narrative representation allows for an illuminating comparative analysis.

The Celestial Church, officially known as the Celestial Church of Christ, is one of the most prominent churches associated with the Aladura movement. The latter is a term used in Nigeria to refer to locally initiated and indigenous forms of Christianity, characterized by a strong emphasis on prayer (from *aláàdúrà*, meaning "one who prays" in Yoruba) as well as other charismatic practices, such as healing and prophecy, and the appropriation of certain indigenous beliefs and rituals into a Christian framework. Aladura Christianity, which emerged from around the 1920s, has been described as a "unique synthesis of biblical belief, Christian liturgical forms, and Yoruba religious and ritual concepts."[36] The Celestial Church was founded in 1947 by Samuel Bilehou Oshoffa (1909–1985), in Port Novo, in what is now known as the Republic of Benin, upon Oshoffa's receiving visions, healing powers, and a "divine order ... of preaching to the world."[37] His church soon spread across the border into Nigeria and became popular throughout Yorubaland (and soon also in the diaspora), with the religious studies scholar Afe Adogame describing it in the year 2000 as "perhaps the most widespread among the Aladura churches in the contemporary period."[38] *The Fishermen* uses the term "white garment church" (26), which is a popular way of referring to the Celestial Church and other Aladura churches, due to the white robes that church members wear during worship, symbolizing their "outward purity as a projection of inner holiness and cleanliness."[39] The term can be seen as reductionist, as it makes the materiality of dress the most distinct feature of this type of Christianity. As the novel suggests, the white robe is also a cause for mockery, as the boys burst into laughter upon seeing a priest from the church with "the white robe flapping against his thin frame ... [as] a child in an oversized coat" (29).

A misconception about the church is reproduced in the novel, when the narrator adds that believers of the Celestial Church "worshipped water spirits" (26). It reflects the popular accusation, often made by Christians from other denominations as part of "polemic exchanges," that the Celestial Church is syncretistic, incorporating indigenous religious beliefs, such as in water spirits, into its belief system.[40] Sometimes, such notions are uncritically adopted by scholars—for instance, when, in a discussion of *The Fishermen*, the Celestial Church is associated with "traditional African animism."[41] However, the blending of indigenous Yoruba religion and Christianity, as found in the Celestial Church, is more complex than that. As much as the church attaches notions of "power" and "life" to water and uses "holy water" copiously in its rituals, as is common in Yoruba religion, Adogame points out that it does not worship indigenous water spirits but in fact diabolizes the latter while believing in Holy Jimata, "the angel of water and of all within the waters."[42]

The Fishermen's reproduction of a popular misconception buttresses the broader narrative point that the Celestial Church tends to be looked down upon. Indeed, the church is described as "a religious sect with a bad reputation in the country" (26), although the reasons for this reputation are not explained, and nowhere does the novel link the church to animal or human sacrifice, or other "fetish rituals," as one critic has suggested.[43] In any case, not only the white robes but also the Celestial worship practices are ridiculed by the boys who, upon discovering the church at the riverbank, peek through the windows and mimic the "frenzied actions and dances" of the worshippers (27). Only the eldest brother, Ikenna, considers this mockery "insensitive to the sacred practice of a religious body," and he tells his younger brothers off for "disrespecting other people's faith" (27, 182). Another example of mockery of practices of white garment churches can be found in the short story "Eko Hotel," by Chinelo Okparanta, where one of the main characters explicitly describes the ritual ceremonies with water on an ocean beach as "ridiculous," rhetorically asking, "How can they really believe that the water will wash away their troubles?"[44] Yet Obioma in *The Fishermen* goes beyond merely representing the wider public's contempt for these churches. Through the figure of Ikenna, the novel rehabilitates the Celestial Church, acknowledging that it is not an obscure syncretistic sect but a community of faith deserving respect.

Reading the narrative representation of the Celestial Church through the lens of the ecology of religion, a few things stand out. The location of the church on the bank of the river Omi-Ala is noteworthy. As the literary scholar Cajetan Iheka points out: "One cannot discuss the spirituality of delta communities without mentioning the significance of rivers."[45] The novel's second chapter, titled "The River," begins by telling how a once-sacred river, "believed to be a god," became desacralized. The narrator says that people of Akure used to worship the river: "They erected shrines in its name, and courted the intercession and guidance of Iyemoja, Osha, mermaids and other spirits and gods that dwelt in water bodies" (25). The novel invokes here the traditional Yoruba belief system where female deities, such as Yemọja and Ọ̀ṣun, are believed to be water goddesses inhabiting rivers and the sea; they are associated with powers of healing, fertility, and prosperity.[46] Across West Africa, and especially among Niger Delta communities, rivers and other water bodies are believed to be enchanted, dwelling places of spirits and deities.[47] Such beliefs, and their related rituals, are central to what Olupona has called "the environmental referentiality of lived religion," which is typical of African indigenous religions in general, and which come with certain "environmental imperatives."[48]

The creative writer Ugochukwu Anadị directly connects these two aspects in a short story in the collection *The Green We Left Behind*: "When the Igbo traditionalist insists on keeping the river clean, on not using it as a dumpsite, or on not felling some rare trees, he [sic] may not have much scientific knowledge on environmentalism and climate, but he believes that a god, a goddess, or some gods reside there and these abodes of the immortals, must not be destroyed or desecrated by mere mortals."[49] Another literary account of the environmental referentiality of indigenous religion can be found in the novella *Luxurious Hearses* by Uwem Akpan (discussed in more detail in chapter 5 of this book). A subtheme in this text is concerned with the effects of oil pollution in the Niger Delta region. The story states in passing that, in response to the symptoms of environmental degradation, such as empty rivers and infertile soil, "ancestral worshippers began asking people to bring animals to sacrifice to Mami Wata and other deities whose terrains were supposedly desecrated."[50] This reflects a perception of the natural environment as sacred and as inhabited by gods, similar to the one narrated in *The Fishermen* with reference to the Omi Ala. Mami Wata, who has been described as a "postcolonial deity," has incorporated features of indigenous goddesses such as Yemọja and Ọ̀ṣun; across West African and diaspora cultures she is believed to be the goddess of water, and in many a literary text and artwork she is invoked to address environmental concerns.[51] The initiative of the adherents of indigenous religion to make sacrifices to her and other deities can be seen as an attempt to restore the relationship with the gods believed to inhabit the natural environment. The Catholic priest in the village—a missionary from Ireland—responds to this by instructing his flock "to forget the pagans," indicating that from his perspective, such rituals, intended to restore an ecospiritual balance, are a form of paganism. This illustrates how missionary Christianity has introduced a disenchanted worldview, in which the natural environment is no longer sacred.

A similar point is made by the narrator in *The Fishermen* when he explains that the river ceased to be the center of communal religious life in the colonial period, from the moment that "the colonialist came from Europe and introduced the Bible, which then prised Omi-Ala's adherents from it, and the people, now largely Christian, began to see it as an evil place" (25). In other words, the suggestion is that Christianization meant a desacralization, and even a diabolization, of the natural environment. Indeed, with regard to the Niger Delta, scholars have argued that the introduction of Christianity brought about a "demythologizing of the cultural myths, which had sustained the ecological balance in the pre-colonial Niger Delta area."[52] To this day, zealous Christian groups in Nigeria frequently engage in crusades against the environment, cutting down trees in sacred groves and forests.[53] However, *The Fishermen* suggests that indigenous ecological worldviews and rituals still endure. For instance, reference is made to "some men at the Omi-Ala . . . in a strange posture, as if worshipping some deity," which seems to be an allusion to a remnant of practitioners of indigenous religion in an otherwise Christianized region (290). As Iheka points out, "although Christianity has spread throughout the [Niger Delta] region, belief in traditional gods and the reverence of ancestors are still commonplace."[54] Moreover, the mention of the Celestial Church located on the riverbank draws attention to an indigenized form of Christianity that does have environmental referentiality. Thus, the novel offers a literary response to the suggestion that African-initiated churches, such as the Celestial Church, by incorporating certain traditional worldviews into their communal life and worship, "have the potential of offering substantial solutions to the environmental challenges on the African continent or at least can offer motivational energies for ecological commitments."[55]

Although it is a misconception that Celestials worship water spirits, as the novel suggests, the church does associate water with "the forces of the Holy Spirit," such as those mediated by the angel Jimata.[56] The abundant use of consecrated water, often derived from rivers and streams, in Celestial Church ceremonies presents a continuity with the Yoruba tradition of using "living water" for healing purposes.[57] In this light, the church's location on the riverbank, as highlighted in the novel, is strategic, as it gives the church direct access to fresh water for consecration and subsequent ritual use. Thus, the narrative about the Celestial Church reflects what Iheka has called an "aesthetics of proximity," as it renders the river an integral component of the ecosystem of this indigenous Christian community.[58] The suggestion is that there are alternatives within Christianity to the desacralization and capitalist exploitation of the natural environment. The novella *Luxurious Hearses* mentioned earlier similarly suggests that Christian practice in the Niger Delta does have environmental referentiality, but that it is under threat because of pollution. The story notes that all rivers in the delta have become "clogged by oil," meaning that they can no longer be used for baptism. It brings one of the characters to the statement that "Dis oil drilling *dey* affect our prayer life *o*," which for her is the reason why Christians "must fight the oil companies for our rivers!"⁵⁹ *The Fishermen* does not engage in any such direct arguments for environmental activism, yet it does make a more subtle ethical case.

From the above, one may also be able to understand the "terror" in the eyes of the priest at the sight of the small fish and tadpoles that the boys had caught and kept in some cans (29). For as much as the Celestial Church associates water with the force of the Holy Spirit, it also recognizes the presence of malevolent forces in natural bodies of water such as rivers. That is why water must be consecrated before it is used for ritual purposes in the church. This ambivalence is also reflected in Yoruba tradition, where water can be both "salubrious and baleful."⁶⁰ In this light, there are several explanations for the priest's terror: Either he takes the ill fate of the small fish as an indication that the boys do not have "any respect for God," as he admonishes them, or he considers catching such fish from the river a taboo because they might be associated with the river's malicious forces, or he comes from a community that considers these fish as totems (28). In any case, it illustrates the point that the environmental referentiality of religion in this Christian context, too, is directly linked to certain ethical "environmental imperatives."⁶¹

Another ecologically relevant aspect is the novel's passing mention of Celestial worshippers walking barefoot. This practice has been explained with reference to "the belief that they are always in the overarching presence of God and therefore, like Moses in the Old Testament, must walk barefoot in his holy presence."⁶² Yet it might also be linked to indigenous notions of the soil of the earth as sacred. In Yoruba tradition, the earth (*ile*) is believed to be "inhabited by a spirit," and some Yoruba sayings pay homage to bare feet, especially "the underfoot, that stays flat to the ground without the hair."⁶³ The creative writer Ernest Ògúnyẹmí, in his autobiographical essay "A Shifting Portrait," recollects a more profane explanation for the practice of barefoot walking in the Celestial Church, which he attended when growing up: "The story goes that Oshoffa had such big feet that no sandals or shoes could fit them. As with several other religions, adherents decided to make a tradition of that situation: when a Celestial member is in the white garment, they do not put on shoes."⁶⁴ Whatever the motivation, bare feet have become a distinct feature of Celestial Church members, and the practice facilitates an unintermittent contact between the human body and the body of the earth.

Where *The Fishermen* represents the Celestial Church as a highly localized and indigenized form of Christianity with obvious environmental referentiality, the Assemblies of God church is depicted as almost deterritorialized. Although its geographical location in the town center of Akure is briefly mentioned, the narrative includes pointers that subtly indicate the transnational nature of this church. These pointers are, for instance, the reference to a young female lead singer in the church with a "foreign accent," the congregational singing of American gospel classics such as "Amazing Grace" and "It Is Well with My Soul," and the use of olive oil for ritual purposes instead of locally sourced holy water (126). Even the name of Pastor Collins is Anglicized. Indeed, historically speaking, the Assemblies of God is a denomination that traces directly to the Azusa Street Revival in early twentieth-century Los Angeles. Although it started in southeastern Nigeria in the 1930s as a local initiative—making it "the first Igbo-founded Pentecostal church"—the local founders soon developed links with, and received support from, Assemblies of God missionaries from North America already active in the West African region.[65] The most detailed church scene narrated in the novel is when Mother, finding out about the prophecy of Abulu and the devastating impact it is having on Ikenna, decides to take her sons to church "to be cleansed from every evil spell Abulu has cast on you" (122). Both Ikenna and Boja refuse to join, saying that they "don't have any demon" and do not need "deliverance from anything" (123). Once at church, Pastor Collins, in a typical Pentecostal question-and-answer form, gets the congregation to declare that Abulu's prophecy is of the devil and needs to be refuted, which the churchgoers respond to with "a rapturous session of fierce prayers" (127). Yet despite this collective performance of spiritual power, the absent Ikenna is not delivered, and Mother's efforts to seek his healing and deliverance "were wasted on him" (127).

While the middle-class Agwu family participates in a globalized Pentecostal form of Christianity, through the character of Mother—who is narratively depicted as leading the family's devotional life—the novel also demonstrates the continued prevalence of traditional beliefs even among Pentecostals who are supposed to have made "a complete break with the past."[66] For instance, after Boja's death by suicide, Mother perceives the presence of Boja's "restless spirit" disturbing the house (213). She also insists that Ikenna's and Boja's possessions be burned, to avoid Abulu's curse being "transferred to the rest of us," and that Boja's body not be buried but cremated, in line with the traditional Igbo belief that burial of a person who committed suicide or fratricide would be a "sacrilege to Ani, goddess of the earth" (226, 231). Although Father considers these beliefs "superstition" and a "contraption by illiterate minds," he gives in "for Mother's sake" (214, 231).

As the narrator explains: "Although Christianity had almost cleanly swept through Igbo land, crumbs and pieces of the African traditional religion had eluded the broom" (231). Yet such beliefs are not just leftovers from the past; they are actively reproduced in Pentecostal settings, as Pentecostalism "preserves traditional spiritual ontologies at the same time that it demonizes them."[67] In other words, the break with the past among born-again Christians is never complete, and one of the ways the past of indigenous beliefs continues to have salience is through diabolization, associating the powers of indigenous spirits with the Christian symbol of the devil. This process is reflected in Pastor Collins, when he declares that Abulu's prophecy is not a form of superstition but comes from the devil. This demonstrates how Pentecostalism takes people's existential fears and spiritual anxieties seriously by considering them real. In that sense, the globalized branch of classical Pentecostalism as represented by the Assemblies of God has also become locally meaningful.

The River as a Prophetic Witness

Earlier, I mentioned the novel's depiction of the river Omi-Ala, which was once considered sacred by local communities but, as a result of colonial and Christian modernity, had been desacralized and is now considered an "evil place." The perceived evilness of the river, associated with malevolent forces, has generated "dark rumours" about "fetish rituals" involving animals and even human bodies taking place at its banks, in response to which the local authorities in 1995 placed a curfew on the river, leaving the once-central communal stream abandoned (25). Thus, the novel conveys the point that spiritual desecration comes with social degradation, as well as with environmental pollution. The Omi-Ala may once have been "a pure river that supplied the earliest settlers with fish and clean drinking water," but in the present day it is no longer a source of life: Its waters have "become a bed of darkening grey" with a "nauseating sight of algae and leaves," turning the river into a "filthy swamp" (25, 28, 51). On their daily fishing expeditions, over a period of six weeks the boys only once catch a fish that was "big enough to sell," while usually the fish were "insignificant, weak, and barely ever survived beyond the day of their catch" (23, 33). The environmental degradation narrated here reflects the actual situation of the Ala river in Akure, which has become heavily polluted as a result of poor waste management practices and urban development.[68] Narrating a similar story of a river, in his hometown, Benin City, that was once held sacred but is now polluted and "a pitiable shadow of its former glory," Orobator has commented that it is a "painful reminder that the earth is crying out, and so are millions of its poor women and men with reduced access to fresh water and food sufficiency."[69]

Against the background of the perception of the river as a site of danger and taboo, the novel conveys that the brothers' fishing was far from an innocent leisure activity but a profound moral transgression of religio-cultural codes. Inspired by a classmate and enabled by their father's long-term absence from home because of work and by their mother's long days at her market grocery store, Ikenna and Boja discover the pleasures of fishing and soon allow their two younger brothers to accompany them. For six weeks, they go there daily after school, despite knowing that their punishment would be severe if their parents ever found out. Doing so is initially narrated as a step into freedom. Reflecting on what happened after their strict father was transferred from Akure to Yola, a thousand kilometers away, Ben says: "Then we broke free. We shelved our books and set out to explore the sacred world outside the one we were used to" (16). Yet sensitive readers might already see the warning here, because sacred worlds tend to center around a dualism of purity and danger.[70] The priest of the Celestial Church appears to have understood this risk, as he advises the boys to leave the river. Yet like the tree of knowledge of good and evil in the Genesis Paradise story, the river's attraction might be exactly in that it had been declared taboo. And where for Adam and Eve eating the fruit from this tree became the "original sin" for which they were cursed by God, for the brothers, fishing at the river turned into a watershed moment of cataclysmic proportions and with ontological significance. As the narrator puts it, in a mythical style: "For it was here that time began to matter, at that river where we became fishermen" (24).

When the brothers are finally spotted at the river by a neighbor who reports it to their mother, the latter is not just angry but deeply anguished. That night, she "paced about with heavy footsteps, wounded … her hands unsteady, her spirit broken" (34). Like Adam and Eve who, according to Genesis, had been seduced by a serpent (symbolizing the devil), Mother believes that her sons had "been pushed into doing it by bad spirits that must be exorcised" (38).[71] She sends the boys to sleep without dinner, stuffing them instead with a biblical quotation from the book of Proverbs: "The eye that mocks a father, that scorns an aged mother, will be pecked out by the ravens of the valley, will be eaten by the vultures," which for Ben is "the most frightening" passage in the entire Bible (35).[72] When Father comes home the next weekend and learns about "the worst, the very, unimaginable worst" that his sons have been up to, he gives them a severe beating, the blows carried out on their "bare flesh, the way you come into this sinful world" (41, 46). Yet as in the Genesis creation story, no punishment can revert the damage that has been done. During these six weeks, the journeys to the river had already turned out to be a "doomed path," with "the mysteries" surrounding Omi-Ala having cast a spell of evil, in the form of Abulu's prophecy (33).

The boys encounter Abulu, known locally as a "madman," one evening on the path alongside the river. The people of Akure recognized that he was not just insane—apparently as a result of brain damage due to an accident—but could reach a "second realm of insanity [that] was extraordinary" (116). In that state he became a mediator between visible and invisible worlds, declaring visions and conveying messages that people had come to believe in as inevitable, breeding "fear of the dark fate awaiting them" (116–17). Abulu is in such a state on the evening that the boys run into him and when he addresses his prophecy to Ikenna, predicting the latter's death caused by a fisherman. Despite their friends' admonishing them to walk on and not listen because doing so would be dangerous, Ikenna does stand still, astonished by the fact that Abulu knows his name, and he allows for Abulu's words to reach his ears and sink into his heart, where they begin to work a "metamorphosis [that] became cataclysmic" (93).

The Fishermen uses the term prophecy and suggests that Abulu can see into the future and predict things that are to happen, yet when such predictions are believed to be inevitable, they become something like a curse, or at least the effect is very similar. Exploring the fluid boundaries between the categories of prophecy and curse, the novel narrates the persistent belief in "potent speech" in African religious settings.[73] In indigenous belief systems, "curses are associated with the African concept of metaphysical causality and symbiotic interaction between the spiritual and the physical realms."[74] Highlighting the continuity of such a worldview in Christian contexts, the novel puts an identical belief in the mouth of Pastor Collins, saying that "whatever happens in the physical already has happened in the spiritual" (247). Traditionally, people who believe they have been cursed would seek divination through which the cause and type of the curse would be identified and its power ritually undone. In contemporary contexts, many Christians would instead seek deliverance from curses in Pentecostal-Charismatic churches, which is what Mother proposes but Ikenna refuses.[75] In the latter's absence, the deliverance prayers in their Assemblies of God church prove to be powerless. The novel directly engages the question asked by the Nigerian theologian Godwin Adeboye—"Can a Christian can be cursed?"—which is a debated issue among Nigerian Christians.[76] Both Ikenna's friend, Kayode, and his brother, Boja, suggest that there is nothing to fear, saying that Abulu "is of the devil, but we are Christians," and "I know you believe the prophecy, but you know we are children of God" (103, 140). Yet these words fall on deaf ears, as Ikenna is losing his faith and professes to "no longer believe there's a God" (136). Thus, Mother's prayers for Ikenna and Ben's prayers against Abulu are of no avail, and they come to believe that Ikenna "has gone mad" and is "imbued with an impregnable power of destruction" (149, 168).

According to the philosopher Molefi Asante, in African belief systems, a curse is "an utterance whose cause it is to do damage to the intended victim," with the person uttering the curse needing to be seen as having the capability of making the curse happen.[77] The novel is somewhat ambivalent about whether Abulu had the intention, and the capability, of destroying Ikenna, or whether he was merely conveying a vision. While some people in Akure considered him relatively harmless and recognized that his prophecies sometimes were actually useful, others perceived him as "an evil spirit manifesting in bodily form" (257). Ikenna himself, perhaps because "his *chi*, the personal god the Igbos believe everyone had, was weak," becomes convinced of "the unquestionable inescapability of Abulu's prescient powers" (133, 178). And for the people around Ikenna, witnessing the profound impact of the prophecy on their son's and brother's life, Abulu becomes a personification of evil, and they hold him responsible for his death. After her son's tragic death, Mother curses Abulu, saying, "You will die a cruel death" (242). Obembe and Benjamin endeavor to make this curse come to pass, and when they finally succeed, they utter the same words as Jesus on the cross, "It is finished" (John 19:30), to highlight the ontological significance of their revenge (297). Upon hearing the news of Abulu's death, Mother (then unaware that two of her sons had a hand in this) sings, "My God has finally vanquished my enemies" (305).

The Omi-Ala plays a central but manifold role in the unfolding tragedy. First, the river is the place where Abulu utters his prophecy. If the river, in Obioma's words, can be seen as a character, it is a witness at the scene. Yet the river is not only a quiet witness to the tragedy but also in a way the cause of it. After all, if the boys had not been enticed to go fishing at the river, they would not have crossed the taboo, and they would not have encountered Abulu and been cursed. Ikenna is said to have been perceptive of "all the dangers . . . lurking like shadows around Omi-Ala," but by then it was already too late (33). The river is also a subject of Abulu's prophecy, as it included an utterance about Ikenna swimming "in a river of red" from which he "shall never rise" again (104). These words are echoed later in the novel, in the scene about Ikenna lying in a pool of blood, after his fight with Boja got dramatically out of hand. Upon finding Ikenna, Obembe, in shock, repeatedly utters the words, "river of red, river of red, river of red," in what is described as an "enchanted intoning" (173, 197). Lastly, the river is involved in Abulu's tragic death. The madman's body, cruelly attacked by Obembe and Ben, "fell backwards into the water in a wild splash," and the boys watch it "being ferried away spouting blood on the darkening waters" (294–95). When Mother later hears the news of Abulu's body being found in the river, for her it confirms that the Omi-Ala is "a place of evil and horror" (306).

Much earlier in the novel, Obembe tries to persuade Ikenna not to have faith in the prophecy, invalidating the latter as merely the words of a madman by saying: "Listen, he mentioned a red river. He said you will swim in a red river. How can a river be red?" (140). This question might be key to unlocking the multilayered meaning of *The Fishermen*. On one level, the river turns red because of fratricide. If the novel and perhaps specifically the river are read as an allegory of Nigeria as "a dwindling nation," the brothers can be seen as representing the different ethnic groups in that nation caught up in a spiral of conflict and violence. The message then is that interethnic violence can paint the nation red, drenching it in blood. Yet, as stated earlier, I am more interested in an ecological reading of *The Fishermen*. From that perspective, the Omi-Ala is not so much a metaphor for the nation but a symbol of all rivers in Nigeria, which risk turning red, symbolically speaking, because of ecocide caused by various forms of environmental degradation. The novel suggests that at the heart of this ecocide is the desacralization of the river, and the natural environment more broadly, which has led to the cruel exploitation and aggressive pollution of water streams and other natural resources. Thus, the river, especially in its original "pure" form, is a prophetic presence through which Obioma underlines the importance of a notion of the natural environment as sacred.

Different from the prophecy uttered by Abulu, the prophecy embedded in the Omi-Ala is not an inescapable curse. In fact, the novel, in my reading, suggests that both fratricide and ecocide can be transcended and overcome. To make this point, I draw attention to the subtle mention of another river in the text. At the valedictory service held for Ikenna and

Boja, the congregation sings the hymn "It Is Well with My Soul." This nineteenth-century hymn, written by the American lawyer and Presbyterian church elder Horatio Spafford in response to personal tragedy in his life, when his four daughters drowned during a shipwreck, has become very popular in Nigeria, to such an extent that the phrase "It is well" is now a "peculiarly Nigerian English salutation for people in grief."[78] Critically, the opening line of the lyrics reads "When peace like a river attendeth my way," which stands in sharp contrast to the rough sea that took the lives of Spafford's daughters. In the novel, on the way back after the service, David, the youngest son of the Agwu family, renders the song in his own childlike version, singing "*Whe pis lak' a rifa ateent ma so*" (271, 273). Notably, this hymn is sung at a service that commemorates Ikenna and Boja together, which can be seen as a prophecy in itself, that peace between the two brothers shall be restored. It is also significant that at the very moment that the hymn is sung, Abulu walked into the church and is said to start crying while repeatedly mentioning Ikenna's name. Perhaps the madman-cum-prophet was not a person with evil intentions after all.

In my ecological reading, the lyrics of this Christian hymn serve a twofold purpose. On the one hand, they stand in contrast to the depiction of the Omi-Ala as a river of death and destruction, yet they simultaneously confirm the original status of this river as a source of purity and life. As mentioned earlier, in pre-Christian Akure the life-giving nature of the river Ala is linked to the deities Yemọja and Ọ̀ṣun, while in the hymn the peace-giving nature of the river is linked to God. After all, the lyrics are inspired by biblical verses such as those from the prophet Isaiah, who speaks about God extending "peace like a river, and the wealth of nations like a flooding stream," and the book of Revelations, which speaks of "the river of the water of life, as clear as crystal, flowing from the throne of God."[79] Christian hymns are full of these biblical references to rivers and waters, yet these tend to be interpreted symbolically or metaphorically. An intertextual reading of "It Is Well" within the broader narrative of *The Fishermen* connects the divine river of peace centered in the hymn to the actual, but heavily polluted, river Omi-Ala centered in the novel. Such a reading affirms the notion of "ecology as fullness of life," as it affirms a holistic understanding in which human and environmental ecology are interconnected.[80] The suggestion is made indirectly that the Omi-Ala is a sacred river, from the perspective not only of indigenous religion but also of Christianity. It is sacred because the source of its abundance, purity, peace, and life is located in the divine, whatever name one might give to it. Thus, *The Fishermen* subtly points to the possibility of resacralizing the natural environment, restoring the environmental referentiality of Nigerian Christianity, and emphasizing the ethical imperatives that come with that.

Conclusion

Ecology has become a major theme in Nigerian literature over the past few decades, and I have explored in this chapter the ways religion and specifically Christianity are engaged in Nigerian eco-fiction. It is fair to say that Christianity is treated ambivalently. Its dominant expressions—be they missionary Christianity or contemporary Pentecostal-Charismatic Christianity—are associated with a (neo)colonial project of desacralizing the natural environment and exploiting its natural resources. Indeed, a novel such as Okorafor's *Lagoon* is quite blunt in its dismissal of Christianity, at least in its Pentecostal form, as a hindrance to the much-needed changes in human mentality and attitude toward the environment, which are necessary to save the earth. It suggests that the environmental future of Nigeria, and possibly of Africa and the world at large, might be served by the disappearance of Christianity, or at least of its key agents, such as Father Oke.

Obioma's *The Fishermen* shares and echoes these environmental critiques of Christianity yet is more nuanced in its treatment. First, by foregrounding the internal diversity of Christianity in Nigeria, it avoids any monolithic representation and generalizing critique, acknowledging and narratively exploring the plurality of ecological perspectives and environmental attitudes that exist within Christian traditions. Specifically, it features indigenous churches such as the Celestial Church of Christ as harboring a unique archive of ecological knowledge and practice, integrating indigenous notions of the natural environment as sacred within a Christian framework. In doing so, the novel clearly conveys that Christianity can be indigenized, taking on environmental referentiality in local contexts and respecting the subsequent environmental imperatives. Second, beyond a specific engagement with indigenous Christian traditions, the novel also draws on broader Christian texts—biblical and hymnal—to provide a layer of intertextuality to its ecological narrative. In particular, the hymn "It Is Well" is effectively woven into the novel to explore the possibility of resacralizing the natural environment and restoring the environmental referentiality of Nigerian Christianity at large. The divine river of peace alluded to in this hymn contrasts with, but also merges with, the heavily polluted Omi-Ala river that is a prominent character in the novel.

At the beginning of this chapter, I quoted one of Ken Saro-Wiwa's poems, which speaks of "the piteous wail of sludged streams." Obioma gives voice to this wail by telling the story of the Omi-Ala—once a sacred river central to the life of the community, but now desolate, polluted, and cursed. Yet *The Fishermen* can also be read as a prophetic call for restoring the sacredness of rivers like this, and of the natural environment they are part of, and it imagines that possibility within the context of Nigerian Christianities.

Chapter 5

SPIRITUAL WARFARE

Christianity, Islam, and Interreligious Recognition

Nigeria is a religiously plural society where Christianity exists alongside several other religious traditions, most notably indigenous religions and Islam. The relationships between these religions are complex, multifaceted, and ever changing. In contemporary Nigeria, the relationship between Christianity and Islam in particular is widely recognized as having significant political, and even geopolitical, implications.[1] Due to historical reasons, such as the precolonial establishment of Islamic caliphates in the north and the colonial restriction of Christian mission activity to the south, the following of these two religions is unequally distributed between the predominantly Christian southern and the predominantly Muslim northern parts of the country. Subsequently, religion adds an extra layer to, and intersects in complex ways with, the already existing divisions in Nigeria such as those relating to ethnicity, economic resources, and political influence.

There is a long and complex history of interaction and exchange between Christians and Muslims in different parts of Nigeria, which at various times and places has been characterized by relative tolerance and peaceful coexistence.[2] Yet since the latter part of the twentieth century, the relationship between the adherents of these religions has become increasingly fragile and volatile, defined by growing competition and rivalry, leading to a "fractured spectrum" of Christian-Muslim relations in the country.[3] The reasons for this are often explained with reference to the emergence of Pentecostal-Charismatic movements in Christianity and of reform movements in Islam, both of which are seen as having similar yet competing and mutually exclusive religiopolitical ideologies and agendas.[4] Due to these movements' strong missionary drive and their quest for public visibility, social impact, and political influence, Christianity and Islam in contemporary Nigeria are frequently depicted as being involved in a "battle over the soul of the country," although it has also been acknowledged that, due to intrareligious competition, there is a battle within both religions—about the "heart and soul of Islam in Nigeria, as well as Christianity."[5]

Since Nigeria is the most populous country in Africa and is projected to have both the third-largest Muslim and the third-largest Christian populations in the world by 2060, it is "an important test case for evolving patterns of Christian-Muslim relations not only in Africa, but all over the globe."[6] The way these two religions and their mutual relationship develop in Nigeria has ramifications for the religious future of the continent, and possibly for the world at large. Although reliable demographic data are hard to find, the trend appears to be that Islam is growing faster than Christianity in Nigeria; according to the Pew Research Center, the Muslim share of Nigeria's population will grow from 50 percent in 2015 to 60.5 percent by 2060, while the Christian share will drop from 48.1 percent to 37.2 percent over the same period.[7] These figures are percentages, and in absolute numbers Christianity is projected to grow in that period from close to 88 million adherents to an estimated 174 million. Despite this tremendous numerical growth, the faster growth of Islam is giving rise to narratives about a decline of Christianity in Nigeria and has reinforced a concern among Nigerian Christians about perceived growing Islamic dominance and—especially in the northern, Muslim-dominated part of the country—religious persecution of Christians.[8] It has also led to speculation among Christians, especially Pentecostals, that Muslims have an agenda to Islamicize the country and indeed the continent, as reflected for instance in Obinna Udenwe's crime thriller *Satans and Shaitans*.[9]

In this context of religious competition in which both Christians and Muslims "tend toward a totalizing view of the other," some Nigerian Christian leaders, especially from Pentecostal backgrounds, have introduced a rhetoric of spiritual warfare in relation to Islam.[10] Spiritual warfare has become a prominent feature of Nigerian Pentecostalism, offering Christians, in Abimbola Adelakun's words, "powerful devices" to respond to perceived forces of evil that they believe to be linked to the devil.[11] Nigerian Christian spiritual warfare practices are located, according to the religion scholar Nimi Wariboko, "between two regimes of discourse," of missionary

Christianity and indigenous religion, and are mostly concerned with what Christians have come to perceive as the "evil power" of traditional practices, such as witchcraft.[12] However, it has been argued that Nigerian Pentecostal-Charismatic movements, possibly under the influence of the American Christian Right, have increasingly engaged in discursive and ritual practices of spiritual warfare against Islam in general, or militant Islamist groups in particular.[13] This is reflected, for instance, in views expressed by the influential pastor Enoch Adeboye, the general overseer of the Redeemed Christian Church of God, captured by religion scholar Asonzeh Ukah as follows: "For Adeboye, Islam is not simply a conflation of religion and politics, but a spiritual force that opposes the plan of God for Nigeria." Adeboye reportedly is of the view that "the plan and mission of God for Nigeria is that this country should be a Christian nation mandated to preach the second coming of Christ to the entire world," and subsequently Islam as an opposing spiritual force should be fought with all means.[14] This is one example of spiritual warfare rhetoric shaping Christian perceptions of and attitudes toward Islam. A literary representation of this can be found in Emmanuel Iduma's novel *The Sound of Things to Come*, in which an Anglican priest, on the eve of an outburst of Muslim riots against Christians in Jos, reiterates the belief of some Christians, obviously highly offensive to Muslims, that "Prophet Mohammed was a demonic construct ... imagined only to avert gazes from the one true savior, Jesus Christ."[15]

Such rhetoric is not the only, or dominant, way Nigerian Christians relate to Islam and Muslims. In fact, there exists a wide range of Christian responses to Islam in Nigeria.[16] Yet acknowledging that such rhetoric exists and is embedded in broader cultures of religious competition, politicization, and radicalization, I explore in this chapter how the relationship between Christianity and Islam is represented in contemporary Nigerian literature. More importantly, I ask how literary texts address and overcome discourses of othering and demonization. What resources do they offer to promote interreligious understanding and to imagine futures of interreligious coexistence in Nigeria? Or, in the words of the Nigerian theologian Simon Aihiokhai, how can literature help reimagine interfaith dialogue "as a liberational tool for freeing religious identity from the domain of scarcity and to positioning it within the domain of surplus?"[17]

In view of these questions, I will discuss three texts that have Christian-Muslim relations in northern Nigeria as their central theme and which engage this theme from a Christian point of view—that is, told from the perspective of a Christian protagonist or written by an author of Christian origin. These texts are the novel *Buried Beneath the Baobab Tree* by Adaobi Tricia Nwaubani, the novel *Sterile Sky* by E. E. Sule, and the novella *Luxurious Hearses* by Uwem Akpan. Together, these texts present a nuanced, multilayered depiction of Christian-Muslim relations in Nigeria's northern region, and they complicate simplistic representations of interreligious relations and one-sided narratives about Islamic radicalization and violence. As much as they offer insight into Christian rhetoric of spiritual warfare against, and demonization of, Islam, their underlying quest is to promote interreligious understanding and coexistence and to transform a politics of religious alterity into what Aihiokhai describes as an "interfaith theology of recognition." Importantly, these texts do imagine such recognition not through any formal interfaith dialogue but through an everyday praxis of interreligious neighborliness. This is essential because, as another Nigerian theologian, Marinus Iwuchukwu, has put it, "being good neighbors to each other is indispensable for peaceful coexistence between northern Nigerian Christian and Muslim residents."[18] The chapter begins with discussing Nwaubani's novel, which explicitly uses the term "spiritual warfare" to frame Christian-Muslim relations in the context of the rise of Boko Haram, and then continues by discussing two texts with more nuanced accounts.

The "Beasts" of Boko Haram

Centering around a young girl nicknamed Ya Ta (Hausa for "my daughter," as she is the only girl among her five brothers), *Buried Beneath the Baobab Tree* offers a narrative account of the spread and impact of Boko Haram, the Islamist militant group that is widely seen as posing "a credible threat" to Nigeria's democratic and multireligious order.[19] Inspired by the well-documented Chibok crisis of April 2014, when Boko Haram kidnapped 276 girls from their secondary school in the town of Chibok, northeast Nigeria, this novel tells the story of Ya Ta and two of her close friends, Sarah and Aisha, who are abducted during a Boko Haram raid of their village. Although Nwaubani has also worked as a journalist and in the process of writing this novel conducted interviews with young women who were kidnapped by Boko Haram, she chose to write about these events in fictional form.[20] In contrast, the novelist Helon Habila opted to write a book-length nonfiction report about the same events, published as *The Chibok Girls*. Yet highlighting the fluidity between these two genres, Nwaubani describes her novel as "a piece of journalism masquerading as fiction," while explaining her choice to write fiction by saying: "Fictionalizing the experiences of the thousands of women and girls kidnapped by the Boko Haram terrorist group is sort of my way of hijacking the interest of people who normally don't pay attention to the news."[21] Published by an imprint of the American publisher HarperCollins Children's, the novel aims at a global audience of young readers. The intended readership is reflected in the book's style, written in accessible English and with short chapters, many just a page long.

Nwaubani is of Igbo origin and grew up in a Christian family in Abia state, southeast Nigeria, and so her writing on this subject is perhaps sensitive, as it touches on the question "Who speaks for Boko Haram's victims?," given that these victims are mostly from Nigeria's northeastern ethnic communities.[22] Yet given that the Chibok crisis was widely reported in Western media and gave rise to a global movement under the hashtag #BringBackOurGirls, *Buried Beneath the Baobab Tree* is an important text, as it offers a unique, creative Nigerian perspective. As has been pointed out, "There is much to learn from the way Nigerians themselves speak to the Boko Haram crisis, often in ways that point to a deep longing for a peaceful multireligious and multiethnic society."[23]

The first part of the novel is set in a village in Borno state, in north eastern Nigeria, which borders Cameroon, Chad, and Niger, which is also the region where Boko Haram emerged in the early 2000s and has caused what has been described as "a new phase of violence" and even a "total war."[24] Village life is narratively depicted as an idyllic case of interreligious coexistence between Muslim and Christian families, with adherents of both faiths coming together to share life events such as naming and wedding ceremonies; the village school caters for Christian and Muslim pupils alike, and both Christian and Muslim children use the Hausa/Arabic word *Allah* for God. Thus, the novel draws attention to the presence of indigenous Hausa-speaking Christian communities in northern Nigeria, which "does not readily fit the usual political narratives" according to which Hausa and other northern groups, such as the Fulani and Kanuri, are Muslim, with Christianity being associated with immigrants from the south.[25]

Moreover, it narratively portrays neighborliness as happening "in the local context where religious people interact daily" and as leading to friendship that "diminishes the distorted perception of mutual mistrust and suspicion."[26] Thus, Ya Ta and Sarah, both from Christian families, are close friends with Aisha, a Muslim girl who dropped out of school after being married to her husband, Malam Isa, at a young age. Malam Isa, in turn, is happy for Ya Ta and Sarah to come to watch movies with Aisha, with whom he is deeply in love, and is also friends with Malam Emmanuel, who is a youth leader at the local church. This peaceful harmony is possible, the novel suggests, because Muslims in the village are moderate. Malam Isa, in particular, is portrayed as representing a mild version of Islam. He interprets his faith as "a religion of peace" and invokes the memory of the Prophet Muhammad living peacefully with Christians and Jews to make the case that "all Muslims are to love all and be just to all regardless of religion" (81). Ya Ta describes him as "a good Muslim man" who takes the instructions of the Quran seriously by giving alms generously (161). Clearly, the novel seeks to interrogate the "prominent notion in Nigeria" that "northern Muslims are, by definition, violence prone" by highlighting cultures of religious tolerance between Muslims and Christian minorities in the region.[27] Notably, the novel does not engage in a similar apologetic about Christianity, seemingly taking for granted this religion's peaceful character.

The idyll of village life is threatened by rumors of Boko Haram activity in the region, causing anxiety among Christians and Muslims alike but also causing tensions between the two groups.[28] Ya Ta's growing concern about the situation is reinforced by the radio reports on BBC Hausa, which her father listens to daily, illustrating that "millions of Nigerians, particularly those in the North, religiously listen to the BBC."[29] These reports make her increasingly worried whether her childhood dream—studying at a boarding school in Maiduguri, the capital of Borno state, for which she sat the admission exams—will ever be realized. In the village, speculation about the threat posed by Boko Haram becomes the talk of the day. Pushed by a question from Malam Emmanuel about Boko Haram's claim to be representing true Islam, Malam Isa is forced to defend his religion by arguing that "they are not reading the same Quran that I read every day" (82). This echoes a point made by Aisha to Ya Ta that Boko Haram's version of Islam is "from inside their heads, not from the holy Quran" (52).

Indeed, a common theme throughout the novel is the question of what "true" Islam is, which narratively demonstrates the notion of Islam as a "discursive tradition."[30] On the one hand, there is Malam Isa, who argues that Muslims are not allowed to attack others except as a form of defense and that killing people of other faiths is "a great sin against Allah" (81). There is also Malam Shettima, who takes issue with Boko Haram's rejection of Western types of education, arguing that "the very first revelation from Allah to the Prophet Muhammad was the word *Read*" (82). On the other hand, Boko Haram fighters are cited as claiming that they are "doing the work of God," because "we must make a river for Allah with the blood of infidels" (132, 215). Boko Haram militants, called *rijale*, are repeatedly described in negative terms, such as "bandits," "ruffians," "hooligans," "criminals," and "human beasts," to convey the evil that they represent (78, 81, 82, 134). Yet while Ya Ta's friend Aisha, who after the kidnapping is raped by one of the fighters, processes her trauma by reminding herself that "this is not Islam," Sarah (by then renamed Zainab) gradually adjusts to her new situation, embraces her new identity as a *rijale* wife, and defends the fighters by saying: "BH are not really bad people. They are only trying to change the world for Allah" (155, 227).

The novel portrays not only northern Nigerian Muslim responses to, and debates about, Boko Haram but also, and more prominently, Christian perspectives toward the imminent threat of Islamist militant violence. When the news reports about Boko Haram activity in the region are multiplying, one Sunday morning Pastor Moses disrupts the usual order of the service in the village church, calling upon the congregation to join in prayer: "Let us lift our voices in prayer for our brothers and sisters in other parts of Borno State who are being killed by Boko Haram. . . . Let us pray that God will deliver them from this evil" (52). The pastor himself asks God to send angels to watch over, and protect, those in danger and to "deliver them from this present darkness" (53). The belief in angels is quite common in Nigeria, among Christians and Muslims alike, and interestingly it has been suggested as a possible "panacea to religious harmony" between adherents of the two faiths.[31] As the reports of raids are coming closer and closer to the village, Pastor Moses underlines the need for more intense spiritual mobilization, announcing a full month of "urgent prayer and fasting for the entire church," saying: "We must rise up together and wage spiritual warfare against the forces of darkness behind Boko Haram" (83). In these pages there is a shift from a discourse of deliverance to a discourse of spiritual warfare. The language of deliverance is used in relation to the threat posed by Boko Haram to others—fellow Nigerians in other parts of Borno state—while the notion of spiritual warfare is used when the threat comes to the village itself. This suggests that deliverance and spiritual warfare operate on a similar discursive and ritual register—they are both "powerful devices," as the Africanist scholar Adelakun calls it, seeking to mobilize spiritual power in the face of perceived evil—but that there is a scale of intensity, with spiritual warfare being more forceful and concerned with combating the demonic forces believed to be behind evil.[32] As Ya Ta contemplates in response to Pastor Moses's call: "I hope that Boko Haram will be annihilated with our prayers" (83). Notably, the denominational background of the village church is undefined in the novel, the implicit suggestion perhaps being that it can be a church of any denomination in the Protestant spectrum.

The month of prayer and fasting does not actually take place—Boko Haram raids the village before the preparations are finished, with the shooting of machine guns replacing the utterance of any "machine gun prayer," as spiritual warfare prayer has been described.[33] Nevertheless, the novel's invocation of spiritual warfare rhetoric is significant in the light of the aforementioned discourses of spiritual warfare against Islam in which the latter is sometimes directly or indirectly depicted as a "religion of Satan" or "a spiritual force that opposes the plan of God for Nigeria."[34] *Buried Beneath the Baobab Tree* clearly seeks to stay away from such a demonization of Islam and Muslims generally—as discussed earlier, it painstakingly makes the case that there are many "good" Muslims and that "true" Islam is peaceful. It also shows that these "good" Muslims, such as Malam Isa and Aisha, are victims of Boko Haram, too—Isa is killed during the raid, while Aisha does not survive her period of abduction. In fact, through the repeated claims made by the "good" Muslim characters that Boko Haram is "not Islam" and has "nothing to do with Islam" (155, 157), the novel reinforces the view that the sect and its members are not genuinely Muslim, merely "appropriating Islam as their ideology" to support their political agenda while "misrepresenting the Islamic faith and community."[35] Indeed, conveying this point is explicitly part of Nwaubani's agenda, as she reflects in an interview: "It was essential for me to show in my novel that Boko Haram is not Islam." Interestingly, she links this to her own identity as a Christian, which has opened her eyes and led to a realization that "the most wicked people in this world are religious people," as they find ways to use the teachings of their faith— be it Christian, Islamic, or otherwise—to "perpetuate their cruelty."[36]

Yet while the novel seeks to "save Islam" from the association with violent religious extremism, there is a clear tendency to demonize Boko Haram, describing the movement as "evil" and its fighters as "human beasts" (52, 134). Interestingly, this conflicts with Nwaubani's own warning, in a 2014 opinion piece, about the risk of depicting Boko Haram fighters as "superstar monsters."[37] The trope of demonization becomes rather explicit in the narrative about Ya Ta's (by then renamed Salamatu) first night with the *rijale* she has been forced to marry, when there is a flashback to Pastor Moses warning that "the devil, the devourer, will often come to you in the form of a man," the implication being that the devil manifests itself in this Boko Haram fighter (193). It echoes the language used by one prominent Nigerian Pentecostal pastor, David Oyedepo, who, in a sermon preached in 2014, referred to Boko Haram forces as "demonic devils" and "Islamic demons" who should be killed.[38] Adelakun, in her book about spiritual warfare, has made the following general observation: "Given that Nigerian churches operate in a society where the contending forces of other religions (a.k.a. Islam) [are] strong, they were self-conscious about being perceived as weak people who could be bullied and beaten."[39] This might apply even more to churches in Muslim-dominated northern Nigeria, as represented by the fictive Christ the King church where Pastor Moses calls for spiritual warfare, if only to overcome any perception of weakness and powerlessness in the wake of militant threats.

By including this demonizing narrative, the novel also subscribes to what has been identified as a problematic "subframe" in Nigerian media discourses about Boko Haram—that is, a frame invested in "the othering of Boko Haram and in presenting it as an enemy of the Nigerian people."[40] This framing risks turning a blind eye to the social, economic, and political conditions that have led to the emergence of the group in the first place, as well as to the violence enacted by military forces against communities associated with Boko Haram. The Africanist scholar Abiodun Alao, in his book about religious violence in Nigeria, has observed that "Boko Haram is a grossly misunderstood movement, due in part to their own secrecy and in part to the media trivializing its messages."[41] *Buried Beneath the Baobab Tree* does not so much seek to enhance the public understanding of Boko Haram, its beliefs, and its motivations; rather, it reiterates widely known notions of the movement being against Western education and democracy. Instead, the novel seeks to represent the impact of the group's violent activities on local communities from the perspective of its victims, Christians and Muslims alike, especially female youths who "bear the brunt of insurgency-induced traumas the most."[42]

During the raid, most male villagers are killed by Boko Haram, including Muslim men such as Malam Isa. Women and young boys, on the other hand, are kidnapped and taken deep into the Sambisa Forest, which is the setting of the second half of the novel. Having seen her father and brothers killed before her eyes, Ya Ta is abducted, together with her friends Sarah and Aisha. Upon arrival in the camp, the Christian girls are forced to abandon their faith and convert to Islam, after which they are trained to become "good" Muslim women and wives to the *rijale*. The one girl who refuses and instead sticks to her faith in Jesus is killed before the eyes of the others. Ya Ta, although "happy with being a Christian," prioritizes the desire to save her life (114). If the narrative point here is that martyrdom is exceptional and that most believers are likely to abandon their faith to save their lives, it stands in stark contrast with a passage earlier in the novel, where Pastor Moses preaches: "As a Christian, you have Jesus Christ living in you. This makes you a victor in life, irrespective of what you pass through. You're unconquerable. Every challenge you pass through is just a springboard to your next level of glory, no matter how dire the situation" (32). The novel's suggestion seems to be that this gospel of "victorious living" turns out to be somewhat shallow in the face of persecution, as the latter requires pragmatism in order to survive.[43]

Indeed, at the moment of their forced conversion, Ya Ta wonders whether Pastor Moses would be ashamed of members of his church abandoning their faith. Ashamed or not, Pastor Moses might also take some pride because Ya Ta, even after her forced conversion, refuses to accept the notion of Boko Haram as representing "true" Islam, and she, having finally managed to escape from the camp in the forest, still remembers the Lord's Prayer. After her escape, Ya Ta—by then pregnant—ends up in a UNICEF camp, where Pastor Moses finds her. The moment he recognizes her, the pastor exclaims that Ya Ta's mother—who escaped kidnapping as she was away from the village during the raid—"never stopped praying that God would bring you back home to her" (291). With these words on its closing page, the novel suggests that prayer, after all, might be effective—especially the prayer of a mother, which in popular Nigerian Christian belief is considered particularly powerful.[44]

Where Ya Ta survives her abduction, her two friends do not. Aisha dies after giving birth in the camp, while Zainab tragically dies in a suicide bomb attack for which her husband put her forward. The story of Ya Ta's survival illustrates that the new name she was given while in the camp—Salamatu, meaning "safety"—turned out to be a "good omen," after all (143). Yet who ensured her safety? Pastor Moses believes it is thanks to God, in response to her mother's unyielding prayers. Yet another key to this question might be found in the reference to the baobab tree in the novel's title. On several occasions, the novel features this tree as an important part of social life in the village but also attaches sacred meaning to it. The baobab is referred to as the "tree of life" (8), echoing a tradition in West African literature in which the baobab is associated with the biblical story of the paradisal tree of life (Genesis 2:9).[45] At the same time, the novel invokes indigenous mythology about the baobab being thrown down from the sky by one of the gods, landing upside down, yet continuing to grow, to explain its unique form. It further alludes, early in the story, to the popular belief that the fruits and leaves of this tree have healing powers and offer protection against evil spirits—beliefs that are dismissed by Pastor Moses as "superstition" (9). Later in the novel, the baobab features again. Ya Ta / Salamatu and her friend Sarah/Zainab, while in the camp, are searching for vegetables in the forest to still their hunger, and they are excited to find a baobab tree. Yet instead of picking its nutritious fruits, they are made to vomit by the pungent smell of rotting flesh—the bodies of those who have been killed and thrown in a mass grave beneath the tree. The tree of life has become a tree of death. Paradise has become hell. The novel, so to speak, turns upside down the symbolic meaning of the baobab to evocatively capture Boko Haram's devastating impact on life in northeastern Nigeria. Yet the story of Ya Ta's survival can also be seen as a hopeful suggestion that, perhaps, the forces of protection, healing, and harmony, as symbolized by the baobab, in the end will be stronger than the destructive powers of religious radicalization.

In her journalistic writing, too, Nwaubani has argued that there is an alternative to the rhetoric of spiritual warfare between adherents of different religions, most notably Christianity and Islam, in northern Nigeria: dialogue, as a way to rebuild trust and to "begin the healing process."[46] Although Nwaubani, in this novel as well as her journalistic writings and media contributions, clearly expresses alarm about the potential of religion to cause division, tension, and violence, she is not a critic of religion altogether. Instead, she is convinced that religion, be it Christianity or Islam, "could turn out to be one of Africa's greatest assets."[47] The key to religion being an asset lies in its ability to promote peace, harmony, and coexistence, as depicted in the novel's opening chapters. The limitation of the novel, however, is that it takes the peaceful nature of Christianity, and its ability to embrace religious pluralism, for granted, while Muslim characters have to defend these values in relation to Islam. Written by an author from a Christian background and told from the perspective of a Christian protagonist, the novel misses the opportunity for a self-critical introspection on the ambivalent role that Christianity has played in building a culture of interreligious neighborliness in northern Nigeria. It illustrates a critical observation by Iwuchukwu that "there is a tendency for many Christians [in Nigeria] to be defensive and in denial of the existence of any so-called Christian militancy," which he argues is because "Christians will traditionally lay claims to the injunction for peace, love, and forgiveness that are paramount teachings of Christ."[48]

Beyond "the Death-Dance of Violent Religions"

From *Buried Beneath the Baobab Tree* one might get the impression that the emergence of Boko Haram is to be blamed for disturbing the hitherto peaceful coexistence of Muslims and Christians in northeastern Nigeria. However, the crisis caused by the Boko Haram resurgence is only a recent chapter in a longer history of religious tension, conflict, and violence in postindependence Nigeria. In his study of this complex history, Alao critically observes that "contrary to what is often assumed, no religion in Nigeria has a monopoly on violence, and all three main sectors in the country—Islam, Christianity, and traditional religions—have engaged in violence and threatened to use it, although the scale of their actions has been different."[49] The novel *Sterile Sky*, by the writer E. E. Sule (pen name of Sule Emmanuel Egya, an established literary scholar), seeks to acknowledge this reality, especially in relation to violence between Christians and Muslims in northern Nigeria, which Sule experienced himself when growing up in Kano and belonging to an ethnic minority, making the novel "somewhat autobiographical."[50] Published in 2012, in the prestigious African Writers Series that had just been relaunched by Pearson Education, the novel won the 2013 Commonwealth Book Prize (Africa Region). Although written for an international audience, the copious use of Nigerian English gives the novel a local flavor. The story is set in Kano, the second-largest city in the country and the capital of Kano state in northern Nigeria. It is also a city that, since the Maitatsine riots of the early 1980s—"the first major violence attributed to Islam"—has been at the center of religious violence in the region.[51] The novel, described by the author as "a story of a destitute family in a time of ethno-religious crisis," focuses on a later phase in this history.[52] It opens with a horrifying story of mob violence by Muslims against Christians that was incited by a crusade of the German evangelist Reinhard Bonnke, in Kano, which took place in October 1991.

Sterile Sky's opening pages capture two important developments in Nigerian Christianity in that period. First, the revivalist campaigns of European and American evangelical figures, such as Reinhard Bonnke, Billy Graham, and Benny Hinn, from the late 1980s had become "an increasingly important element in African Christianity" in general, and Nigerian Christianity specifically.[53] Bonnke was the founder and director of Christ for all Nations, and his ministry was particularly focused on Africa.[54] From the mid-1980s, he began to visit Nigeria, initially the southern part of the country, until in 1991 he announced a crusade in Kano, hosted by the local branch of the Christian Association of Nigeria, reportedly under the theme of "tearing down the strongholds of Islam."⁵⁵ Illustrating the negative impact of international evangelical actors on a volatile interreligious environment, the announcement of this crusade was, understandably, ill received by the majority Muslim population. Initially peaceful protests led to riots in which reportedly about three hundred people were killed. According to Ezekiel Ajani, "this negative incident earned Bonnke a ban from that part of the country, and contributed to make him popular elsewhere."⁵⁶ Thus, second, the opening of *Sterile Sky* captures this tragic incident, which heralded a new phase of religious violence in northern Nigeria, described by the historian Toyin Falola as "the age of warfare" in the 1990s.⁵⁷ The episode in question can be classified, in Alao's words, as "Islamic violence as a reaction to the perceived provocation of other religions."⁵⁸ In this case, the provocation was caused by an evangelizing campaign that was believed to be aimed at converting Muslims and undermining the historical Islamic character of Kano.

Written in a gripping style, the novel's opening pages tell how the teenage protagonist, Murtala, suddenly sees violence erupt on the streets around Sabon Gari, a high-density part of Kano city with a mostly Christian population originating from other parts of the country.⁵⁹ A kiosk covered with Bonnke's posters is set on fire by a chanting mob, while the vendor cries for God to save her life. A fruit hawker standing close to Murtala explains what is going on: "Dem say dey no wan Bonnke to come Kano. I no know why the man come by all means sef" (2). Once he has managed to make it home safely, Murtala overhears his parents debating Bonnke's visit. His father, Baba, expresses a similar skepticism as the hawker, arguing that this "white man" should rather have stayed in his home country and preached to his own people, instead of causing unrest in Kano. His devout mother, Mama, on the other hand, says that "a man sent by God to perform miracles" should be welcomed, reflecting the strong emphasis of Bonnke's campaigns on staging miracles (3). The next day, Murtala wakes up to news of Christian residents having set the main mosque in Sabon Gari on fire, and he overhears a neighbor Muslim boy threatening: "We'll burn all their churches! We'll kill them" (6).

Chapter 2 narrates how this threat becomes reality, with Muslim rioters moving from house to house in the neighborhood. Murtala's family is hiding in their home, with Mama whispering prayers for protection to "Jehovah our Lord" as the chanting of rioters and the screaming of their victims become louder (7). They hear the family next door being killed ruthlessly, including Murtala's friend, Helen, but Murtala's family narrowly escapes death, thanks to a Muslim neighbor who convinces the rioters that the residents have left the house. The family finds safety at the police station, flooded with refugees, yet tragedy catches up with them as Murtala's younger brother, Ukpo, is hit by a car in the chaos and dies. This is the beginning of the family falling apart. In the aftermath of the events, Murtala's parents become estranged and the struggle for economic survival intensifies, with his mother (a petty trader) seeking refuge in her faith and his father (a police officer who loses his job) becoming increasingly depressed. Murtala, as the oldest son, tries to keep the family together while coming to terms with his own trauma and loss.

Sterile Sky offers a complex, nuanced, and insightful account of Christian-Muslim relations in the context of religious violence in northern Nigeria. The novel addresses the question of the cause of such violence while avoiding simple answers. Although opening with a portrayal of a Muslim mob rioting against Christians, the story also alludes to the possibility that this was a response to Christian provocation, as Bonnke's crusade had undermined the delicate balance of interreligious coexistence in Kano at a time of increasing religious competition between Christianity and Islam in the region and in the country at large. Thus, the novel appears to sympathize with the point that "any careful observer of Kano's social and political reality would not fail to conclude that things were not likely to go well with Bonnke's proposed visit."[60] Moreover, the novel makes repeated mention of Christian violence against Muslims, too, first suggesting that it was a "counter-offensive" in response to Muslim violence, but later—when narrating a conversation among Murtala's school friends—also alluding to the possibility that Christians may have initiated it (6, 42).[61] Whoever started it, Baba's take is that the mutual killings are the result of people "using their loud religions" (44), the plural indicating that radicalization among Christians and Muslims alike is to be blamed for an ongoing cycle of violence, with religious beliefs being instrumentalized as a justification. Another character, named Omodiale, goes even further, referring to Christians and Muslims as "children of Cain," thus turning around the racist myth that associates the mark of Cain with Blackness and instead associating it with the curse of monotheistic religions, in particular Western Christian colonial and colonizing forces that "killed all our Jesuses so that they could use their Jesus to rob us" (89–90). He further argues that violence is not the result of recent processes of religious radicalization but is an inherent part of any religious tradition, and indeed of human civilization. In his cynical view, "the tradition of killing people and taking their land, rooted in Christianity and Islam, has continued throughout all ages.... The foundation of the world and its religions is laid on violence. Even our primitive societies were founded on violence" (88, 91). As a "vernacular intellectual," Omodiale deconstructs religious difference by identifying violence at the heart of any religion.[62]

Where the novel *Buried Beneath the Baobab Tree* invokes the notion of spiritual warfare as a discursive practice, *Sterile Sky* shows how easily spiritual warfare can turn into physical violence. For instance, one of Murtala's neighbors announces that he is about to join an "army" of Christians who have "sworn they would confront the jihadists in what threatened to be a total war" (257–58). As much as the idea of such a "Christian militia," according to Alao, may long have been considered an "oxymoron" in Nigeria, in 2011 such a group did actually emerge, in Kaduna state.[63] Preempting this development, the novel conveys the key point that Christianity is not too distant from violence either. The novel's refusal to point at one religious group as the wrongdoers is perhaps best summarized in the observation by Murtala that "the crisis was between Christians and Muslims," which avoids blaming either of the groups (42). Notably, the rioters in *Sterile Sky* are depicted as belonging to the youth and disenfranchised, and perhaps religion is only the veneer to express their much more deeply rooted social, economic, and political frustrations. This aligns with another theme in the novel, a critique of structural adjustment programs, mainly expressed by Baba, who sees these international donor–imposed programs as a set of policies through which people are "adjusted into poverty and violence" (46). By alluding to this broader socioeconomic and political-economic context, the novel also indirectly asks to what extent religious violence is, actually, religious.

Sterile Sky further conveys the point that tensions and violence between different religious groups in northern Nigeria are intricately connected to ethnic divisions, especially between the predominantly Muslim Hausa, who originate from the region, and the predominantly Christian Igbo and other southerners who migrated to the north during and after the colonial period. For instance, a connection is made in passing between the current Muslim-Christian conflict and the history of the Nigerian Civil War, during which "Hausa people had fought strangers" and "killed many Igbos" (44). And later in the novel, there is a story of Igbo Christian youth hunting two women they believe to be Hausa and Muslim, setting them ablaze. Thus, the novel clearly illustrates that in Nigeria, "religion has become interwoven with the politics of the nation's ethnopolitical divide."⁶⁴ Interestingly, the ethnic group that Murtala belongs to is not stated, although his parents are said to come from a village in Plateau state, central Nigeria, which is populated by various ethnic minority groups.

As much as *Sterile Sky* addresses religious and ethnic divisions, it also seeks to disrupt monolithic representations of particular groups as evil. As the literary scholar Nathan Suhr-Sytsma has observed, the novel seeks to deconstruct a binary, oppositional representation of religious identities by presenting "Christians and Muslims not as doubles of each other but as diverse members of a shared community."⁶⁵ Thus, the story about Murtala's family having narrowly survived the killings by Hausa rioters tells how on their way to the police station they pass many Hausa people in the neighborhood watching them, "looking sad and sympathetic" (14). This is reiterated later in the story, when the family flees to the police station again, to escape another eruption of violence. As mentioned earlier, the family's life is saved thanks to the intervention of one Muslim neighbor who later explains his motivation by saying: "Prophet Muhammadu *sallalahu alaihum wassalam* enjoins us to welcome strangers and live with them. It's the strangers that bring the things we need that we don't have" (71).

This neighbor exemplifies the "good Muslim," motivated by his faith to respect and protect the lives of others, thus undermining any simple equation of Islam to violence. When Murtala's family, after the first riots, moves to a new place, they end up at a tenement house with residents from diverse ethnic and religious backgrounds—Hausa, Fulani, Yoruba, Igbo, Christian, Muslim—who live together as a very ordinary example of what has been called "dialogue of life"—that is, "the ongoing social phenomenon where people are required to interact healthily with neighbors, friends, family, and co-workers of different religions," which Iwuchukwu considers key to religious pluralism in northern Nigeria.⁶⁶ Thus, their daily interactions are narratively depicted as peaceful and playful, with their joint enemy being the landlord who frequently visits to collect rent. At the moment that the next riots break out, one of their neighbors, Baba Fatima, tells the Christian residents that there is no need for them to run anywhere because "Na Muslim I be. And oder Muslims dey here. We go protect you people wey be Christians. Na one big family we be" (251). When the family decides to seek safety at the police station anyway, their Hausa Muslim neighbors express their sympathy. Thus, through these characters—*pace* Omodiale—the novel suggests that interreligious and interethnic neighborliness is possible, even in the face of threats of violence, and that the underlying values enabling this can be inspired by religious traditions.

Another division addressed in the novel is that of social class. Murtala's school friend Ola comes from an upper-class and mixed-faith family, his father being Christian and his mother Muslim; when Murtala first hears about this, he is astonished that such an arrangement is even possible and asks: "How did they come to like each other? Christians and Muslims always hate each other," to which Ola simply answers that it is about love (73). Ola's father pays for Murtala's school fees when his own father is unable to, although the latter does not accept this easily. In the aftermath of the second round of riots, the family is offered refuge at Ola's house, with Murtala initially managing to persuade his mother to accept until she decides a few days later that they will move to the village instead. Thus, as much as this thread conveys the point that interreligious marriage and cross-class friendship, empathy, and support are possible, it also narrates the difficulties of transcending deeply rooted social divisions.

Lastly, and perhaps most intimately, the novel offers a profound insight into religious meaning-making in the midst and the aftermath of interreligious violence. The most devout character is Murtala's mother, who leads family devotions at home and is an active member of her church women's fellowship. The church that she and her family attend is not described in any detail. Brief references to the practice of multiple offerings and paying tithes; to posters of the Virgin Mary, a crucifix, and Jesus with a halo hanging in the pastor's office; and to the pastor's concern with the devil indicate a combination of Catholic, Protestant, and Pentecostal elements that, probably deliberately, makes any straightforward denominational identification impossible. In any case, Mama is depicted as a devout, praying, and Bible-reading Christian woman. When the riots break out and the family is in acute danger, she calls upon "Jehovah our Lord" and "the God of Abraham, Isaac and Jacob" for protection, while expressing her faith that "God forbid, they'll not kill us, in Jesus' name" (7, 8, 10). The latter statement can be seen as a positive confession, which is an utterance of faith through which God's promises—in this case, the promise of protection—are claimed in the present. After the death of her son Ukpo, we read that she started "accusing God of bringing such sorrow upon her" (30). One might think that she is losing her faith as a result of her grief. Yet uttering accusations to God in situations of profound loss and existential crisis is not uncommon in Nigerian Christian cultures, especially in indigenous churches where the language from the biblical books of Psalms and Lamentations has shaped everyday spirituality.[67] Against the same background, one can read the harrowing cries that Murtala overhears when the neighboring family is being slaughtered during the first riots—"Jesus, where are you?," and "God na you I blame!" (9, 10)—as echoing the language of biblical lament Psalms, which, for instance, read "My God, my God, why have you forsaken me?"[68] These raw utterances of the classic question of divine presence in the face of evil are not necessarily an expression of unbelief but, in indigenous religions as well as in indigenized forms of Christianity, reflect a dynamic relationship with the divine in which believers may confront God about any afflictions they face.[69]

Another example of local Christian vernacular is reflected in Mama's prayer for the well-being of her children, in which she says: "God, are you there? Do you see what's happening to my children? Do you want to disgrace me, God? Come to our aid, Almighty God, you who led the children of Israel through turbulent times, you who saved us from the killers in Kano. Come to my aid. If it is witches that are after us, let the fire from above consume them. If it is the spirit of sickness that is after my children, God prove that you exist for me as you do for others" (83). What stands out here is the language of lamenting and petitioning God, the way the memory of God's activity in the past, as narrated in the Bible, is evoked to call for God's intervention in the present, and the invocation of God's curse and wrath on the forces of witchcraft believed to be behind the threats that the family is facing. The prayer exemplifies what the biblical scholar David Adamo has described as "African cultural hermeneutics at work," particularly in situations of pain, suffering, and distress.[70] Where Mama keeps pleading with God, as an expression of her strong faith, other characters in the novel demonstrate skepticism toward religion, and indeed to faith in God. Baba, never a fervent churchgoer anyway, becomes more and more cynical as his depression deepens. For him, God acts, at best, randomly, telling Christians and Muslims to kill one another when he likes, while further musing that "even God forgets people" (202). He, as well as Omodiale, list several "black saviours" (90, 284) to suggest that African resistance to and, possibly, redemption from the cycle of religious violence come from the continent and its diaspora rather than from any imported religion.

At the end of the novel, Baba experiences some sort of enlightenment, and he implores Murtala to stay away from people who are "enslaved to Islam and Christianity, two foreign religions tied together by violence" (283). Murtala himself, repeatedly referred to by his mother as "the rational one" because of his intelligence and his tendency to think about things, increasingly questions his mother's faith. On the day he returns to school after the riots, and the names of students who died are being commemorated, with both Christian and Muslim prayers being offered, he is unable to join in: "I did not wish to pray anymore with the religions that had triggered the violence in which Ukpo and Helen perished" (40). Later in the story, when his father has gone missing and Mama spends the whole night praying for her husband to return, Murtala considers it a waste of time, and he wonders whether God will ever listen to his mother's persistent prayers. From his point of view, "If I ever met God, if I ever convinced myself that he would actually listen to me, I would ask him just one question: why did things never go right for my family?" (221). In response to his growing skepticism, Mama admonishes Murtala for his "tendency to blaspheme" and warns him "to be careful the way you talk about God" (265). Yet by then it is already clear that her son has departed from the Christian faith of his mother. Given Sule's comment that *Sterile Sky* is "somewhat autobiographical" and that his own childhood experience of religious violence in Kano has "profoundly influenced" his "attitude towards religion today," one wonders about the convergence between Sule's standpoint and that of Murtala as his main protagonist.[71]

In the closing chapter of the novel, Murtala finds his father in a desolate place out of the city, after he has a dream in which his deceased brother, Ukpo, reveals himself through a whirlwind and tells him where Baba is hiding. The whirlwind could well be a reference to the Wind, which is central in the spirituality of Murtala's grandmother (and, to some extent, Baba), which we read about earlier. For instance, Grandmama refers to Murtala as "Son of the Wind" and underlines the need for him to come to the village for initiation "so that we connect you to the Wind and the Wind will be your eternal companion and protector" (119). This narrative thread alludes to the belief in the spirit or goddess of the wind, known in Yoruba tradition as Oya but also found in other West African indigenous religions.[72] For Grandmama, the spirituality of the Wind is the alternative to what she calls "the death-dance of violent religions," and she implores Murtala to connect to this ancestral wisdom of the past and to embrace the dreams through which the ancestors reveal their wisdom to him (123). When, on the novel's closing page, Baba blesses Murtala with the words "your path is that of light," it is a confirmation of Grandmama's earlier prophecy that Murtala is "the regenerative spirit of our ancestors" (286, 123). On a meta level, the narrative suggestion is that reclaiming indigenous spirituality may offer a way out of the cycle of interreligious violence that has kept northern Nigeria in a deadlock. This suggestion, which is not developed in any detail, aligns with arguments put forward by the prominent Nigerian intellectual Wole Soyinka that indigenous religions could remedy the current climate of religious competition and rivalry. Referring to Yoruba religion, Soyinka writes: "This ancient religion . . . proposes that 'warfare' between religions need not be."[73] Although historically, indigenous religions have indeed been defined by a sense of "inclusive pluralism," this suggestion overlooks the fact that, in recent years, these religions have also become associated with Nigerian cultures of violence.[74]

Interestingly, it is the male characters in *Sterile Sky* who represent a severe critique of religion, particularly of the monotheistic religions of Christianity and Islam. Mama, as the central female character, is the one who retains her Christian faith, even if she laments God for the catastrophe of violence and suffering happening to her family and community. Sule appears to deliberately narrate contesting voices and views regarding religion—Christianity, Islam, and indigenous religion—in *Sterile Sky*, using the novel as a dialogical space to explore and critique the way religion in northern Nigeria has become intricately connected to economies of violence. Clearly, the novel reflects the author's self-stated commitment "to deconstruct anti-human religious and cultural conventions," which he considers key to the work of northern Nigerian Anglophone writers, and it promotes a vision of neighborliness as key to human recognition across religious boundaries.[75]

"One of Us Be One of Dem"

A fascinating example of complicating simple binaries of north versus south, and Christian versus Muslim, is offered by Uwem Akpan's *Luxurious Hearses*, which is a novella included in the collection *Say You're One of Them*. It has been argued that Catholic social teaching served as an inspiration for the collection—Akpan was a Jesuit-trained Catholic priest at the time of writing the novella—as he explores various social justice concerns, with two of the five stories dedicated to the theme of Christian-Muslim relations.[76]

The reference to the "new democratic government" in the opening line of *Luxurious Hearses* indicates that the story is set around the year 2000 (Nigeria transitioned to democracy in 1999). This is confirmed by a later reference to the "Sharia crisis" (155, 158), a term generally used to refer to the riots between Muslims and Christians in Kaduna, which broke out after the state governor in February 2000 announced the introduction of Islamic law, and during which an estimated one to five thousand people were killed, and many more were forced to flee.[77] Although Kaduna was not the first state in northern Nigeria to Islamicize its legal system, it was a particularly controversial case given the state's considerable Christian minority population.

The narrative setting is a bus, the type of coach used for cross-country travel; in this case, it is used by southerners to flee from the north after the outbreak of riots. As has been observed in relation to the Nigerian context, "Those experiencing religious persecution are likely to decide to flee an area when and where they are the targets of violence," resulting in society becoming more religiously segregated.[78] The story centers on one of the passengers, Jubril, who, intriguingly, is introduced on the first page as "a Muslim [who] had done a good job disguising himself as a Christian fleeing south" (155). This sets up the plot of the story. Why would a sixteen-year-old Muslim man from the north embark on a bus journey with Christian southerners who seek to escape violence? And how is this young Muslim man going to endure such a journey, in the context of overheated interethnic and interreligious tensions? As the narrator observes: "Because of the religious conflict in the country, nobody would expect a northerner or Muslim to risk travelling with Christians to the south or the delta" (155–56). The story narrates, with great affect, the interactions between the passengers, with the bus becoming a microcosm of a country in turmoil. Through flashbacks, it also narrates how Jubril came to find himself on this bus for a journey that is supposed to bring him to safety but, at the very end, leads to his death.

Jubril is fleeing from Khamfi, a fictional city in the north that, not unlike Kaduna, is described as multireligious and multiethnic, with "as many Christians as there were Muslims" (181). Akpan's choice for a fictional name might reflect a wish to "distinguish his fiction from ethnography."[79] In Khamfi, Jubril lived in a neighborhood dominated by a "very conservative brand of Islam," with which he identified himself to such an extent that, when his hand was amputated as a punishment for stealing, he accepted it with an "unparalleled confidence in his faith" (156, 177). Having been part of the demonstrations in support of the introduction of Sharia law, he was prepared to face the consequences. In the past, he had joined fellow Muslim youth when they went to "wage war with the Christians," and he had set churches on fire (182). When his elder brother had converted to

Christianity and became a "firebrand Deeper Lifer," with a strong evangelizing zeal, Jubril realized that it was up to him to "protect the honor of his family, neighborhood, and Islamic faith"; he did not mourn when his brother was stoned to death for apostasy, and this earned him the recognition as a "true Muslim" by his friends (175, 176, 177).[80]

Yet in a tragic turn of events, the same friends, not too long after, were prepared to kill Jubril during the outbreak of the riots, calling him a "pake [fake] Muslim," a "traitor," a "souderner [southerner]," and an "inpidel [infidel]" (181–82). The reason for this sudden suspicion about his religious credentials was that Jubril, although having grown up in Khamfi from the age of two with his mother's Hausa Muslim family, had actually been born in the southern delta region, out of his mother's short-lived interethnic and interreligious marriage with a Catholic from the south. Never having cared about his infant baptism, Jubril suddenly found this element of his biography used against him to question his Muslim credentials. He painfully discovered the truth in the argument that his mother had used to persuade his brother after converting to Deeper Life Church—that he actually was a Catholic, rather than a Pentecostal, because "according to Catholic theology, baptism leaves an indelible mark on a person's soul" (175–76). On a meta level, Jubril is presented as modeling Nigeria at large. As the narrator points out: "Like his multireligious, multireligious country, Jubril's life story was more complicated than what one tribe or religion could claim" (172). Yet for his fellow Muslim friends in the spur of interreligious violence, there is no room for nuance and complexity; there is only black-and-white thinking. From their point of view, it is unimaginable that "one of us be one of dem," and thus they beat him up and intend to kill him, with Jubril only narrowly managing to escape (182). That is how he ended up on this bus with southern Christian refugees, hoping to make it safely to his father's village and present himself as a prodigal son.

The journey on the crowded bus turns out to be an ordeal. Not only is his paid-for seat taken by a chief who refuses to give it up, but also the driver takes many hours to secure enough fuel before they can finally set off, and the police have to intervene repeatedly to deal with commotion among the passengers. More critically, Jubril has to hide anything that might reveal his identity as a Hausa Muslim—his name, his accent, his amputated wrist—while praying for Allah's help to avoid all the things considered *haram* he is surrounded by—women passengers, one breastfeeding her baby in touching distance, and a TV screen in eyesight. In the meantime, existential questions about his identity force themselves upon Jubril's mind, articulated in the form of a prayer:

> Allah, is it true that once a person is baptized, as my mother said I was at birth, he remains a Christian forever, never able to remove the mark from his soul? Are you punishing me for this infant baptism that I did not choose? You know that as long as I can remember, I have always felt every inch a Muslim, and to prove my steadfastness, I did challenge Yusuf's apostasy and sacrificed his brotherhood to you.... If the world will not accept me as a southerner-northerner, will you also condemn me as a Christian-Muslim? Though I was attacked by Musa and Lukman for being a fake Muslim, Allah, please, give me the wisdom to convince the Christians in this bus that I am truly one of them. Lead me home, merciful one, lead me to peace.... Allah, your religion of Islam is a religion of peace. (199)

Petitioning Allah for sympathy with his delicate situation and for understanding of his religious boundary crossing, Jubril evokes the notion of Islam as a religion of peace, implicitly reminding Allah that peace is one of the names of Godself. Simultaneously, attempting to convince the Christian passengers that he is one of them, Jubril memorizes his baptism name, Gabriel, and wears a Marian medal (given to him by a Muslim who helped him escape) around his neck. In the quest for survival, he has to embrace the "pre-Muslim, Christian roots" he had always been ashamed of (197).

As a microcosm of Nigeria, the bus is depicted as a space of religious contestation, and even of spiritual warfare, resulting in a somewhat bizarre narrative with multiple twists. On one level it serves as a satirical commentary on the volatile nature of Nigeria's religious climate, but on another level it can be seen as a "a prophetic introspection into the contents and contours of the religious consciousness operating in post-colonial Nigeria."[81] The chief, as an adherent of indigenous religion, argues that "Britain arbitrarily joined the north and south together [and] ... forged the Muslim-majority north and the Christian-majority south into a country" (228). A similar point is made by a soldier who, traumatized by fighting in the Liberian civil war and considered a "mad man" by his fellow passengers, states, "It's you Christians and Muslims who've charmed Khamfi with your evil politics! ... Jour faiths are interlopers on this continent!" (230). Yet although the chief and the soldier seem to share the view that Christianity and Islam, as foreign religions, have brought trouble to Nigeria, they are also at loggerheads with each other, the former accusing the latter of practicing "madman's worship" and "juju," a false version of the "religion of our ancestors," while also heatedly debating the legacies of the military government and the recent turn to democracy (232).

When the soldier reveals to his fellow travelers the talismans he carries on his body, the Christians deploy their own rituals to neutralize the space. One of them, a Catholic woman called Madam Aniema, uses holy water, makes the sign of the cross, and invokes a litany of saints, while another one, a Pentecostal man called Emeka, becomes possessed by the Spirit, starts praying in tongues loudly, and invokes the power of the blood of Jesus to "cleanse this bus spiritually." Prophesying that "there's an enemy in this bus," Emeka then points not at the soldier but at Jubril, saying: "You've betrayed Christ!" (237). When Jubril, in self-defense, shows his Marian medal and refers to his infant baptism, Emeka flings the medal out the window and argues that "Mary is an idol in Catholic worship" and that Jubril's baptism as a child is invalid (238). The Catholic passengers are offended by Emeka's denigration of their faith, and Madam Aniema sprinkles him with holy water to bring him to his senses. Yet Emeka—a self-declared member of the "Pentecostal Explosion Ministries" and a representative of what has been described as the growing number of "militant Christians in northern Nigeria"—gets carried away by the Spirit.[82] He invokes the blood of Jesus, as a protection not only against the juju of the soldier but also against all Muslims as an imagined enemy. Deploying a biblical trope as a curse against Muslims, he says: "May the Muslims drown in Khamfi, like Pharaoh and his army in the Red Sea" (240).[83]

Emeka and the colonel end up fighting what the passengers consider "a spiritual fight" (which becomes quite physical), till some police officers intervene and restore calm. Yet this peace does not last long. Soon after the bus has finally embarked on its journey, the TV reports "reprisal violence" in southern cities against Muslim northerners living there, and Jubril alarmedly realizes that "the madness had spread to the south" (255–56). The Christian passengers welcome the news. Even Madam Aniema, depicted as a "sympathetic female character" devoutly reading the Christian classic *The Imitation of Christ* (by the fifteenth-century mystic Thomas à Kempis), says: "We're tired of turning the other cheek" (257).[84] Apparently, the instruction of Jesus in the Gospel to offer one's other cheek to someone slapping you (Matthew 5:39) is no longer applicable. With this fictional reference to reprisal violence, Akpan satirically conveys the point that Christian claims of being peaceful and forgiving may be a thin veneer; as much as there may exist a "pacifist streak" in some Nigerian Christian traditions, it is difficult to maintain in a context of interreligious conflict and violence.[85] At the end of the story, when Jubril inadvertently removes his amputated wrist from his pocket and thus is finally discovered to be a Muslim northerner, it is ironically the non-Christian chief who holds up a mirror to his Christian fellow passengers, asking them how "our Lord Jesus" would have reacted to a situation like this (258). The question is to no avail, as the Christians have forgotten that "Christianity is pure forgiveness" (206).[86] For the second time, Jubril finds himself trying to save his life by telling the complicated story of his "Christo-Muslim identity," yet the "murderous looks" of the Christian passengers remind him of the Muslim friends who tried to kill him earlier (259). Only, this time, there is no escape for him, apart from a spiritual one, as his tragic death fulfills Jubril's "yearning for oneness" with Allah (260). In Suhr-Sytsma's reading, Jubril becomes a scapegoat, with the Christian passengers sacrificing him as "a momentary solution" to their "divisions along ethnic, class, and denominational lines."[87]

Luxurious Hearses offers an insightful, simultaneously hilarious and tragic narrative of interreligious relationships in Nigeria and of the breakdown of neighborliness—between Christians and Muslims; between indigenous religion, Christianity, and Islam; and between Catholics and Pentecostals. Yet the novella does do more than that. It counterbalances the main story about conflict and violence with narrative depictions of interreligious solidarity. Thus, the novella includes a flashback of Jubril, together with a group of Christians, hiding in the house of a Hausa Muslim, Mallam Yohanna Abdullahi, while a mob of rioters is looking for them. In their hiding place, the Pentecostal Christians are praying in tongues, using "rapid-fire prayer" to beseech God's protection, while the Catholics are whispering Hail Marys, their prayers not competing but complementing each other (208). They are hidden away under the prayer mats of Mallam Abdullahi's family, with the mats proving to be "holy enough for all," saving the lives of Christians and one Muslim refugee alike (211). It makes Jubril realize that "every life counted in Allah's plan" (213). Furthermore, it is Mallam Abdullahi who later reminds Jubril that Islam is "a religion of peace," admonishing him not to "go around trying to terrorize the Christians" (223).

The story about Islamic prayer mats saving the lives of Christians is paralleled later in the novella by the testimony from a Hausa-Fulani Muslim living in the south that his life was saved by a Christian family hiding him under their Sacred Heart altar while Christian-associated vigilantes (the Bakassi Boys) stormed their house.[88] By including these stories of "good Muslims" and "good Christians," Akpan offers an alternative to the spiral of violence and suggests, in the words of the narrator, that the nation could "rise above all types of divisiveness" if only people would connect "at a deep, primordial level, where one's life was irreversibly connected to one's neighbor" (256). This insight is put in the mouth of Jubril to illustrate his transformation—perhaps a conversion—from religious zealotry and extremist views to a recognition of a shared humanity and an ethic of neighborliness. Interestingly, the references to prayer mats, Marian medals, holy water, the blood of Jesus, talismans, and the like also draw attention to the materiality of religion in the context of religion-related violence—that is, how sacred objects serve complex roles as they can both instigate, protect against, and help overcome violence between adherents of different religious groups.[89] As Suhr-Sytsma has commented with reference to Chimamanda Ngozi Adichie's short story "A Private Experience," these references also serve to decenter belief as a site of difference and instead draw "parallels between embodied religious practices" across faiths.[90]

In the character of Jubril, Akpan thematizes the complexity of religious identity and belonging in Nigeria. The novella offers a literary version of the argument put forward by various scholars that the Nigerian religious context is characterized by constant interactions and boundary crossing.[91] While this argument is usually made with reference to the southern part of the country, especially Yorubaland, Akpan suggests that something similar applies to the north and that even the boundary between northern and southern Nigeria is not as rigid as is often suggested. After all, "the average modern city or growing town in northern Nigeria consists of residents from different parts of Nigeria," making the north a highly "pluralistic geopolitical society."[92] Thus, through the persona of Jubril, Akpan explores whether "one of us [can] be one of dem" (182)—can a northerner be a southerner, and can a Muslim be a Christian? Clearly, the narrative suggests that such multiple religious and ethnic belonging is a biographical and social reality for many Nigerians and that a greater awareness of this can help the country and its citizens to embrace religious and ethnic pluralism. Yet it also conveys that the latter has become difficult in the context of increasing religious radicalization and divisive ethnopolitics. The painful irony is that where Jubril finds death at the hands of Christians after failing to disguise his Muslim identity, his brother Yusuf finds death at the hands of Muslims after converting to Christianity. Finally, like Sule in *Sterile Sky*, Akpan in

Luxurious Hearses points to the socioeconomic dimension of what is easily framed as religious conflict. The reference to the rioters as "hungry-looking *almajeris*" used by politicians to serve their interests suggests that religion is only one factor in a much broader economy of violence (191).

In his discussion of the novella, the literary scholar Oby Okolocha concludes that "both Muslims and Christians presented in this narrative appear to be incapable of any deep-seated feelings of attachment, affection or love in any meaningful way—it is all about religious identity."[93] It is true that *Luxurious Hearses* problematizes and critiques the rigid politics of Christian and Muslim identities in Nigeria. However, the novella also narratively explores the complexity of religious identity in the Nigerian context, demonstrating how "religious identity" itself is not static and monolithic but ambiguous, multifaceted, and flexible. Moreover, the novella does include exceptions to the rule of incapability of human recognition: As mentioned above, there are several characters who do stay true to the moral tenets of their faith by engaging in practices of neighborliness. Akpan's underlying message may exactly be that rediscovering this practice, and the religious values underlying it, may offer a way out of the cycle of violence and put Nigeria on a path toward religious coexistence.

Conclusion

Engaging the theme of Christian-Muslim relations from a Christian point of view—that is, told from the perspective of a Christian protagonist or written by an author of Christian origin—the novels under discussion also offer a distinct contribution to the representation of Islam in African literature.[94] They avoid a singular association of Islam with religious radicalization, extremism, and violence by explicitly featuring "good" Muslim characters and by reiterating that Islam is a "religion of peace." In doing so, they complicate and nuance any monolithic representation of Islam, and instead they foreground the multiple possibilities within Muslim worlds, as well as the various ways Muslims and Christians can relate to one another.

Discourses of spiritual warfare against Islam, which can be found in some Nigerian Christian circles, are informed by a politics of alterity in which the religious Other is seen negatively, as an existential threat, and even as demonic. As Aihiokhai has pointed out, such an "apologetic posturing" needs to be abandoned in the quest for what he calls an "interfaith theology of recognition."[95] The literary texts discussed in this chapter contribute in various ways to this quest. Where interfaith dialogue is often seen as a "dialogue of action"—that is, organized initiatives for people from different religious groups to come together and collaborate for the common good—these texts instead foreground the importance of "dialogue of life"—that is, the day-to-day interactions of people from different religious backgrounds and their sharing of everyday life, be it in the family setting, the workplace, or local neighborhoods.[96] Thus, Akpan, Nwaubani, and Sule in their respective fictional narratives offer accounts of everyday life as a site of fostering mutual understanding and interreligious coexistence, which in the narrated situations of violence engender concrete acts of neighborliness, empathy, and solidarity. In doing so, they narratively demonstrate that there is an alternative to the ongoing cycle of violence, centering around interhuman recognition and recognizing the "sacredness of all life," beginning with the life of religious and ethnic others.

Through the deployment of the symbol of the baobab tree, and the reference to the spirituality of the Wind, Nwaubani and Sule draw on resources from indigenous religious lifeworlds that can promote such a recognition, while Akpan's intertextual reference to *The Imitation of Christ* alludes to Christian traditions directed toward the same end. None of the texts under discussion explicitly point in the direction of a "de jure religious pluralism," in which other religions are recognized as revealing the divine, perhaps because such an inclusive theology of religions is too far-fetched in the contemporary Nigerian Christian landscape.[97] Yet they do suggest that a de facto pluralism, in which adherents of different religious traditions share life together in peace and harmony, is possible. One does not need a theology of religious pluralism to acknowledge, in the words of Murtala's Muslim neighbor in *Sterile Sky*, that "the breath of life is the same for every person" (13). Yet it is exactly this basic recognition of a shared humanity that allows for neighborliness across and beyond religious difference.

The problem in contemporary Nigeria is that the possibility of interreligious neighborliness has been severely constrained by recent histories of violence and the subsequent tendency toward greater separation of and suspicion between religious groups. The texts under discussion do not necessarily provide a solution to this problem. Yet they do invite their readers on a journey of introspection and reflection on the values and resources that enable living neighborly with religious others.

Chapter 6

PROSPERITY

Pentecostalism, Charismatic Leadership, and the Prosperity Gospel

The figure of the charismatic "man (and occasionally, woman) of God" has become a popular character in Nigerian literature. Already in the 1960s, Wole Soyinka dedicated a full theater play to Brother Jero (shorthand for Jeroboam), a self-declared "prophet by birth and by inclination" who leads a ministry on a beach in Lagos, competing for worshippers, or "customers," as he refers to them, with other prophets.[1] In Soyinka's satirical account, Brother Jero is a moral hypocrite and a religious charlatan who runs his prophetic ministry as a business and deceives his followers in pursuit of his own interests while appealing to their hopes and aspirations with fake prophecies. Dressed in a white gown and using paraphernalia such as bottles, a mirror, a rosary, and a cross, Brother Jero is depicted as a representative of Aladura Christianity. This is an indigenous charismatic movement that became popular in mid-twentieth-century Nigeria, but whose popularity in later decades was gradually overtaken by the more modern Pentecostal-Charismatic movements. As Jero himself observes in the play: "The worshippers have dwindled to a mere trickle and we really have to fight for every new convert. They all prefer High Life to the rhythm of Celestial hymns. And television too is keeping our wealthier patrons home."[2] This comment reflects a transition in the musical cultures of Nigerian Christianity, as "celestial hymns" refer to the "indigenous and neotraditional Yoruba song and dance performances" that are typical of the Celestial Church and other Aladura churches, while "High Life" refers to

Nigerian popular music that was introduced in Pentecostal-Charismatic churches particularly to appeal to youth.³

However, in spite of the musical and other differences between Aladura churches and Pentecostal-Charismatic churches, one can easily identify several similarities as well. One of them is the notion of prosperity, which is mostly associated with late twentieth-century neo-Pentecostal Christianity, but which is already reflected in the preaching of Brother Jero, as most of his prophecies are about career prospects, business opportunities, and life expectancy. Another one is the concern with pastoral entrepreneurship in which the prophet or pastor must build a distinctive brand to gather and keep a following on a competitive religious market. Yet another is the risk of deception and exploitation, with charismatic religious figures misusing the power they hold over their followers for personal gain. Thus, Soyinka depicts the figure of Brother Jero as a "Machiavellian con artist" in order to "satirize and deride the repercussions of the rapid spread of Christianity across West Africa" in general, especially the many Pentecostal movements that, notwithstanding significant differences, have in common that they center around and depend on charismatic leadership.⁴

In the light of the aforementioned similarities, it is no surprise that more recent Nigerian literary texts engage similar themes as Soyinka does in *The Jero Plays*, but in relation to Pentecostal-Charismatic churches, which, in the early twenty-first century, have come to define the Nigerian Christian landscape. Indeed, one could easily argue that the satirical representation of moral and religious hypocrisy among "men (and women) of God," as charismatic pastors and prophets are popularly called, has become a prominent trend in the engagement with Christianity in twenty-first-century Nigerian literature—for example: Chika Unigwe's novel *The Middle Daughter*, about a smooth-talking preacher luring and raping a vulnerable young woman and forcing her into an oppressive marriage; Tola Rotimi Abraham's novel *Black Sunday*, about a family being exploited by a fraudulent prosperity preacher; Timendu Aghahowa's novel *The Bishop's Prodigal Daughter*, about a succession and family drama in a Pentecostal megachurch; the thriller *Gaslight* by Femi Kayode, about a money-laundering megachurch pastor arrested for murdering his wife; Olukorede Yishau's novel *In the Name of Our Father*, about a Pentecostal pastor deriving his power from a black magic brotherhood; and Elnathan John and Àlàbá Ònájìn's graphic novel *On Ajayi Crowther Street*, about the family drama of a sexually abusive and homophobic Pentecostal pastor who fakes deliverance rituals. Other examples are the novella *Fattening for Gabon* by Uwem Akpan and short stories such as "Under New

Pastoral Management" by Tanure Ojaide, "The Anointed Wife" by Damilare Kuku, and "Miracle" by Chimamanda Ngozi Adichie (later included in her novel *Americanah*). Most of these literary texts associate Pentecostal leaders with excesses such as sex scandals, domestic violence, decadence and self-enrichment, money laundering and fraud, moral hypocrisy, and religious deception. These literary accounts complement the existing popular tales in Nigeria that link charismatic pastors to various forms of moral corruption.[5]

Where scholars of African and global Pentecostalism have called for a "cultural turn" in the study of this religious movement, my contention is that, as part of such a turn, we need to examine not only the ways Pentecostal actors engage in cultural production but also how other cultural actors, such as literary writers, represent and engage Pentecostal beliefs and practices critically and creatively.[6] Nigeria is a particularly productive place for such an endeavor: Having become one of the epicenters of Pentecostal Christianity globally, with Lagos in particular being described as the "Pentecostal capital of the world," Nigerian literature has emerged as an important site for the cultural critique of Pentecostalism as a public religion in the country.[7] While the sociologist Ebenezer Obadare has argued that contemporary Pentecostal pastors as "Men of God" have taken over the social status and public influence that "Men of Letters" used to have in Nigeria, I suggest that it may be too early to declare the latter as being "of yesterday."[8] A new generation of literary writers—male and female—has emerged who use their pens to not just represent but also critique the power that Nigerian Pentecostal pastors have undoubtedly accumulated. In this chapter, I focus on one key example of this trend: Okey Ndibe's 2014 novel, *Foreign Gods, Inc.* I consider this text particularly rich and fascinating, because it is one of the most detailed and multifaceted fictional representations of Nigerian Pentecostalism, the prosperity gospel, and charismatic leadership. In this representation it also revisits some of the long-standing issues relating to Christianity in Nigerian and African literature, most notably the question of the relationship between Christianity and indigenous religions. With *Foreign Gods, Inc.*, as well as through other writings, Ndibe has positioned himself as a perceptive commentator on religion in Nigerian public life.[9]

Reading *Foreign Gods, Inc.*

Set in the early 2000s and framed in a transnational context of migration, globalization, and neoliberal capitalism, *Foreign Gods, Inc.* tells the story of a Nigerian immigrant, named Ike, living in the United States. His name is a shorthand for Ikechukwu, meaning "God's strength" in Igbo, and although Ike does not seem to be a strong believer, the novel's plot does indeed center around a contestation about divine power, albeit in a different way from what his name might suggest. Making a meager living as a taxi driver, while struggling to overcome his gambling and drinking problems, Ike is far from living the American dream. Yet one day he gets a brilliant idea about the key to his success and wealth (or so he believes). Reading in a magazine about a top-notch New York art gallery specializing in gods from across the world, and selling them for exorbitant prices, Ike is reminded of the ancestral shrine in his home village, Utonki, in southeastern Nigeria, where his uncle serves as the priest. The statue of the god of his people, named Ngene—"a majestic god with a rich legend and history"—certainly would make good money (3). Utonki is a fictive village, but it might somewhat resemble Ndibe's own hometown, Amawbia, which is also in Igboland and where Ndibe, like the character of Ike, during his childhood also spent time at the shrine of the local deity even though he was born into a Catholic family.[10]

Upon arrival in his home village, Ike gets caught up in a drama of social and religious affairs. First, he has to face his widowed mother, who accuses him of having neglected her all the years he lived in America, leaving her to "chew sand for food" (127). Then, he finds out that his mother, after the death of his father, joined a recently opened Pentecostal church. Under the influence of its pastor, whom she considers "a real man of God," she has broken ties with her in-laws, who she believes live in "darkness" (134, 131). She forbids Ike from visiting his paternal uncle and grandmother, and she insists that he should join her at church instead. Giving in, Ike does accompany his mother to church, resulting in a confrontation with Pastor Uka. When Ike, against his mother's instructions, does visit his grandmother and uncle, he is warmly welcomed by both, and Uncle Osuakwu initiates him into the worship of Ngene. Determined to complete his mission, Ike realizes that the religious strife in the village might work in his favor: Pastor Uka is likely to be blamed if the statue of Ngene were to disappear. And so it happens. However, by the time Ike has managed to steal the statue, bribe his way through customs, and bring it to America, his fortunes have turned sour: He is told at the gallery that "African gods are no longer profitable" (318). To make things worse, when the deity is sold off to a customer in Japan, its spirit continues to haunt Ike. The literary scholar Katherine

Hallemeier captures it succinctly: "Ike, in the end, does not so much possess Ngene as he is possessed by him."[11]

Described as a "masterfully-woven tale of human frailty and moral ineptitude," *Foreign Gods, Inc.* has received considerable attention from literary critics who have read the novel through such theoretical lenses as cosmopolitanism and postsecularity.[12] Recognizing that this is a satirical text that makes one "laugh about religion," in this chapter I read the novel as a commentary on Christianity, especially in its neo-Pentecostal form, in contemporary Nigeria.[13] In doing so, I explore three central themes: the relationship between Pentecostal Christianity and indigenous religion, the risks of charismatic leadership, and the nature of the prosperity gospel, which are among the most conspicuous aspects of Pentecostalism in contemporary African contexts and are widely debated among scholars. The subsequent discussion highlights the productive effects, as well as the possible limitations, of satire as a literary style to engage religion. Drawing attention to the novel's comical but also somewhat stereotypical representation of Nigerian Pentecostalism as a form of religious manipulation and exploitation, I underscore the need to acknowledge the nuances and complexity of this form of Christianity and to understand its appeal to, and popularity among, its many followers in contemporary Nigeria.

Pentecostalism and Indigenous Religion

Foreign Gods, Inc. continues a tradition in African literature where Christianity at large is problematized for its impact on traditional society and indigenous cultures and religions. The theme of Chinua Achebe's classic *Things Fall Apart*, about the arrival of European missionaries in Igboland, is extended and reframed by Ndibe in the contemporary period, when Pentecostalism has become the dominant expression of Christianity. Moreover, by weaving a second storyline into the novel, about the Anglican Reverend Walter Stanton as the first missionary to arrive in Utonki in 1898, Ndibe narratively points to the historical continuities between early missionary Christianity and contemporary Pentecostalism in their antagonism toward indigenous religion. Although there is more than a century between them, Reverend Stanton and Pastor Uka use similar language, such as when they speak about indigenous religious worshippers as "people in darkness" and "heathens" in need of salvation; they also have a similar zeal for "dethroning the deity," as they consider Ngene "a powerless, inert idol" and a "fallen god" (97, 131, 115, 197). Thus, both these Christian preachers are representatives of the ongoing process of the Christianization of Igboland, in which Christianity continues, in the words of the historian Ogbu Kalu, to "embattle local gods."[14] Ironically, in the novel it is Ike, an unbeliever, who in the end succeeds in bringing Ngene down, although he soon regrets this as he discovers the god is not powerless after all.

However, there is a difference in their language, too, as Pastor Uka more explicitly demonizes the worship of Ngene—for instance, when he refers to Ike's uncle and grandmother as "grandmasters in the demonic world" and "agents of Satan" (161). He also uses the rhetoric of spiritual warfare when speaking about the confrontation between the powers of good (Christianity) and evil (indigenous religion): "I'm awake every night. I pray. I call down Holy Ghost fire. I break spells and yokes. I unbind the bound. Without me, this village wouldn't know peace at night" (162). Indeed, Uka invokes the biblical narrative of the prophet Elijah in his battle with the prophets of Baal, claiming to carry Elijah's mantle himself and to possess the prophetic powers that will cause fire from heaven to consume the traditional worshippers and their "false god." Ironically, at the end of the novel, after Ike has stolen the statue from the shrine and the news breaks in the village, Pastor Uka claims it to be a success of his warfare: He "proclaimed it an act of the God he served" and organized an overnight prayer service "to praise the true God that had vanquished a false idol" (309).

Thus, *Foreign Gods, Inc.* suggests that Pentecostalism has only reinforced the existing tensions between Christians and indigenous worshippers, and the alienation between both traditions, by intensifying the demonization of indigenous religion. Whereas some of the historic mission churches in the later decades of the twentieth century went through a process of inculturation (see chapter 3 in relation to the Catholic Church), the attitude of Pentecostal churches toward indigenous traditions has been interpreted as "moving the hand of the clock back," and *Foreign Gods, Inc.* gives that criticism narrative form.[15] The novel thus illustrates the point made by many scholars that Pentecostalism in Nigeria, as in Africa more broadly, engages in a process of "repudiating and demonizing Nigerian deities, spirits, and ancestors and waging war against them," and that in doing so it "is undermining or destroying the social fabric of African societies."[16] The painful truth, as the novel indirectly conveys, is that the agents of this repudiation of African indigenous cultures and religious traditions are no longer European missionaries but local Pentecostal pastors who, in a way, are continuing the colonizing project, as subtly indicated by the word *efulefu* (see below).

Through flashbacks, we learn that during Ike's own upbringing the antagonism between Christianity and indigenous worship had been supplanted by his father's tolerant religious attitude. Although his parents used to be "devout Catholics," his father remained close to his older brother, Uncle Osuakwu, after the latter "answered the call to serve Ngene" and became the priest of the ancestral shrine (252, 191). As a teenager, Ike (like the young Ndibe) was a "devoted mass server," but when the Catholic parish priest chastised him for hanging around at his uncle's shrine, his father told the priest that his son had permission "to visit his uncle as many times as he wishes" (130–31). Thus, the novel suggests that there is an alternative to an antagonistic relationship, one that centers around mutual respect and coexistence. In the light of the memory of his father, Ike is astonished when, upon his return to the village many years later, he finds out that his mother has broken ties with her in-laws and talks about them in a way that would have pained and angered her late husband. Uncle Osuakwu tells Ike that his mother's attitude changed after she came under the influence of Pastor Uka, who convinced her that her in-laws were using witchcraft to bring death into her family. Indeed, Ike's mother echoes her pastor's rhetoric of demonization, such as when she refers to her late husband's brother as "the servant of Lucifer" and "Satan's biggest agent" (130). As several scholars have pointed out, by demonizing the spiritual forces of indigenous religion, Pentecostalism also recognizes the power that they hold.[17] This is clearly reflected in Ike's mother, who deeply fears the powers of witchcraft she ascribes to her in-laws. For her, discerning these powers is not a form of superstition but a sort of "spiritual vision" guided by the Holy Spirit, with protection being offered through "the blood of Jesus" (133). Arguably, Pastor Uka is the person who both instilled this fear in her and who makes her believe that his "anointing" offers her much-needed protection. This illustrates how "the spell of the invisible," which according to the religion scholar Nimi Wariboko is at the heart of Nigerian Pentecostalism, can establish a religious economy of fear, vulnerability, and dependence, with the risk of exploitation.[18]

Notably, in the conversation between Uncle Osuakwu and Ike, Pastor Uka is referred to as an *efulefu*—an Igbo word meaning worthless or irresponsible person but one that can also mean traitor—which is described in the novel as "a man blown about by the wind" (193, 205). Interestingly, in *Things Fall Apart* Achebe uses the same word to refer to the first group of converts who built a church in the Evil Forest, thus transgressing the religio-cultural taboos of their community.[19] Another subtle allusion to

Achebe's classic can be observed when Uncle Osuakwu makes the following comment about Pastor Uka: "A stranger has arrived in our midst with a basket of stories he plucked from the air—and he has used these to drive many apart" (196). Note the use of a more active phrase here: It is not about things *falling* apart but about Uka—as the main embodiment of Pentecostalism in the novel—actively *driving* people of different religious orientations apart and causing social division.

The question whether Nigerian Pentecostalism has "community-forming power" is debated among scholars, with Ndibe clearly erring on the pessimistic side.[20] However, in the novel it is not only Pentecostalism, as embodied by Uka, that threatens social cohesion. A similar, though disguised, threat is presented by Ike, who, having fallen prey to consumer-capitalist temptations and a postmodern logic about the globalization of sacred artifacts, does succeed where Stanton and Uka could not: dethroning the deity that, for ages, was the center of communal life in the village. When Ike first arrives at the shrine, his uncle greets him with a question that makes him go mute: "Ikechukwu, the journey that brought you home, is it a good one?" (190). As the story unfolds, it turns out that Ike can be considered an *efulefu*, too, not because he converted to a zealous and divisive form of Christianity but because he has been seduced by a secular "god of mammon." Thus, on a meta level the novel suggests that not only Pentecostal Christianity and its logic of demonization but also a neoliberal capitalist ideology in which local deities are commodified and commercialized in a global economy pose a threat to the heritage and continuing tradition of indigenous religions.[21]

As much as *Foreign Gods, Inc.* offers narrative insight into the ongoing Christianization of Igboland, which, with the spread of Pentecostalism, has entered a new chapter, it also portrays the resilience of indigenous religion. As Kalu has noted, "The gods in Igboland have become increasingly embattled and yet resilient."[22] This resilience of indigenous gods is evocatively captured in the novel's ending, when the spirit of Ngene continues to haunt Ike to such an extent that the latter realizes—too late—that the statue "must return to its shrine—or trouble continues" (329). It reflects the Igbo notion that "a god whose artefact is stolen or desecrated ... descends with vengeance."[23] The novel also narrates the practice of indigenous worship, not as a relic of the past but as something that continues to attract a following and that is relevant in modern times. When Ike arrives at the shrine, he finds a Mercedes-Benz parked with a driver and police officer waiting, indicating that some "Big Man" is visiting; moreover, half the worshippers are "much younger" than the priest (175), suggesting that the extensive prayers and ritual ceremonies performed at the shrine continue to resonate with a younger generation (although the number of worshippers at the shrine is much smaller than at Uka's church); when Ike expresses surprise about the priest having a cell phone, the latter responds that "a man must dance the dance that reigns in his time" (184). Yet none of these issues are developed in a substantial way, and as such the novel does not offer narrative insight into the modernization or revitalization of indigenous religion in contemporary Nigeria.[24] Moreover, Ndibe himself has commented, with reference to the character of Uncle Osuakwu and the way he performs the traditional prayers and ceremonies authentically, that "the art of enchanting talk is a waning art" in contemporary Igboland.[25] The question whether there is anyone who could succeed the elderly priest in leading the worship of Ngene is underlined in the novel by the allusion to the possibility that Ike might be "favored" by the deity, which makes the plot about him stealing the very god he might be called to serve all the more ironic but also painful (17).[26]

Problematizing Charismatic Leadership

Pentecostalism, in its various manifestations, is a form of religiosity that centers around charismatic leadership—that is, a form of religious authority that depends on what are believed to be gifts of the Holy Spirit expressed as "supernatural endowment."[27] Especially in neo-Pentecostalism, such gifts are associated with the pastor's ability to perform miracles of prosperity, healing, and deliverance. Pastors who are believed to have such a "special anointment" are likely to attract a large following. Subsequently, with the rise of Pentecostalism, charismatic pastors, in the words of Obadare, have come to "enjoy an unprecedented prominence" in contemporary Nigeria, and they have "captured politics, public policy, popular culture, and, crucially, the moral imagination."[28] *Foreign Gods, Inc.* can be seen as a literary critique of the social prestige and power that pastors have gained in Nigeria, specifically of the risks these entail for their followers and for society as a whole. As such the novel can be read as a companion to Obadare's book *Pastoral Power, Clerical State*, which offers a critical sociological analysis of the same. A contemporary version of Soyinka's character Brother Jero, Pastor Uka, too, is depicted as a religious charlatan duping people through a carefully crafted aura of "anointing." As a character, Uka stands for the broader phenomenon of "rogue pastors" who, in Wariboko's words, "have diverted God's grace . . . for filthy lucre."²⁹ As Ndibe has commented in an interview, "There are too many so-called men and women of God who hustle the most vulnerable, most desperate members of society out of their miserable feeding money. These ostensible holy men—among them priests, pastors and imams—specialize in selling high-priced fantasies of prosperity to the deprived and desperate. And to the sick, they vend schemes of magical release. This disheartening phenomenon—what I call deformation of faith—is terribly widespread in Nigeria. In my novel, I wanted to bring into focus some of the forms, and consequences, of this modern-day plague."³⁰

The portrayal of Pastor Uka in *Foreign Gods, Inc.* problematizes two aspects of Pentecostal pastorship. One is what Obadare has conceptualized as the "Pentecostal erotic economy," a term he uses to analyze how the relationship between pastors and their congregations is characterized by gendered affect, desire, and control and subsequently is erotically charged.³¹ The second is the moral corruption of Pentecostal-Charismatic leadership (discussed in more detail below). With regard to the former, Obadare even goes so far as to refer to the Pentecostal pastor as a "charismatic porn-star."³² The following passage from *Foreign Gods, Inc.*, about Pastor Uka entering his church during a Sunday service with the congregation welcoming him, might illustrate what Obadare means by this: "The congregation shook with excitement. They stampeded to meet the pastor at the entrance. 'Daddy! Daddy!' they sang, young and old alike. They massed around the man, enveloped him. They bawled, hands upraised, like fans at a soccer game. Some uttered inaudible supplications, speaking with diarrheic rapidity. Others just droned, emitting sounds that were a cross between a quiet wail and a crazed groan. . . . Had God descended through the clouds and into the shaggy church, the frenzy could scarcely have been more delirious" (146). At first sight, this passage assigns the pastor the aura of a pop star, his fans welcoming him enthusiastically as their idol. However, the language and imagery used here to describe relationality ("Daddy"), sound ("crazed groan"), and bodily movement ("enveloped him") also create the impression of an "intimate aesthetics of embodied social interaction," which the anthropologist Rudolf Gaudio has argued is typical of contemporary Nigerian urban life, of which Pentecostalism is a central part.³³ Even though the intimate interaction described here may not be explicitly erotic, it certainly depicts the pastor as an object of desire and captures the affective feeling of the faithful toward him.

The last sentence in the quote—saying that if God had descended into the church, the congregation would not have responded more deliriously—captures exactly the point that the pastor is believed to be a "man of God," a representative of God on earth, and a performer of divine power or "divine libido," to use critical theorist Achille Mbembe's term. While Mbembe argues that "there is no *religious act* not, at the same time and in some respect, also an erotic-sexual act," the fluid boundaries and overlap between the religious and the erotic are particularly obvious in Pentecostal-Charismatic worship, which is embodied, sensual, and ecstatic, and of which the pastor can be seen as the "throbbing erotic heart."[34] Uka is one of those pastors who, as the performance studies scholar Abimbola Adelakun argues, "spectacularize themselves and make their embodied self the visual focal point and point of contact to divine power."[35]

As soon as Pastor Uka has entered the church and freed himself from the envelopment by his congregation, he proclaims God's promises of prosperity. He himself is seen as "anointed" by God, and he is also believed to make "powerful anointing" flow around him (134, 148). This expectation and performance of anointing is central to the erotic economy of Pentecostalism. Key to the successful performance of such anointing is, in Obadare's words, the pastor's "drama of self-fashioning in which dressing, mode of preaching, aesthetics, personal 'tone,' automobile; as a matter of fact, a vast personal entire repertory, is sexually charged."[36] Uka's self-fashioning is explicitly narrated in *Foreign Gods, Inc.* Wearing a yellow shirt, a dark jacket, a maroon tie, python-skin shoes, a gold chain around his neck, and rings on eight fingers, his appearance is described as a "study of gaudiness" (142). As such, the pastor stands in sharp contrast to his church building, which is a "shabby, ramshackle establishment" in a "dilapidated state," as if to underline that this form of religiosity centers around the figure of the pastor (144). The performativity of Uka's preaching, too, is outlined in detail: "Pastor Uka began to strut about the room. Circling and circling, he randomly threw punches at the air. His bulgy body quivered, as if some kinetic force had crept into it" (148). It is an erotic performativity, indeed, with congregants pressing forward, forming "an ever-tightening circle within which the pastor moved." Ike's mother turns ecstatic, her tossing and writhing body taking a posture described in the novel with the sexually charged word "wantonness" (151), as if to illustrate the "orgasmic pleasure" that participating in the spectacle of Pentecostal worship can bring about.[37]

In the character of Ike, the novel voices a clear skepticism toward this erotic economy centered on the pastor. Faced with Uka's fashionable appearance, Ike silently nicknames him "peacock pastor" (147). Observing the spectacle of Uka's performance and the congregation's excited response with "boisterous prayers," Ike further concludes that "the chaos before his eyes was the very substance of the event," while also discerning that "there was a peculiar brand of logic to this madness" (148–49). Although Ike does not spell out this logic explicitly, from the way the novel narrates his skeptical observation of, and visceral response to, Pastor Uka's charismatic performance, he appears to discern the logic of the erotic that, in Obadare's analysis, is at the heart of Pentecostalism.

A key question to be raised, then, is whether embodied and ecstatic Pentecostal worship and its dependence on the charismatic pastor can be reduced to this erotic dimension. Is it the "very substance" of the event, as Ike concludes, or can it be read, in religion scholar Ashon Crawley's term, as an "aesthetic of possibility," perhaps even the possibility for "more embodied, real, and sexed experiences of the divine"?[38] The novel does not explore such alternative interpretations, probably because Ndibe, like Obadare, is primarily concerned with the risk of the erotic economy of Pentecostalism, as reflected in the above quote where he warns against "the deformation of faith" at the expense of "the most vulnerable, most desperate members of society." As Obadare puts it: "For me, although it is necessary to stress that the faithful derive fulfillment from the erotic charge, it is arguably more important to emphasize how this makes them potentially susceptible to emotional, hence political, manipulation."[39] The result of Obadare's decision to give more weight to the latter is that the former aspect remains somewhat underexposed in his work, and the same can be said of Ndibe's novel. Little effort is made to critically grasp the emotional, spiritual, and possibly even cognitive appeal of Pentecostal worship and charismatic leadership from the perspective of believers; instead, this appeal tends to be represented as deception, as if Nigerian Pentecostalism is the latest illustration of the Marxist adage of religion being the opiate of the masses.

Although manipulation and exploitation in religious circles can happen in various, and often quite subtle, ways, *Foreign Gods, Inc.* narratively emphasizes this risk without subtlety by depicting Pastor Uka unequivocally as a crook. We read that Ike, when facing the pastor, sees constantly blinking eyes and a roguish smile, as if he is "bemused at the gullibility of the crowed he'd duped" (147). Thus, the novel suggests not only that Pastor Uka is a charismatic performer of religio-erotic spectacle but also that he exemplifies morally corrupt Pentecostal-Charismatic leadership. In the words of Ike (who himself is not the most morally upright character either), Uka is "a trickster garbed in the visor of a religious seer," a fraud who has been exploiting his mother while she was grieving the death of her husband, making her susceptible to his influence (133). Where his mother believes that Uka is "anointed, a real man of God," Ike sees him as "an anointed liar" and "a shameless exploiter of people," a "con artist," and a "bloody charlatan" (134, 158, 225). Uncle Osuakwu, too, sees through Pastor Uka, describing him as "a madman" and, as mentioned earlier, an *efulefu* (194, 205). Investigating the true identity of Uka, Osuakwu finds out that the pastor is the grandson of a robber who was widely known and feared in the area and that Uka himself also has a history of theft, for which he ended up in jail, adopting a new name after his release and when founding his church. Thus, the narrative suggests that the church is just a scam, a pretext for Uka to steal money from people. Similar literary representations of Pentecostal pastors as frauds, and their churches as vehicles of money laundering, can be found in novels such as *Gaslight*, by Femi Kayode, and *Black Sunday*, by Tola Rotimi Abraham.

The suggestion of Uka being morally corrupt is repeated later in *Foreign Gods, Inc.*, in the story about the pastor siding with criminal drug smugglers and taking lots of money from them in exchange for his prayers that could "save them from arrest" (225). The wife of one of the smugglers, Regina, was not only battered at home by her husband but also subjected to a horrifying deliverance ritual by Uka, as the pastor claimed that she was "bonded to the water mermaid" and would bring bad luck to her husband (224).[40] When her husband dies after the packets of heroin that he has swallowed burst open in his stomach, Uka accuses Regina of witchcraft, and her in-laws chase her away from her house, leaving her and her children homeless. Uka's shameful behavior is contrasted with that of a Catholic priest, who supports Regina and her children "with food and a little money" (227). As much as this brief sympathetic mention of a religious leader may reflect Ndibe's self-expressed "profound respect for Christianity and religious faith when they are concerned with . . . the establishment of an order in which we care for others," it can also be seen as giving the impression that such care for others cannot be found in Pentecostalism and as reflecting the writer's more favorable disposition toward Catholicism, the tradition he grew up with and identifies with himself.[41]

The novel by Kayode, focusing on a fraudulent and murderous pastor of a megachurch, is more nuanced in this regard. The detective investigating the case expresses his own ambivalence about Pentecostalism when he reflects: "Prosperity preachers like Bishop Dawodu have been criticized for living in luxury off the widows' mites of a congregation whose average income is less than ten dollars a day. Yet looking at the prayer team,

I'm reminded again how much good churches can do. Giving back, building a sense of community and, most of all, offering hope in a nation that's stripped its people of every reason to have it."[42] Yet despite this comment made in passing, Kayode's novel, like Ndibe's, is predominantly concerned with unmasking Pentecostalism as a fraud. This illustrates that there is not yet a balanced and nuanced literary representation of Pentecostalism in Nigerian literature that acknowledges the internal complexity and diversity of this mass religious movement, as for instance Adichie does with regard to Catholicism in *Purple Hibiscus* (see chapter 3).

The Prosperity Gospel

The message of Uka's preaching reflects the all-too-familiar prosperity gospel (also known as the faith gospel or the health-and-wealth gospel). According to the Africanist scholar Karen Lauterbach, it has become "one of the most prominent characteristics of charismatic Christianity in Africa, and also one of the most contested."[43] Subsequently, it also features in literary texts, not only in *Foreign Gods, Inc.* but also, for instance, in Adichie's novel *Americanah* and Akpan's novella *Fattening for Gabon*. Although several scholars have argued that there exists a "plurality of prosperity theologies" within and beyond Pentecostalism, *Foreign Gods, Inc.* does not explore such nuances and complexities. In the character of Pastor Uka, the novel clearly offers a negative and perhaps stereotypical portrayal of this strand of Christianity, with the intention to highlight the risks inherent in it.[44]

Invoking the biblical promise made by God to Abraham, and suggesting that this promise applies to the faithful today, Uka tells his congregation that "Abraham's prosperity is your prosperity," and he promises them "double portions and triple blessings," to which they respond by shouting, "We claim it" (149).[45] This preaching reflects the notion, central in prosperity theology, that God's covenant with Abraham has been inherited by, and thus extends to, all Christian believers, and this covenant is believed to offer material blessings as part of a "spiritual contract."[46] Theologically speaking, at the heart of this message is the belief, as Uka puts it, that "the God who owns all the seas and lands, all the gold and diamonds, wants to prosper you" (159–60). In Adichie's *Americanah*, this theological conviction is captured succinctly by the character of Pastor Gideon, when he tells his congregation: "Our God is not a poor God, amen? It is our portion to prosper, amen," while in Akpan's *Fattening for Gabon*, Pastor Adeyemi preaches, "Our God is a rich God, not a pauper."[47] In other words, divine abundance is available to those who claim it in faith. Pastor Uka concretizes this message of prosperity by relating it to a variety of things, such as having children, finding husbands, securing jobs, getting promoted at work, and being freed from evil spirits and witchcraft. It demonstrates the range of social, economic, and spiritual benefits with which "prosperity" is associated. With his earlier-discussed fashionable appearance, Uka is also a "testimony to the self-evidential truth" of the gospel he preaches.[48]

Yet the promise of these various divine blessings comes with a condition, as Uka reminds his congregation: "God said only those who tithe will be blessed" (151). Tithing is a term used in the Bible for the instruction that a tenth of the harvest should be returned to God as an expression of gratitude.[49] In many Pentecostal churches today, this is understood as church members being expected to share 10 percent of their income with the church. In the logic of the prosperity gospel, or at least in one of its dominant strands, tithing is not just a donation but an investment that unlocks future blessings. As expressed in the rhetoric used by Pastor Uka, tithes are like seed money that must be sown to reap a bountiful harvest of fruits in the future. It illustrates the point made by Wariboko that "prosperity theology emphasizes financial contributions as the key to prosperity and wealth."[50]

The risk of this emphasis is that such a message facilitates the enrichment of preachers and their churches who capitalize on the dreams and aspirations of their followers. Ike discerns this risk in Pastor Uka's preaching when he accuses the pastor of having exploited his widowed mother, thus echoing a broader criticism of the prosperity gospel as targeting those who are economically deprived and socially vulnerable. This accusation is made at the end of a heated private conversation between the two. Assuming that Ike must have a well-stocked bank account in the United States, the pastor tells him that a "mighty harvest" of "divine millions" is waiting for Ike, if only he is prepared to sow: "God is asking you to sow fifty thousand dollars to build him a church here [in Utonki]. If you obey, you'll become a millionaire. As simple as that" (159, 162). Seeing through the pastor's intentions, Ike discerns that the pastor has devised this scheme to enrich himself, and Ike subsequently confronts him: "You call yourself a man of God, but you're rotten. Rotten inside and out! You say your God wants me to sow fifty thousand dollars. But fifty thousand, in truth, is the size of your greed" (165). The irony of Ike accusing the pastor of greed is, of course, that he himself has also set his mind on accumulating wealth and is prepared to cross moral boundaries for that purpose. The difference between the two men is only that they pursue different paths to reach a similar goal.

In the above passage, *Foreign Gods, Inc.* draws critical attention to the popular association of prosperity preachers with enrichment and indeed greed. The prosperity gospel is widely associated with a culture of consumption that, in the Nigerian context, is morally ambivalent. Whether wealth and consumption are seen as legitimate or illegitimate depends, as the anthropologist Davide Casciano has argued, on the question of its contribution to the well-being of the wider community. This is reflected in Uka's own attempt to justify himself by claiming that God has used him "to prosper a lot of people" (163). Yet the problem for Uka, in the context of this novel, is that it appears as if "the pastor's consumption has no positive outcomes for society or is entirely selfish," which makes his figure "dangerously resemble that of other evil forces, which secretly consume to the detriment of others."[51] In other words, his embodiment of the prosperity gospel is similar to witchcraft. As a crooked pastor, Uka fails to adequately maneuver the moral tension that, according to Lauterbach, is central in prosperity-oriented Pentecostalism, "between accumulation [of wealth] for the individual and the community."[52]

What if the promise of prosperity does not come through for the congregation? Some prosperity preachers might offer a moral explanation. For instance, in *Fattening for Gabon*, the pastor preaches: "You're poor because your ways aren't straight before the Lord; if you do good, then your Heavenly Father, who is rich, will make you rich."[53] In this understanding, it is up to the individual believers to realign their lives with God's commandments in order for the promise of prosperity to be fulfilled. However, Pastor Uka in *Foreign Gods, Inc.* offers a spiritual explanation instead, thus effectively "demonizing poverty."[54] He claims that the reason is that "Satan blocked your way" out of jealousy, while also suggesting that witchcraft can block the flow of prosperity (160). In this context he points Ike to his uncle and grandmother who, as agents of the devil, would work against him. In doing so, Uka presents himself as having not only the anointing powers needed to make prosperity flow to his followers but also the power to combat and overcome any spiritual obstacles that hinder such flow. In this twofold way, he puts himself at the center of a spiritual economy of prosperity.

One of the scholarly debates about the prosperity gospel that *Foreign Gods, Inc.* implicitly engages centers around the question whether this form of religiosity is a "foreign element in African Christianity" and is "basically an American invention."⁵⁵ According to the religion scholar Paul Gifford, among other scholars and commentators, prosperity-oriented Pentecostalism became popular across Africa from the 1970s—thanks to the televangelism, writings, and crusades of mostly American prosperity preachers like Kenneth Copeland and Kenneth Hagin—and is another example of Western dominance in the development of African Christianity.⁵⁶ Yet other scholars have highlighted the prominent role of local actors, such as Benson Idahosa in Nigeria, who may indeed have had connections to American Pentecostalism but who demonstrated considerable agency and creativity in introducing and developing the prosperity gospel in their own context and in response to the challenging socioeconomic situation in the 1980s.⁵⁷ Moreover, these scholars have argued that the prosperity gospel was widely embraced in Nigeria and across Africa, not simply because it was American but because it resonated deeply with indigenous ideas about salvation.⁵⁸ *Foreign Gods, Inc.*, as well as other Nigerian literary accounts of the prosperity gospel mentioned earlier, do not seem to be concerned with the question of the historical origins of prosperity-oriented Pentecostalism and do not engage the debate about its possible American orientation. Yet by featuring local prosperity preachers, these texts narratively portray it as a homegrown phenomenon—that is, as something that, regardless of its origins, has become rooted in the Nigerian socioreligious milieu—and they highlight the agency of its local proponents.

Moreover, this novel does something interesting by showing that Pentecostal Christianity and indigenous religion operate on a somewhat similar discursive and ritual register of prosperity. Thus, the lengthy account of Ike's visit to the shrine of Ngene narrates in detail how the priest, Uncle Osuakwu, leads the traditional ceremony of breaking the kola nut and makes the corresponding invocations. It is noteworthy that the opening line of the prayer addresses the deity, Ngene, as "the hand of splendor, the hand of riches," thus associating him with wealth and abundance (178). The subsequent text of the prayer is full of proverbial language reflecting the notion that divine riches will be shared with humans and that this includes material blessings. This is most obvious at the end of the prayer, when the priest breaks the kola nut and interprets the four lobes as "the sign of prosperity," meaning that "hunger will never dog you; your journey will always be filled with success" (183). The novel invokes here an Igbo religio-cultural framework in which the kola nut–breaking ceremony is highly significant and serves several purposes, with the number of the lobes thrown up during the ceremony being taken as a symbolic message. A four-lobed nut is seen as a "good omen," as it symbolizes "the blessings attached to the principle of the four market day cycle" of the traditional Igbo calendar.[59] By putting the same language of prosperity in the mouths of both an indigenous priest and a Pentecostal preacher, *Foreign Gods, Inc.* suggests a similarity and continuity between both. It alludes to the possibility, in Wariboko's words, that the prosperity gospel has found "widespread support and acceptability" in Nigeria exactly because it has "incorporated several dimensions of local cultural and social aesthetics," including the belief that "salvation is about wholeness, embracing physical and spiritual blessings."[60]

Nevertheless, the novel suggests that although indigenous religion and Pentecostal Christianity are somewhat similar in their understanding of salvation as including material blessings, they are not identical. Ike's visit to the shrine and his participation in the kola nut ceremony is narrated much more empathetically than his visit to Pastor Uka's church. The portrayal of the pastor as a rather unsympathetic character is connected to the repeated suggestion—by Ike and Uncle Osuakwu—that he is selfish, greedy, and manipulative. The novel's evident suggestion is that in the Pentecostal context, as represented by Uka's church, the emphasis on prosperity on the condition of tithing is so strong that it becomes exploitative. Ike observes the "expressions of hope" etched on the faces of worshippers, yet it is a "hope worn thin" because of "repeated disappointment" as the promised breakthroughs fail to materialize (152). Thus, the only one who gets to enjoy prosperity is the preacher himself, while his followers remain impoverished. The suggestion is that in Pentecostalism prosperity is about an individualistic and materialist quest for wealth, while in indigenous religion it is about a communal and holistic quest for well-being. As Kalu has noted, "Pentecostal prosperity theology, when properly exegeted, is rich in its capacity to re-imagine the gospel from an indigenous idiom."[61] In the light of this point, Ndibe's critique appears to be that the prosperity gospel is not a "properly exegeted" contextualization of Christian faith vis-à-vis indigenous religious understandings of prosperity but is a neoliberal capitalist diversion of it. Thus, without explicitly thematizing this, the novel seems to align with broader sociological and theological critiques that problematize the perceived "spirit of capitalism" in African neo-Pentecostalism.[62] Phrased more positively, by including the indigenous idiom of prosperity in the context of the traditional kola nut ceremony and contrasting this with the excesses of the prosperity gospel in a Pentecostal context, the novel points to the possibility of a more authentic, meaningful, and constructive reimagination of prosperity teaching in Nigerian Christianity, although it does not indicate what that would look like.[63]

Conclusion

Foreign Gods, Inc., as a creative work of fiction, does not claim to offer a fair or balanced representation of Pentecostal Christianity in Nigeria. Yet with this novel, Ndibe as a social thinker and a satirical writer does clearly aim to draw critical attention to some of the excesses of this religious culture. The novel exemplifies a recent trend in which Pentecostalism as a public religion is made the subject of public critique and in which literary writers engage in social critique of this highly popular religious movement. In an interview with the literary scholar Rebekah Cumpsty, Ndibe has indicated that in *Foreign Gods, Inc.* he "wanted to dramatise some of the reprehensible ways in which the true meaning of faith is distorted and mocked, and believers deceived."[64] This comment elucidates two things.

First, for Ndibe, Pentecostalism, at least in the version represented by Pastor Uka, is morally reprehensible. Further explaining this, he says: "I'm troubled, then, by the commercialisation of religion. I execrate scam artists like Pastor Uka who usurp the name of religion to terrorise or terrify people, to sunder relationships and to dupe the unsuspecting. Far too many unscrupulous 'men and women of God' prey on their congregants, including the most wretched ones. I find these predatory habits, masked as the bestowal of material riches by supernatural means, to be contemptible." Ndibe echoes here a concern expressed by many commentators of religion in Nigeria: that the Pentecostalization of Christianity has been a major force in turning religion into a marketplace, pastors into entrepreneurs, religious beliefs and practices into commodities—all at the risk of manipulating and exploiting ordinary people.[65] Ndibe's *Foreign Gods, Inc.* is a brilliant example of the way Nigerian literature offers a satirical criticism of Pentecostalism as a religious movement that arguably has become a major social and political factor in Nigeria, Africa, and the diaspora. Yet as much as Ndibe's representation of Pentecostalism is a humorous piece of satire, it is also somewhat stereotypical at times. This runs the risk of reinforcing the accusation of elitism that literary writing in the Afropolitan tradition, with which Ndibe often is associated, has received.[66] The Afropolitan writer, typically based in the diaspora, may fail to acknowledge that Pentecostal Christianity can be seen, as Mbembe has argued, as a form of "practical cosmopolitanism" on the continent.⁶⁷ Seemingly endorsing a Marxist notion of popular religion as an opiate of the people, little effort is made in this novel to seriously understand the appeal of Pentecostalism on a grassroots level and to explain this beyond allusions to the charismatic posturing of Pentecostal leaders and their false promise of prosperity to desperate followers. In other words, Pentecostalism can only be seen in terms of deception and exploitation, and not as an "aesthetic or a particular poetic of the world," to use a phrase from Mbembe.⁶⁸ A novel like *Foreign Gods, Inc.* offers an important mirror to a society where Christianity has become deeply Pentecostalized and, as part of that process, has become deeply intertwined with money, power, and popular culture, with all the risks that entails. However, if Wariboko is right that "*only some* rogue pastors have diverted God's grace for filthy lucre," then the question that remains unanswered is how we can understand the authentic motivation and ethics of Pentecostal pastorship beyond the stereotype of a character like Pastor Uka.⁶⁹ The simple dichotomy between Pentecostalism being either a financial scam or a genuine form of religiosity also needs to be problematized in the light of the long and complex historic relationship between Christianity and money, in which spiritual and financial concerns have often been intricately connected.

Second, the above-quoted statement by Ndibe makes clear that, despite his strong critique of popular religion in Nigeria, he does not reject organized religion and Christian faith altogether. Having grown up in a "devout Catholic home," he has written that, after a break from practicing it, he returned to Catholicism after the death of his father.⁷⁰ Subsequently, he expresses a concern about "the true meaning of faith," which for him is linked to a religious-humanistic vision: "Belief in God ought to come with a deepened humanity, with fidelity to the idea of doing unto others as you'd wish them to do unto you."⁷¹ Thus, Ndibe here demonstrates that, as a literary writer, he is not only a social thinker but also a religious thinker—thinking *about* but also *with* religion. Ndibe's own commitment to Catholicism, and his indebtedness to the tradition of Catholic social thinking, is not explicitly reflected in *Foreign Gods, Inc.* but does manifest in his critical portrayal of Pentecostalism. Many of the social and religious excesses in Pentecostal culture that the novel draws attention to, such as the antagonism toward indigenous traditions, the corruption of charismatic leadership, and the problematic nature of the prosperity gospel, have been discussed extensively by Nigerian and other African Catholic thinkers.⁷² There is one short passage, early in the novel, where Ndibe's Catholic aesthetics and spirituality perhaps show most visibly. In this scene, Ike, at that time still in the United States, walks into a church on a weekday evening, and while seated on one of the empty pews he fixes his eyes on a large wooden crucifix hanging above the altar. "After a while," the narrator says, "he felt himself the focus of its expressionless stare. He gazed back, disquieted" (23). The suggestion here is that Ike, when faced with the crucifix as a symbolic representation of the redemptive suffering of Christ, is led into a moral and spiritual introspection. The quiet and tranquil environment evoked in this scene reflects a Catholic aesthetic that contrasts sharply with later narrative portrayals of ecstatic Pentecostal worship. It can be seen as implicitly echoing one of the main Catholic theological critiques of Pentecostalism, that its gospel of "victorious living" does not acknowledge the role of the crucified Christ in history. Perhaps this scene can be seen as Ndibe's suggestion that society could benefit from being subjected to the discomforting staring gaze of the crucified Christ, as a mirror to reflect on human vices such as greed, exploitation, and neglect of the Other.

CONCLUSION

Nigerian Literature as African Religion and World Christianity

In the introduction to this book, I made a case for the importance of contemporary Nigerian literature as a prolific, fascinating, and innovative lens for studying and thinking about Christianity in Nigeria, and as a rich resource for understanding and reconstructing Nigerian religious and social thought. In this conclusion, I return to this idea, with a particular focus on two subjects of academic inquiry—the study of African religions and of world Christianity—although doing so will, of course, also be relevant to the other fields this book is positioned in, as outlined in the introduction. Following the close reading of a range of Nigerian literary texts in the six main chapters of *Decolonizing Christianities in Contemporary Nigerian Literature*, what critical insights have we gained, and what scholarly contributions can be identified? My response to these questions is organized around the threefold purpose of studying religion in African literary texts that I identified in the introduction and will revisit and develop here: representation, critique, and imagination.

Representation: The Plurality and Publicness of Nigerian Christianity

The aim of fiction is not to offer an ethnographic representation of empirical phenomena. Yet this does not preclude fictional writing from providing any insight into social reality. In the subfield of literary anthropology it is recognized that literary texts, particularly social realist fiction, can provide "ethnographic source material."[1] It has even been claimed that the works of creative writers can offer "more compelling, more accurate, and more profound accounts of the social worlds they explore" than the writings of social scientists.[2] Admittedly, in the same subfield there is an ongoing debate about the extent to which, and the ways in which, novels and other forms of fiction—precisely because of their creative and imaginative nature—can be read as truly and accurately representing reality. I am not entering the latter debate here, but I echo Ngũgĩ wa Thiong'o's suggestion that the novel "gives a view of society from its contemplation of social life, reflecting it, mirror-like, but also reflecting upon it, simultaneously."[3] Following Ngũgĩ's proposition, in this book I have read the selected Nigerian literary texts as both a creative reflection *of* and a critical reflection *upon* Christianity as part of Nigerian social life. One clear value of fiction in this sense is a pedagogical one. Readers who may not be familiar with the social, cultural, and religious context or with the form of Christian belief and practice narrated in the text are introduced to that context, and its social and religious lifeworld, through the power of narrative imagination. In the preceding chapters of *Decolonizing Christianities in Contemporary Nigerian Literature*, I have demonstrated, with the help of Nigerian literary texts, how this pedagogical value can be deployed for the study and teaching of African religion and world Christianity. At least three key insights have been gained through that exercise.

To begin, the fictional writings discussed in this book reflect the plurality that has come to define Nigerian Christianity, or indeed, following Asonzeh Ukah's suggestion, "Christianities," and the dynamics within and across various Christian denominations and traditions.[4] The various categories of Christianity discussed in the introduction are all represented—for instance, the historic mission (or mainline) churches in *Purple Hibiscus* with its focus on Catholicism; African independent or indigenous churches in *The Fishermen*, with its account of the Celestial Church of Christ; and Pentecostalism in *Foreign Gods, Inc.* Perhaps more importantly, the novels demonstrate how the boundaries between these categories have become increasingly blurred. *Purple Hibiscus*'s concern with inculturation shows how the traditional antagonism toward indigenous religion and culture, typical of missionary Christianity, is gradually replaced with respect for indigenous traditions, something that used to be associated with independent/indigenous churches. If Susan VanZanten's discussion of *Purple Hibiscus* focuses on the hybridity of Christianity and traditional religion and culture, this hybridity has come to characterize, in various ways, other Christian denominations, too.[5] Various novels also foreground the overall Pentecostalization of Nigerian Christianity in the twenty-first century. For instance, *Buried Beneath the Baobab Tree* features spiritual warfare rhetoric, and *Under the Udala Trees* narrates deliverance practices, without specifically locating these in Pentecostal churches but instead suggesting that such phenomena have come to define Nigerian Christianity more generally.

Furthermore, the literary texts discussed in this book narratively demonstrate Simon Gikandi's point that Christianity has become part of "the social and cultural fabric" of postcolonial African societies, what other scholars have referred to as Christianity's role in Nigerian public culture and its status as a public religion and a political spirituality.[6] As far as the church as an institution is concerned, *Buried Beneath the Baobab Tree* centers village life around the local parish church, while *Purple Hibiscus* suggests that the Catholic Church is well established and influential in society, and *Foreign Gods, Inc.* narrates how a Pentecostal church is popular enough to cause major division in the community. These texts also show the ways the church shapes children and youth, such as through Sunday school (*Beasts of No Nation*), prayer sessions at school (*Under the Udala Trees*), and university chaplaincy (*Purple Hibiscus*). Beyond an interest in institutionalized Christianity and the role of the church, many texts also offer a much broader and more diffuse picture of how Christian language, texts, rituals, and symbols have infused Nigerian social life. They do so, for instance, by including references to popular Christian practices, such as praying the Angelus in public (*Song for Night*); to Christian-influenced popular culture, such as soap series and music (*The Fishermen*); and to mass religious events, be they the evangelizing crusades of Reinhard Bonnke (*Sterile Sky*; *The Fishermen*), Marian pilgrimage sites (*Purple Hibiscus*), or miracle campaigns (*On Ajayi Crowther Street*). The heated religious conversations and contestations on a bus, as narrated in *Luxurious Hearses*, further portray narratively how Christianity is part of, and shapes, social interactions in the public domain.

Lastly, these texts demonstrate the argument, put forward by scholars such as Kwame Bediako and Lamin Sanneh, that Christianity has become an African religion.[7] Contemporary Nigerian Christian faith and religious practice are associated with local agents and actors, rather than with foreign missionaries. When the latter are part of the narrative account, either it is in the form of a flashback to the colonial period as in *Foreign Gods, Inc.*, or they are presented as the last of the Mohicans, as in *Purple Hibiscus*. Indeed, the latter novel offers an up-to-date picture of mission in the current era by the storyline about a Nigerian priest becoming a missionary in Germany, which may be the first literary account of what in scholarly literature is often conceptualized as "reverse mission."[8] The texts discussed in the previous chapters further depict Christian faith and practice as rooted in, and appropriated by, local communities, and as blending with local vernacular, idiom, and cultural styles. The way *The Fishermen* draws on indigenous and Christian sources to promote an understanding of the river as sacred and how *Under the Udala Trees* merges the sacred udala tree from Igbo tradition with the biblical tree of knowledge are examples of the development of a deliberate literary effort to narrate Christianity as localized and culturally meaningful. Even a novel like *Foreign Gods, Inc.*, in which the contestation between Pentecostal Christianity and indigenous religion is a central theme, foregrounds significant continuities and similarities between both religions, such as by highlighting their shared emphasis on prosperity.

Critique: Nigerian Christianity, Coloniality, and Alterity

Earlier, I quoted Ngũgĩ as saying that literature is not simply a reflection *of* but also—and perhaps primarily—a reflection *on* social life. Part of the task of African writers as social thinkers, in the words of Wale Adebanwi, is to offer "critical reflections on the African lifeworld."[9] And as Afe Adogame has pointed out, "African novels principally communicate the African milieu's experiences in its historical setting but also critique it." Hence, he underlines the need to examine the "literary criticism of religion," given how central religious belief and practice are to African social milieus.[10] One of the key arguments of this book is that engaging seriously with African literary critiques of religion is important for the study of African religions as well as world Christianity. In both these fields, the status of Christianity as a public religion in African societies is widely recognized and subjected to scrutiny.[11] However, little attention has been paid to the flip side—that is, to the ways Christianity, as a public religion, is also made the subject of cultural, social, and political critique. This book has demonstrated that in contemporary Nigeria, literary writing has emerged as a distinct and important site for the public critique of Christianity as a public religion.

As discussed in the introduction, the critique of Christianity, and specifically the relationship between Christianity and European colonialism, is a central characteristic of twentieth-century African literary writings, including in a Nigerian classic like Achebe's *Things Fall Apart*, and this theme has long dominated the scholarly discussion of the representation of Christianity in African literature.[12] From my close reading of literary texts in the previous chapters, it appears that critique is still a distinct—though not necessarily the primary—feature of the way Christianity is engaged in contemporary Nigerian literature. This includes a critique of the ongoing colonial legacies and colonizing tendencies of Christianity. I have shown how the characters of Papa Eugene in *Purple Hibiscus* and Mama Adaora in *Under the Udala Trees* are narratively depicted as "colonized minds," for example.[13] In Eugene's case, he has internalized the hatred toward indigenous culture and religion induced by European missionaries, making him reject his own father; in Adaora's case, she has adopted a conservative and homophobic interpretation of the Bible according to which homosexuality is an "abomination," which makes her forget about the traditions of gender and sexual diversity in her own culture. In different ways, both represent an African Christian postcolonial amnesia in which the memory of precolonial traditions is consciously or unconsciously suppressed or erased. The novel *Foreign Gods, Inc.* critiques Pentecostal Christianity for continuing this colonial project of erasure in the contemporary era, depicting Pastor Uka as a Nigerian Christian leader who completes the mission of the British missionary Reverend Stanton to combat local deities and demonize indigenous religion. Thus, these texts narratively underline the need for an ongoing "decolonization of the mind" among Nigerian and other African Christians.

As much as the critique of Christianity in contemporary Nigerian literary texts is concerned with colonialism, its legacies, and its aftermaths, the texts discussed in this book also revisit and broaden this critique. It is revisited because European missionaries and colonial agents are no longer seen as the key representatives of Christianity's colonizing tendencies. Instead, the agency of Nigerian Christians is acknowledged, and their role in maintaining and perpetuating certain internalized colonial logics is interrogated. It is also broadened because the texts under discussion acknowledge intersectionality and demonstrate the pluralization of critique toward Christianity. *Purple Hibiscus* offers a gendered critique of the patriarchal nature of colonial and colonizing Christianity, while *Under the Udala Trees* offers a queer critique of the heteronormative and homophobic character of Christianity. Obioma's *The Fishermen* problematizes how the colonial and missionary desacralization of the natural environment continues to hamper contemporary Nigerian Christianity, thus offering an ecological critique. The novels

Foreign Gods, Inc. and *Sterile Sky*, like the novella *Luxurious Hearses*, further interrogate the exclusivist and violent tendencies of Christianity in its relationship to religious Others, specifically those who practice indigenous religion or Islam. In different ways, the literary texts discussed in this book draw critical attention to the ways Christianity in contemporary Nigeria continues to be invested in a colonial and neocolonial politics of alterity that maintains and reinforces structures of power, inequality, and injustice toward those who are seen as Other on the basis of ideologies such as patriarchy, heteronormativity, anthropocentrism, and religious superiority.[14]

In the introduction, I quoted the theologian Tinyiko Maluleke about what he calls the "tragic nature of Christianity in Africa"—a tragedy stemming from the violence of colonialism and its legacies and afterlives.[15] Contemporary Nigerian writers portray this tragedy by narrating how the violence of Christianity turns toward certain groups that are marginalized or excluded within hegemonic Christianity, such as women and same-sex-loving people, or even members of indigenous churches who are looked down on because of their "syncretism." These writers also portray this tragedy by narrating how Christianity continues to cause division and disruption in communities, along such lines as ethnicity, religion, and social class. Drawing critical attention to the ways Christian politics of alterity allow for an ongoing "evasion of justice" in Nigeria, the literary texts discussed in this book exemplify the importance of critique as a central mode in the literary engagement with Christianity.[16] Lastly, we have seen how several novels take on Christianity, in particular in its Pentecostal-Charismatic forms, for its association with a culture of corruption in Nigeria, thus offering a moral critique of the various excesses—sexual, financial, and otherwise—with which Christian leaders and churches are popularly linked. Both *Purple Hibiscus* and *Foreign Gods, Inc.* combine this with a criticism of Nigerian Big Man culture, as represented by the characters of Papa Eugene and Pastor Uka.

Compared to the literary classics from the mid-twentieth century, which have long dominated the perception of Christianity in Nigerian and African literature, the twenty-first-century texts discussed in this book demonstrate that the scope of critique to which Christianity is subjected has significantly broadened and diversified. Moreover, the main concern is no longer with Christianity as a foreign religion imposed by outside forces, but by the sometimes violent and otherwise harmful forms that Christian belief and practice may take at the hands of local actors. Thus, contemporary literary writers acknowledge that Christianity has become a homegrown phenomenon in Nigeria, and they engage it critically precisely because it has become a powerful public religion embedded in the fabric of postcolonial society. Lastly, and importantly, a number of writers engage Christianity critically from what can be described as an insider's perspective. For instance, Adichie, Akpan, Ndibe, and Obioma confess to be Christians themselves, and this positionality motivates their concern with what they see as certain excesses within their own religion. Thus, contemporary Nigerian literature offers a space not just for the critique *of* but for critique *from within* Christianity.

Imagination: Nigerian Christianity Toward a Humane and Just Future

It follows from the latter observation that contemporary Nigerian writers not only think *against* Christianity in the mode of critique but also often think creatively *with* Christianity and its imaginary resources. Religious, alongside social and political, imagination is, after all, central to African literary traditions.[17] The texts discussed in the previous chapters draw on the rich universe of Christian texts, beliefs, and symbols, as part of what Nimi Wariboko describes as the literary quest for "social transformation for a humane world."[18] Thus, we have seen how, for instance, the symbol of the Virgin Mary is deployed in *Song for Night* in a theopoetic quest for healing from civil war–induced trauma and in *Purple Hibiscus* in a feminist quest for the affirmation and empowerment of women. Biblical texts and stories are invoked directly, such as in *Beasts of No Nation*, in order to express the longing for salvation in the context of violence and atrocity, and are made the subject of debates about their interpretation, such as in *Under the Udala Trees* with regard to same-sex relationships and in a quest to affirm sexual diversity. *The Fishermen* draws on the lyrics of a hymn as an intertextual resource supporting its quest to resacralize the natural environment, while sacred objects such as crucifixes and Marian medals are referred to in various texts as symbols mediating divine presence and protection.

These literary texts recognize that Christianity is not intrinsically connected to the violence of colonialism and its aftermaths but can be redeemed and has decolonial possibilities. If decoloniality, in the words of Sabelo Ndlovu-Gatsheni, is about "a necessary liberatory language of the future for Africa," the writers under discussion suggest that Christianity is one of the discursive archives offering the idiom for such language.[19] As much as they acknowledge that realizing these decolonial possibilities is a work in progress, they contribute to that work through their creative writing. They do so by dissociating Christianity from its European missionary and colonial heritage and by reimagining it in the Nigerian context, indeed as a Nigerian and African religion, as discussed above. *Purple Hibiscus*'s exploration of Catholicism as an inculturated religion and *The Fishermen*'s foregrounding of the indigenous Celestial Church of Christ are two key examples of this. These novels link the decolonization of Christianity to issues of gender and ecology, respectively, thus acknowledging how coloniality intersects with patriarchy and human-nature dichotomies, and they deploy various resources to reimagine Christianity in feminist and ecological directions. *Under the Udala Trees*, too, demonstrates intersectionality, with a particular concern for sexuality, as it seeks to unlink Nigerian Christianity from its heteronormative and homophobic legacies and reimagine it in queer directions that affirm gender and sexual diversity. If decoloniality begins with acknowledging and processing the trauma of colonialism and its violent aftermaths, both *Beasts of No Nation* and *Song for Night* profoundly contribute to that quest while drawing on Christian imagery and idiom of healing and forgiveness. Addressing the problem of Christian-Muslim relations and interreligious tensions and violence, which itself is both a legacy of colonialism and shaped by postcolonial conditions, the novella *Luxurious Hearses*, among other texts discussed in chapter 5, promotes an ethic of neighborly living; its subtle intertextual reference to *The Imitation of Christ* offers a resource for thinking about what Christian discipleship might mean in the context of religious pluralism. Addressing and seeking to overcome the politics of alterity, the texts discussed in this book interrogate othering on the basis of gender, sexuality, ethnicity, and religion, and they engender an affirmative vision of life that recognizes difference, dignity, and fullness of life for all in Nigeria.

Some literary texts, such as *Under the Udala Trees*, explicitly engage in constructive theologizing in order to interrogate hegemonic forms of Christianity and develop alternative Christian possibilities. Other texts make suggestions without necessarily developing these in depth. After all, these are literary writings, not theological treatises. Nevertheless, it is obvious that the writers discussed in this book are not only social—*pace* Adebanwi—but also religious thinkers.[20] As social thinkers, they think about and with religion, precisely because religion—and specifically Christianity—has become part of the fabric of society. Subsequently, contemporary Nigerian literature as discussed in this book offers a rich and productive interface for conversations about postcolonial African Christian social and religious thought. In the introduction, I quoted Abraham Waigi Ng'ang'a saying that there is a "deep affinity and common ground" between African literature and African theology.[21] In response to this observation, I have begun to outline in this book the contours of an engagement between the two, exploring contemporary Nigerian literature as a starting point for critical, creative, and constructive theologizing. Indeed, in the preceding chapters I have identified various contributions that Nigerian literary writers make to theology in the Nigerian and broader African context, ranging from feminist, queer, and ecological theologies to theologies of trauma and religious pluralism.

Through the lenses of representation, critique, and imagination, in *Decolonizing Christianities in Contemporary Nigerian Literature* I have demonstrated the rich and exciting interface that Nigerian literary writing offers to the study of Christianity and social thought in a postcolonial African context. I have also shown how contemporary Nigerian literature can significantly expand the critical and imaginative resources available to students and scholars in the fields of African religions and theology, African literature, religion and literature, and world Christianity, among others. I offer this book as an invitation to those working in these fields, and I look forward to seeing how the conversation between Christianity and literature in Nigeria, in Africa more broadly, and in other regions of global Christianity will develop and stimulate critical and creative religious and social thought.

Notes

Introduction
1. Achebe, *Things Fall Apart*, 101.
2. Achebe, *Things Fall Apart*, 124.
3. Gikandi, "Christianity and Christian Missions."
4. For more detailed discussions about Christianity in Achebe's work, see Asamoah-Gyadu, "'Evil You Have Done,'" and Yiğit, *Christianity*; on Ngũgĩ's work, see Kamau-Goro, "African Culture," and Kgalemang, "Novel Biblical Translation."
5. Ojo-Ade, "Black Man's Burden," 126, 128.
6. For a book-length study of this in relation to East African literature, see Mugambi, *Critiques*.
7. Johnson and Zurlo, *World Christian Encyclopedia*, 589.
8. Jeff Diamant, "The Countries with the 10 Largest Christian Populations and the 10 Largest Muslim Populations," Pew Research Center, April 1, 2019, https://www.pewresearch.org/short-reads/2019/04/01/the-countries-with-the-10-largest-christian-populations-and-the-10-largest-muslim-populations/.
9. "Key Findings from the Global Religious Futures Project," Pew Research Center, December 21, 2022, https://www.pewresearch.org/religion/2022/12/21/key-findings-from-the-global-religious-futures-project/.
10. See the various contributions to Aderibigbe and Falola, *Palgrave Handbook*; see also Hackett, "Revitalization."
11. For some key texts, see Bediako, *Christianity in Africa*; Sanneh, *Whose Religion Is Christianity?*; Ter Haar, *How God Became African*; Adogame, "How God Became a Nigerian." Arguably, Christianity in Africa pre-dates the era of the European mission, as it has a much longer history in some parts of the continent.
12. Ogungbile and Akinade, *Creativity and Change*.
13. Kalu, *African Christianity*.
14. Gikandi, "Christianity and Christian Missions."
15. Ojo-Ade, "Black Man's Burden," 155.
16. Hawley, "God Who Speaks," 25–26.
17. Hawley, "God Who Speaks," 27.
18. For discussions of the novel along those lines, see Chennells, "Inculturated Catholicisms," and VanZanten, "World Christianity."
19. Adichie, *Purple Hibiscus*, 13.
20. Okyerefo, "Christianising Africa," 64.
21. Okyerefo, "Christianising Africa," 64.
22. See Amaefule, "'My God Tells Me.'"
23. Adeniji, "Nigerian Literature," 121.
24. Adebanwi and Obadare, "Introducing Nigeria," 1.
25. Wariboko, *Social Ethics*, 5.
26. For instance, see Barreto and Sirvent, "Introduction"; Foster and Greenberg, *Decolonization*; Sakupapa, "Decolonising Content of African Theology."
27. Mignolo and Walsh, *On Decoloniality*, 125.
28. Ndlovu-Gatsheni, *Epistemic Freedom*, 3.
29. Barreto and Sirvent, "Introduction," 5.
30. Zeleza, "Disciplinary, Interdisciplinary and Global Dimensions," 199.
31. For a discussion of inter- and transdisciplinarity in African studies, especially in relation to religion, see Bongmba and Oliver, "Challenge," and Bongmba, "Interdisciplinary." In this book, I expand the notion of inter- and transdisciplinarity advanced by Bongmba, by underscoring the importance of literary texts and studies for engaging the public manifestation of religion in contemporary Africa.
32. Knight, "Introduction," 4.
33. Felch, "Introduction," 4.
34. VanZanten, "World Christianity."

35. VanZanten, "African Narrative," 373.
36. Jager, "Reconciliation," 432.
37. For the issue on South African literature, see Levey, "Tracing the Terrain." For articles in the journal about African literary texts, see, for instance, Bongmba, "On Love"; Searle, "Role of Missions"; Stobie, "Dethroning the Infallible Father"; Livingstone, "Unfinished Forgiveness."
38. Nagy, "Recalling," 42, 57.
39. Bauer and Zirker, "Modern Debates," 60.
40. Eze, "Afropolitan Aesthetics."
41. For instance, see van Klinken, *Kenyan, Christian, Queer*. My decision not to engage in such a reflection in this book is related to the different material I am working with here—literary texts, instead of ethnographic material. Although questions of positionality are relevant for the interpretation of both, the need for scholarly self-reflexivity is particularly important in ethnographic research given the issues of power and interpersonal relationships at play here.
42. Chitando, "Fact and Fiction," 80, 92.
43. Adogame, "Religion in African Literary Writings," 3–4.
44. Asamoah-Gyadu, "'Evil You Have Done'"; Kamau-Goro, "African Culture"; Okyerefo, "Christianising Africa."
45. Ng'ang'a, "African Literature," 27. See also Ng'ang'a, "African Theology."
46. For theological engagement with Achebe, see Orobator, *Theology Brewed*, 1–10; Katongole, *Sacrifice*, 125–34. For a theological engagement with Ngũgĩ, see Bongmba, "On Love."
47. Van Klinken, "Religion in African Literature," 3.
48. Adejunmobi and Coetzee, *Routledge Handbook of African Literature*. The chapter in question is Edwin, "Geopolitical and Global Topologies."
49. For the studies of Islam, see Mirmotahari, *Islam in the Eastern African Novel*; Edwin, *Privately Empowered*.
50. Jackson and Suhr-Sytsma, "Religion, Secularity, and African Writing," vii.
51. Suhr-Sytsma, "Forms of Interreligious Encounter."
52. Bediako, *Christianity in Africa*; Sanneh, *Whose Religion Is Christianity?* Both scholars make the important historical point that Christianity on the African continent long pre-dates European colonialism and mission, most notably in countries such as Egypt and Ethiopia.
53. Maluleke, "Postcolonial Theology," 340, 338.
54. Ndlovu-Gatsheni, *Epistemic Freedom*, 1, 11. The biblical verse paraphrased here is Matthew 6:33, which, in the King James version, reads: "But seek ye first the kingdom of God, and his righteousness; and all these things shall be added unto you."
55. Barreto and Sirvent, "Introduction," 5.
56. In this regard, the study of literature is behind that of film. For instance, see Meyer, *Sensational Movies*; Olayiwola, "Nigerian Evangelical Film."
57. Adichie, *Purple Hibiscus*, 5, 208.
58. Knight, *Introduction*, 2.
59. Walls, *Cross-Cultural Process*, 85.
60. Wilson-Tagoe, "West African Literature."
61. Ashcroft, Griffiths, and Tiffin, *Empire*.
62. Gikandi, "Christianity and Christian Missions."
63. Baur, *2000 Years*, 110–52.
64. For in-depth studies of this, see Kalu, *Embattled Gods*; Kolapo, *Christian Missionary Engagement*; Peel, *Religious Encounter*.
65. Vaughan, *Religion and the Making of Nigeria*, 9.
66. Ray, "Aladura Christianity," 266, 267.
67. Lindfors, *Comparative Approaches*, 121.
68. Feldner, *Narrating the New African Diaspora*, 18.
69. Akinpelu, "From Third-Generation Nigerian Literature," 148.
70. Akinpelu, "From Third-Generation Nigerian Literature," 163.
71. Guignery, "Introduction."
72. Hodapp, "Introduction," 3.
73. Ukah, "African Christianities," 2.
74. Frederiks, "World Christianity," 11.
75. For a Nigeria-specific historiography of Christianity with a similar typology, see Komolafe, *Transformation of African Christianity*.
76. See Ukah, *New Paradigm*.
77. With regard to the Anglican Church, see Zink, "'Anglocostalism'"; for the

Catholic Church, see I. Nkwocha, *Charismatic Renewal*; Lado, *Catholic Pentecostalism*.

78. See Adabembe, "Commercialisation of Christianity."

79. Krishnan, *Contemporary African Literature*, 3.

80. Krishnan, *Contemporary African Literature*, 2; Musila, "Part-Time Africans."

81. Gikandi, "Diaspora"; Eze, "'We, Afropolitans,'" 114. About the controversy surrounding Afropolitan literature, see Hodapp, "Introduction."

82. Agbaje-Williams and Adimora, *Of This Our Country*.

83. Adogame, *African Christian Diaspora*. For an in-depth study, see Ugba, *Shades of Belonging*.

84. Effa, "Releasing the Trigger."

85. Of the novels under discussion, only Ndibe's *Foreign Gods, Inc.* explicitly engages themes of migration and transnationalism, yet its representation of Christianity is focused on the Nigerian context.

86. Falola, *Nigerian Literary Imagination*.

87. For instance, see Eze, *Justice and Human Rights*.

88. See Akpome, "Overview."

89. Adebanwi, "Writer as Social Thinker"; Quayson, *Calibrations*.

90. Quayson, *Calibrations*, xv.

91. Englund, "Introduction," 3. For a study of how Christian idiom has changed local language, see Muo, "Recasting Traditional Adages."

92. Marshall, *Political Spiritualities*; Obadare, *Pentecostal Republic*.

93. Adeniji, "Nigerian Literature," 131.

94. Igboanusi, "Igbo Tradition," 53.

95. About Christianity among the Igbo, see Ekechi, "Colonialism and Christianity"; Okwu, *Igbo Culture*; Burgess, *Nigeria's Christian Revolution*.

96. Amoko, "Autobiography," 195.

97. Hoagland, "Postcolonial Bildungsroman," 219.

98. Achebe, *There Was a Country*, 2.

99. Falola and Ezekwem, *Writing the Nigeria-Biafra War*.

100. See Mabura, "Breaking Gods," 221.

101. Soyinka, *Of Africa*, 131, 136–37. About Soyinka and religion, see Joseph, *Radical Humanism*; Waigi, "African Literature."

Chapter 1

1. Nwosu, "Muse of History."

2. Hartwiger, "Orphans of the Nation," 318.

3. In 2015, it was developed into a film with the same title, directed by Cary Joji Fukunaga.

4. Tunca, *Stylistic Approaches*, 148.

5. Egbedi, "Exclusive Interview with Uzodinma Iweala."

6. Falola and Ezekwem, *Writing the Nigeria-Biafra War*.

7. See Aycock, "Interview with Chris Abani"; Egbedi, "Exclusive Interview with Uzodinma Iweala."

8. See, e.g., Hartwiger, "Orphans of the Nation," and Tunca, *Stylistic Approaches*, 146–74.

9. Mackey, "Troubling Humanitarian Consumption," 107.

10. Adogame, "Remembering to Forget." Adogame's notion of "narratives of articulation" is derived from Ashplant, Dawson, and Roper, "Politics of War Memory."

11. See Soyinka, *Burden of Memory*.

12. Addei, "'Body of a Lion,'" 4.

13. Addei, "'Body of a Lion.'"

14. Mackey, "Troubling Humanitarian Consumption," 111.

15. Mackey, "Troubling Humanitarian Consumption," 111.

16. Durrant, "Creaturely Mimesis," 199.

17. Hoagland, "Postcolonial Bildungsroman," 220.

18. Hartwiger, "Orphans of the Nation," 324.

19. Uwaegbute, "Christianity and Masquerade Practices."

20. Nkwoka, "Role of the Bible," 334.

21. Matthew 7:13–14. According to Bernth Lindfors (*Comparative Approaches*, 8), Bunyan's *The Pilgrim's Progress* "was available in Nigeria in a Yoruba translation in 1911 and in a simplified English version at least as early as 1937."

22. I. Okafor, *Toward an African Theology*, 123. See also chapter 4 of this book, about Chigozie Obioma's *The Fishermen*, which

also invokes the biblical story about Cain and Abel.

23. C. Okafor, "Sacrifice and the Contestation of Identity," 35.

24. Although Igbos are overwhelmingly Christian, there is a history and possibly a recent trend of conversion to Islam. See Uchendu, "Being Igbo and Muslim."

25. Aycock, "Interview with Chris Abani," 7. Catholic imagery is also prominent in some of Abani's other novels, most notably *Virgin of Flames*.

26. Walsh, "Taking Matter Seriously," 244.

27. Mercy Oduyoye, "Biblical Interpretation," 34; about the use of the Bible as a source of protection in West Africa, see also Adamo, *Reading and Interpreting the Bible*, 67–84.

28. Adamo, *Reading and Interpreting the Bible*, 73.

29. Lado, *Catholic Pentecostalism*, 123.

30. Ellis and Ter Haar, *Worlds of Power*.

31. About a "material turn" in the study of religion-related violence, see van Liere, "Image of Violence."

32. Ngong, *Senghor's Eucharist*, 82–85.

33. Garner, *Theopoetics*, 5.

34. Akpan, "My Parents' Bedroom," 270, 288.

35. Ikechukwu, *Being a Christian in Igbo Land*, 104.

36. Orobator, *Theology Brewed*, 95. About Marian devotion, see also chapter 3 of this book, in relation to Chimamanda Ngozi Adichie's *Purple Hibiscus*.

37. Katongole, *Born from Lament*, 119, 120. Katongole links the unpopularity of the notion of a vulnerable God to African traditional religious cosmologies in which gods are perceived as powerful and potent forces. Yet an additional factor is the god of missionary Christianity, who was preached to be almighty. Contemporary Pentecostalism can be seen as drawing on both these traditions, as it promotes an image of an interventionist God performing miracles.

38. Adedeji, "Musical Revolution," 238.

39. Katongole, *Born from Lament*, 68n13.

40. Hartwiger, "Orphans of the Nation," 328–29.

41. Okeke, "Human Person, Trees and Spirituality," 98–99. For a literary account blending the sacred meaning of the iroko tree with Christian symbolism of Jesus Christ, see the novel *Dance of the Iroko*, by Aghaegbuna Ozumba and Chineme Ozumba.

42. Drewal, "Introduction," 6.

43. Potts, *Forgiveness*, 14–15.

44. Adichie, "Hiding."

45. Hartwiger, "Orphans of the Nation," 324.

46. Soyinka, *Burden of Memory*, 13.

47. Livingstone, "Unfinished Forgiveness," 46.

48. For a theological exploration of this question, see Katongole, *Born from Lament*, 225–42.

49. Burgess, *Nigeria's Christian Revolution*. About the role of the Catholic Church in rehabilitation and reconstruction efforts in postwar Nigeria, see Omenka, "Catholic Church."

Chapter 2

1. Green-Simms, "Emergent Queer"; Dunton, "Tuning into the Polyphony."

2. Ajayi-Lowo, "Same-Sex Marriage (Prohibition) Act."

3. Awondo, "Politicisation of Sexuality."

4. Van Klinken and Chitando, *Public Religion*.

5. See Oguntola-Laguda and van Klinken, "Uniting a Divided Nation"; Olali, "African Traditional Religion."

6. Hellweg, "Same-Gender Desire," 890.

7. Interestingly, Pentecostal deliverance has also emerged as a central theme in novels concerned with issues of (in)fertility. See, for instance, Ayọ̀bámi Adébáyọ̀, *Stay With Me*, and Abi Daré's *The Girl with the Louding Voice*.

8. Admittedly, he received this award for his second collection, *Nomad*, which was published in 2022. Nevertheless, he is the first openly queer Nigerian writer to receive this prestigious national literary prize.

9. Oriogun, *Sacrament of Bodies*, 37.

10. Oriogun, *Sacrament of Bodies*, 30.

11. For autobiographical accounts, see, for instance, the stories in Azuah, *Blessed Body*.

12. Dibia, *Walking with Shadows*, 175.

13. Iweala, *Speak No Evil*, 48, 79.
14. John and Ònájìn, *On Ajayi Crowther Street*, 120.
15. Emezi, *Death of Vivek Oji*, 76.
16. Papillon, *Ordinary Wonder*, 146.
17. Ibeh, *Blessings*, 119.
18. John and Ònájìn, *On Ajayi Crowther Street*, 120; Iweala, *Speak No Evil*, 72.
19. Van Klinken, "Pentecostal Plurality," 291. For further studies of spirits and sexuality in West African Pentecostal contexts, see Homewood, *Seductive Spirits*; Richman, "Homosexuality."
20. Adelakun, *Performing Power*.
21. Wariboko, *Nigerian Pentecostalism*, 120–21. For further studies of deliverance in West African Pentecostalism, see Hackett, "Is Satan Local"; Onyinah, *Pentecostal Exorcism*.
22. Papillon, *Ordinary Wonder*, 148.
23. John and Ònájìn, *On Ajayi Crowther Street*, 144.
24. Somtochukwu, *And Then He Sang*, 242, 284.
25. Emezi, "Who Is Like God."
26. Quayson, *Calibrations*, xv.
27. I am grateful to Biko Mandela Gray for reminding me of this alternative and more constructive meaning of deliverance, in his thoughtful reflection on my book *Kenyan, Christian, Queer*. See Gray, "Deliverance of Christian Queer," 321.
28. Courtois, "'Thou Shalt Not Lie'"; Osinubi, "Promise of Lesbians"; Pucherova, "What Is African Woman?"
29. Adebanwi, "Writer as Social Thinker."
30. Falola and Ezekwem, *Writing the Nigeria-Biafra War*.
31. Lombardi, "'Where Paradise,'" 23.
32. Lombardi, "'Where Paradise,'" 24.
33. Burgess, *Nigeria's Christian Revolution*.
34. But for an insightful discussion of the religious and biblical aspects of the text, see Stiebert, "Lesbians, Lesphobia and the Bible," and Ofei and Oppong-Adjei, "Sexual Identities."
35. See, e.g., Oguntola-Laguda and van Klinken, "Uniting a Divided Nation."
36. See Ramakrishnan, "Queerness, Womanity and Hope."
37. Gilette, "Chinelo Okparanta."

38. These opening words are echoed in the concluding line of the acknowledgments at the end of the book, where Okparanta expresses thanks to "God and the Universe, for conspiring together to make this book the assured expectation of things hoped for, and the evident demonstration of realities, though not beheld" (320).
39. Pucherova, "What Is African Woman?," 117.
40. For the Nigerian context, see Macaulay, "'Just as I Am'" and "Spreading the News"; Uchechukwu, "Will of God." For African Christianity more broadly, see van Klinken and Chitando, *Reimagining Christianity*.
41. The Sabbath is the seventh day of the week (i.e., Saturday) and is the day of religious observance in the Jewish tradition, as well as in some Christian traditions, which follow the Old Testament instruction. Most Christian traditions observe Sunday.
42. See Burgess, *Nigeria's Christian Revolution*, 75; Kalu, *Embattled Gods*, 298–303;
43. Kalu, *African Pentecostalism*, part 1.
44. In Pentecostal churches, pastors are typically referred to intimately as "daddy," instead of more formally as "father" (see, e.g., Ndibe's novel *Foreign Gods, Inc.*, discussed in chapter 6). Yet note that Okorafor's novel *Lagoon* features a Pentecostal pastor referred to as "Father Oke" (see chapter 4).
45. Ogoti, "Soundscape and Narrative Dynamics," 296.
46. Courtois, "'Thou Shalt Not Lie,'" 129.
47. Stinton, *Jesus of Africa*, 165.
48. Mercy Oduyoye, *Introducing*, 57, 60, 63.
49. See, e.g., Abbey, "I Am the Woman"; for an overview, see van Klinken et al., *Sacred Queer Stories*, 182–89.
50. See, e.g., Burgess, *Nigeria's Christian Revolution*, 84–87.
51. See, e.g., Achebe, *There Was a Country*, 125; Uzoigwe, "Background to the Nigerian Civil War."
52. Richman, "Machine Gun Prayer."
53. Jehovah's Witnesses arrived in Nigeria in 1928, with the country reportedly having the largest population of Witnesses on the African continent to date. See Falola and Genova, *Historical Dictionary*, 180.
54. Nkwoka, "Role of the Bible," 326, 328.

55. Burgess, *Nigeria's Christian Revolution*, 103–9.
56. For a discussion with regard to the Igbo, see Amadiume, *Male Daughters*; Zabus, *Out in Africa*, 44–48. For a broader discussion, see Murray and Roscoe, *Boy-Wives and Female Husbands*.
57. Zabus, *Out in Africa*, 48.
58. Zabus, *Out in Africa*, 46.
59. Dube, *Postcolonial Feminist Interpretation*, 78.
60. See Emenyonu, *Literary History of the Igbo Novel*, 91.
61. Nkwoka, "Role of the Bible," 333–34.
62. See Sullivan-Blum, "'It's Adam and Eve'"; Kaoma, *Christianity, Globalization, and Protective Homophobia*, 91–92.
63. Stone, "Garden of Eden," 66.
64. Dube, "Service for/on Homosexuals," 209.
65. Nkwoka, "Role of the Bible," 326.
66. Dube, "Scramble for Africa," 3.
67. Quoted from West, *Stolen Bible*, 326.
68. West, *Stolen Bible*, 555.
69. Ramakrishnan, "Queerness, Womanity and Hope."
70. Setswana is the language spoken by the Batswana, the people of Botswana.
71. A. Anderson, *African Reformation*; Asamoah-Gyadu, *African Charismatics*.
72. Dube, *Postcolonial Feminist Interpretation*, 42.
73. Dube, *Postcolonial Feminist Interpretation*, 116–17.
74. Okparanta, "Tribute."
75. Achebe, *Arrow*, 480.
76. Achebe, *Arrow*, 480.
77. Courtois, "'Thou Shalt Not Lie,'" 123.
78. Okparanta, "Runs Girl," 83.
79. On the theme of forgiveness, see also chapter 1 of this book.
80. Lombardi, "'Where Paradise,'" 21.
81. Quinn, "Chinelo Okparanta on Faith."
82. Dube, *Postcolonial Feminist Interpretation*, 197.

Chapter 3

1. The first missionaries to arrive in the area now known as Nigeria were Portuguese, in the fifteenth century. Their missionary activity had limited impact and largely faded away, until new Catholic missions were established from the 1860s.
2. The *World Christian Encyclopedia* cites the number of 25,536,000 Catholics in Nigeria in 2020 (12.4 percent of the total population), while the website Catholics and Cultures cites the following official Vatican statistics from 2020 as 32,576,000 (14.82 percent) (see https://www.catholicsandcultures.org/nigeria).
3. For the report about mass attendance, see Jonah McKeown, "Where Is Mass Attendance Highest? One Country Is the Clear Leader," Catholic News Agency, January 29, 2023, https://www.catholicnewsagency.com/news/253488/where-is-mass-attendance-highest-one-country-is-the-clear-leader.
4. Aihiokhai, "Need for Prophetic Voices," 15.
5. Aihiokhai, "Need for Prophetic Voices," 13.
6. Ihenacho, *Eucharistic Inculturation*, 3.
7. Ihenacho, *Critical Study*, 74; Ihenacho, *Eucharistic Inculturation*, 1.
8. Lauterbach and Vähäkangas, *Faith in African Lived Christianity*.
9. VanZanten, "World Christianity," 271.
10. Chennells, "Inculturated Catholicisms," 17. For a reading along similar lines, with a focus on liturgical inculturation in the novel, see Amaefule, "Roman Catholic Church."
11. Stobie, "Dethroning the Infallible Father," 422.
12. Wallace, "Chimamanda Ngozi Adichie's," 467.
13. Dube, "*Purple Hibiscus*," 223.
14. Mabura, "Breaking Gods," 203.
15. Anya, "In the Footsteps."
16. Orobator, *Theology Brewed*, 10.
17. Adichie, "Writing Life."
18. Orobator, *Theology Brewed*, 10.
19. Baur, *2000 Years*, 147–52.
20. See Mabura, "Breaking Gods," 221. Adichie's second novel, *Half of a Yellow Sun*, is explicitly set in the context of the Biafra War.
21. The relationship between Catholics and Pentecostals in Nigeria has been described as "based on mutual suspicion and disregard. While Catholics are accused of worshipping images and idolizing Mary . . . , the

Pentecostals are perceived to be proselytizers and scam artists." See Odeyemi, *Pentecostalism and Catholic Ecumenism*, 29.

22. Ndula, "Deconstructing Binary Oppositions," 33.

23. Mercy Oduyoye, *Daughters of Anowa*, 9.

24. Stobie, "Dethroning the Infallible Father," 424. On Nigerian Big Man culture, see D. Smith, *To Be a Man*.

25. Orobator, *Theology Brewed*, 82. Orobator here references one of the main documents that came out of the council, *Lumen Gentium*, which is about the Church and has a chapter titled "On the People of God."

26. Quoted in Orobator, *Theology Brewed*, 131.

27. For a recent overview, see Magesa, "Theology of Inculturation."

28. Orobator, *Theology Brewed*, 129–30.

29. Orobator, *Theology Brewed*, 129, 131.

30. Orobator, *Theology Brewed*, 134.

31. Papa-Nnukwu's comment on the doctrine of the trinity as a "mad" idea echoes the character of Okonkwo in Achebe's *Things Fall Apart* (103), discussed by Orobator in his attempt to offer an account of the trinity that is sensible in an African cultural context (see Orobator, *Theology Brewed*, chapter 3).

32. Mutambara, "African Women Theologies."

33. Dube, "*Purple Hibiscus*," 232.

34. Odeyemi, *Pentecostalism and Catholic Ecumenism*, 29.

35. Orobator, *Theology Brewed*, 106.

36. Orobator, *Theology Brewed*, 97.

37. Stobie, "Dethroning the Infallible Father," 429–32; Cooper, "Resurgent Spirits," 7–8.

38. Orobator, *Theology Brewed*, 95.

39. For instance, it is not mentioned in a recent overview article on African Catholicism (Lado, "Catholicism as a Lived Religion"), and it is only discussed briefly in a recent handbook (Ilo, *Handbook of African Catholicism*).

40. Orobator, *Theology Brewed*, 95.

41. Venbrux, "Miraculous Medal."

42. For the Association of Our Lady of the Miraculous Medal in Nigeria, see their Facebook page, https://www.facebook.com/groups/1220344568019287/about (accessed December 7, 2020). For the National Shrine of the Our Lady of the Miraculous Medal, Nigeria, see the website http://www.miraculousmedalnigeria.com (accessed December 7, 2020).

43. On the link between Marian devotion and ritual healing in an African context, see Comoro and Sivalon, "Marian Faith Healing."

44. Wilkens, "Mary and the Demons," 306. Wilken's study does admit, however, that the faith of those praying for the patient can also be a defining factor.

45. As Gerrie ter Haar ("Wondrous God," 422) observes, "Ritual drama in Africa is essentially a community affair, and this also affects the performance of miracles. Official church recognition, therefore, is less important than the recognition accorded by the public which, at the same time, constitutes a further reason for the Church to act."

46. Orobator, *Theology Brewed*, 98, 104, 105.

47. For an overview of, and contribution to, this field, see Chigumira, "Mary as a Symbol."

48. Mercy Oduyoye, *Introducing*, 106.

49. The Aokpe apparition is part of a broader trend of Marian apparitions in Africa. Gerrie ter Haar ("Wondrous God," 417) suggests that the first reported case was in Rwanda (1981), with later claims appearing in Cameroon, Burkina Faso, Congo-Brazzaville, and Egypt, among other countries.

50. See http://www.aokpe.co.uk/index.html (accessed December 8, 2020). See also http://www.miraclehunter.com/marian_apparitions/approved_apparitions/aokpe/index.html (accessed December 8, 2020). Information presented here about Aokpe is derived from these two websites.

51. The ongoing debate about this title is reflected by Orobator (*Theology Brewed*, 97), when he comments that Mary should be seen not as mediator but as intercessor: "The role of Christ's unique mediation is neither challenged nor undermined by Mary's intercessory function." For a historic and theological overview of this debate, see Fastiggi, "Mary in the Work."

52. Ter Haar, "Wondrous God," 421. This domestication is not the same as the official recognition of the apparition (which

is a Vatican process). Instead, it refers to a process where the local church tries to exercise control over claims of apparitions and other miracles, embedding those claims and the popular devotion they give rise to into the structures of the church.

53. Ilo, "Theology and Literature," 122.
54. Stobie, "Dethroning the Infallible Father," 429.
55. VanZanten, "World Christianity," 273.
56. Ter Haar, "Wondrous God," 420.
57. This may be the first literary reference to the phenomenon often described as "reverse mission" (see Ojo, "Reverse Mission").
58. Mercy Oduyoye, *Introducing*, 106.
59. Orobator, *Theology Brewed*, 132.
60. Stobie, "Dethroning the Infallible Father."
61. Wallace, "Chimamanda Ngozi Adichie's," 481n13.
62. Chitando and Chirongoma, *Redemptive Masculinities*.
63. Adichie, *We Must All*, 48.
64. Dube, "*Purple Hibiscus*," 224, 226.
65. Chitando and Chirongoma, "Introduction," 2.
66. As Chitando and Chirongoma acknowledge, "the notion of redemptive masculinities can thus be problematic in a world dominated by men" ("Introduction," 1).
67. Fwangyil, "Reformist-Feminist Approach," 269.
68. "Global Catholicism," 2.
69. Lado, *Catholic Pentecostalism*.
70. Stobie, "Dethroning the Infallible Father," 423.

Chapter 4

1. Iheka, *Naturalizing Africa*, 89.
2. Adepitan, "Ken Saro-Wiwa," 177.
3. See https://zocalopoets.com/2015/03/24/poems-of-protest-from-prison-nigeria-1995/ (accessed April 18, 2025).
4. Orobator, "Ken Saro-Wiwa," 79; see also Adepitan, "Ken Saro-Wiwa."
5. Egya, *Nature, Environment, and Activism*, 1.
6. For a study thereof in Niger Delta ecopoetry, see Erhijodo, "Traumatogenic Metaphors."
7. Kanu, *African Eco-Theology*, 4.
8. Omenyo, "Man of God Prophesy."
9. Jue, "Intimate Objectivity."
10. See https://nnedi.blogspot.com/2019/10/africanfuturism-defined.html (accessed April 18, 2025).
11. Otu, "When the Lagoons Remember," 31.
12. See, for instance, Okey Ndibe's *Foreign Gods, Inc.*; Casciano, "Popular Tales of Pastors." See also chapter 6 of this book.
13. Orogun, "Agencies of Capitalism."
14. Sakupapa, "Spirit and Ecology," 424; Golo, "Groaning Earth," 213.
15. Clarke, "New Waves," 154.
16. See https://nnedi.blogspot.com/2015/09/insight-into-lagoon.html (accessed April 18, 2025).
17. Curtin, "2, 2 and 2: Chigozie Obioma."
18. Curtin, "2, 2 and 2: Chigozie Obioma."
19. Curtin, "2, 2 and 2: Chigozie Obioma."
20. Courtois, "'Revolutionary Politics' and Poetics"; Emelone, "Literature, History and Contemporary Development," 21. The notion of Nigeria as a "dwindling nation" is from Obioma himself; see https://www.edbookfest.co.uk/writers/chigozie-obioma/ (accessed February 19, 2024).
21. Harlin, "'How Can a River Be Red?'"
22. Anuonye, "Writing, the Gambler's Art," 45; Iheka, *Naturalizing Africa*.
23. Olupona, "Religion and Ecology," 259.
24. Matthew 4:18–20; Mark 1:16–20; Luke 5:1–11.
25. Genesis 4:1–16. See also chapter 1 of this book, about Uzodinma Iweala's *Beasts of No Nation*, which references the same bible story.
26. Heinz, "Revision as Relation," 113–14.
27. For a discussion of Ngũgĩ and the Bible, see Kgalemang, "Novel Biblical Translation."
28. Gikandi, "Christianity and Christian Missions."
29. C. Smith, "Two Worlds"; see also Obioma, "Pistols and Repentance."
30. Adogame, *African Christian Diaspora*, 159; Adelakun, "Pentecostal Panopticism," 103. Adelakun dates the start of the series to 1993.
31. Omobowale, Akinade, and Omobowale, "Ember-Months and Disaster Beliefs"; Udeagha, "African Belief Systems."
32. Wariboko, *Nigerian Pentecostalism*.

33. Datta, "Silence Is the Tool," 57.
34. Fagunwa, *Nigerian Pentecostalism*.
35. C. Smith, "Two Worlds."
36. Ray, "Aladura Christianity," 267.
37. "Short Biography," 6. For a book-length study of the Celestial Church, see Adogame, *Celestial Church*.
38. Adogame, "Doing Things with Water," 60.
39. Adogame, "Ranks and Robes," 20.
40. Adogame and Omoyajowo, "Anglicanism and the Aladura Churches," 91; Marshall, *Political Spiritualities*, 78. For a critique of the term "syncretism" in relation to the Celestial Church and more generally, see Adogame, "Aiye loja, orun nile," 25.
41. Harlin, "'How Can a River Be Red?,'" 694.
42. Adogame, "Doing Things with Water," 69.
43. Harlin, "'How Can a River Be Red?,'" 694.
44. Okparanta, "Eko Hotel," 218; for another reference to Celestials worshipping on the beach, see Ehirim, *Prince of Monkeys*, 57.
45. Iheka, *Naturalizing Africa*, 89.
46. In Yoruba religion, Yemoja (also known as Mami Wata) is a universal goddess, believed to be the mother of all *orisha* (deities), including Òşun. See Àsáwálé, "Màmí-Wàtá"; Canson, "Yemonja." A similar belief is reflected in the novel *Foreign Gods, Inc.* (see chapter 6) in an Igbo context, when it narrates the traditional belief that the local river "belongs to Ngene," the local deity, and that "the god's spirit lives in the river" (Ndibe, *Foreign Gods, Inc.*, 101).
47. M. Anderson, "Enchanted Rivers."
48. Olupona, "Religion and Ecology," 259–60.
49. Anadị, "Fragments of Being," 63.
50. Akpan, *Luxurious Hearses*, 174.
51. Ojaide, "Toward a Bioregional," 20.
52. Ijaola, "From Colonialism to Neo-colonialism," 168.
53. Ikeke, "Christianity, Sacred Groves and Environmental Sustainability."
54. Iheka, *Naturalizing Africa*, 89.
55. Werner, "Challenge of Environment," 53.
56. Adogame, "Doing Things with Water," 69.
57. Victor Turner, as quoted in Adogame, "Doing Things with Water," 71.
58. Iheka, *Naturalizing Africa*, 21–56.
59. Akpan, *Luxurious Hearses*, 242.
60. Adogame, "Doing Things with Water," 71.
61. Olupona, "Religion and Ecology," 260.
62. Ludwar-Ene, *New Religious Movements*, 20.
63. Ukpokolo, "Visible and Invisible Forces," 337; Afọláyan, "Homage," 155.
64. Ògúnyẹmí, "Shifting Portrait," 126.
65. Burgess, *Nigeria's Christian Revolution*, 71–72; Kalu, *African Pentecostalism*, 42–43.
66. Meyer, "'Make a Complete Break.'"
67. Robbins, "Anthropology of Religion," 160.
68. Butu et al., "Impacts of Poor Solid Waste Management Practices."
69. Orobator, *Religion and Faith*, 106–7.
70. Douglas, *Purity and Danger*.
71. See Genesis 2:4–3:24.
72. The cited verse is Proverbs 30:17.
73. Modupe Oduyoye, "Potent Speech."
74. Adeboye, *Can a Christian Be Cursed?*, n.p.
75. About deliverance in contemporary Nigerian Christianity, see also chapter 2 of this book.
76. Adeboye, *Can a Christian Be Cursed?*
77. Asante, "Curse," 1:188.
78. Kperogi, *Glocal English*, 183. See also Unuabonah and Kupolati, "Pragmatics of 'It Is Well.'"
79. Isaiah 66:12; Revelations 22:1 (NIV).
80. Orobator, *Religion and Faith*, 115.

Chapter 5
1. Falola, *Understanding Modern Nigeria*, 200–217.
2. Nolte, Ogen, and Jones, *Beyond Religious Tolerance*; Peel, *Christianity, Islam, and Orisa Religion*; Shankar, *Who Shall Enter Paradise?*
3. Akinade, *Fractured Spectrum*. See also Mustapha and Ehrhardt, *Creed and Grievance*.
4. Loimeier, *Islamic Reform*; Marshall, *Political Spiritualities*; Obadare, *Pentecostal Republic*; Ojo, "Pentecostal Movements."

5. Nweke, "Religious Peacebuilding," 17; Dowd, *Christianity, Islam, and Liberal Democracy*, 99–100.

6. Akinade, "Sacred Rumblings," 3.

7. Jeff Diamant, "The Countries with the 10 Largest Christian Populations and the 10 Largest Muslim Populations," Pew Research Center, April 1, 2019, https://www.pewresearch.org/short-reads/2019/04/01/the-countries-with-the-10-largest-christian-populations-and-the-10-largest-muslim-populations/.

8. Gideon Para-Mallam, "An Existential Threat to Christianity in Nigeria? Systematic Persecution and Its Implications," Lausanne Movement, https://lausanne.org/content/lga/2019-07/existential-threat-christianity-nigeria/ (accessed March 26, 2024).

9. On Christian conspiracy theories, see Kalu, "Sharia and Islam," 101.

10. Iwuchukwu, *Muslim-Christian Dialogue*, xi.

11. Adelakun, *Powerful Devices*.

12. Wariboko, *Nigerian Pentecostalism*, 163.

13. Brouwer, Gifford, and Rose, *Exporting the American Gospel*; Marshall, "Destroying Arguments."

14. Ukah, "Contesting God," 106. See also Marshall, *Political Spiritualities*, 214–15.

15. Iduma, *Sound of Things*, 85.

16. Akinade, *Christian Responses to Islam in Nigeria*.

17. Aihiokhai, "Alterity and Religious Violence," 570.

18. Iwuchukwu, *Muslim-Christian Dialogue*, 175. Other Nigerian theologians working on interreligious relations also have promoted interreligious neighborliness. See, for instance, L. Nkwocha, *At the Feet of Abraham*; Umaru, *Christian-Muslim Dialogue*.

19. Akinade, "Sacred Rumblings," 9. See also Anugwom, *Boko Haram Insurgence*.

20. She has also written more journalistic reports; for instance, see Nwaubani, "Killing for Airtime."

21. Dunn, "Four Questions."

22. Kendhammer and McCain, *Boko Haram*, 156–89.

23. Kendhammer and McCain, *Boko Haram*, 156.

24. Alao, *Rage and Carnage*, 115; Thurston, *Boko Haram*, 197.

25. Shankar, *Who Shall Enter Paradise?*, xv.

26. L. Nkwocha, *At the Feet of Abraham*, 136, 146.

27. Mustapha, "Introduction," 3.

28. These tensions are implicit in the novel but can be discerned in the narrative sections about Christian villagers, who question their fellow Muslim villagers and push them into a position of defense. This is reminiscent of the likelihood that the emergence of Boko Haram can easily deteriorate Christian-Muslim relations; see Onapajo and Usman, "Fuelling the Flames."

29. Kendhammer and McCain, *Boko Haram*, 158.

30. Asad, *Formations*, 226.

31. Oluwafemi, "Comparative Analysis."

32. Adelakun, *Powerful Devices*. Admittedly, this distinction can be observed in Nwaubani's text but not necessarily in other literary texts. For instance, as discussed in chapter 2 of this book, many Nigerian texts narrate deliverance in relation to the perceived "demon" of homosexuality.

33. Richman, "Machine Gun Prayer." Richman derives the term from the prominent Nigerian Pentecostal pastor Daniel Olukoya.

34. Ukah, "Contesting God," 106.

35. Adeleke and Omobowale, "Representations of Sectarian Extremism," 38; Olojo, *Nigeria's Troubled North*, 8. For a balanced discussion of whether Boko Haram is an Islamic movement, see Vaaseh, "Political Uncertainty."

36. Dunn, "Four Questions."

37. Nwaubani, "Media Turns Boko Haram."

38. Quoted in Alao, *Rage and Carnage*, 83.

39. Adelakun, *Powerful Devices*, 125.

40. Uwazuruike, "Reporting Terrorism," 109.

41. Alao, *Rage and Carnage*, 119.

42. Ajibola, "Trauma Continuum," 37.

43. On the notion of victorious living, see Gifford, "Healing."

44. Oluchi, "Prayers of a Mother," https://steemit.com/parenting/@oluchi/the-prayers-of-a-mother/; Evangelist Joshua, "Prayers to Break the Curse of a Mother,"

https://evangelistjoshua.com/prayers-break-curse-mother/.

45. See Thompson, "Myth of the Garden of Eden."

46. Nwaubani, "Nigeria Community Divided."

47. Nwaubani, "Power of Religion."

48. Iwuchukwu, *Muslim-Christian Dialogue*, 77.

49. Alao, *Rage and Carnage*, 14–15.

50. See https://moonchild09.wordpress.com/2016/12/19/why-i-deliberately-worked-violence-into-my-novel/ (accessed April 18, 2025).

51. Alao, *Rage and Carnage*, 46.

52. Osofisan, "E. E. Sule."

53. Gifford, "Reinhard Bonnke's Mission," 13.

54. Gifford, "'Africa Shall Be Saved,'" 63.

55. Marshall, *Political Spiritualities*, 228.

56. Ajani, "Reinhard Bonnke's Crusades," 110; see also Iwuchukwu, *Muslim-Christian Dialogue*, 124.

57. Falola, *Violence in Nigeria*, 193.

58. Alao, *Rage and Carnage*, 57.

59. *Sabon gari* means literally "new town" in Hausa and refers to sections of cities in northern Nigeria that in the colonial period were designated for nonnative residents, mostly Yoruba and Igbo. See Fourchard, "Dealing with 'Strangers.'"

60. Mu'azzam and Ibrahim, "Religious Identity," 71.

61. The notion of "counter-offensive" comes from Deegan, "Religious Conflict in Kano," 88.

62. Suhr-Sytsma, "Forms of Interreligious Encounter," 684.

63. Alao, *Rage and Carnage*, 87.

64. Alao, *Rage and Carnage*, 11.

65. Suhr-Sytsma, "Forms of Interreligious Encounter," 684.

66. Iwuchukwu, *Muslim-Christian Dialogue*, 176.

67. Adamo, "Use of Psalms in African Indigenous Churches"; U. Dike, "Lament Psalms."

68. Psalm 22:1.

69. Idowu, *Olodumare*, 178–79; Mbiti, *African Religions and Philosophy*, 43–45. For a more detailed discussion, see Cordeiro-Rodrigues and Agada, "African Philosophy of Religion."

70. Adamo, *Explorations in African Biblical Studies*, 6.

71. See https://seeingthewoods.org/2019/06/18/uses-of-environmental-humanities-sule-emmanuel-egya/ (accessed April 18, 2025).

72. Olajubu, *Women in the Yoruba Religious Sphere*, 82–83.

73. Soyinka, *Of Africa*, 134.

74. Iwuchukwu, *Muslim-Christian Dialogue*, 167; Alao, *Rage and Carnage*, 101–13.

75. Egya, "Not Yet Season of Blossom," 349.

76. See Szolosi, "Uwem Akpan's *Say You're One of Them*." The other story about Christian-Muslim relations in the collection is "What Language Is That?," which is set in Ethiopia.

77. For a background to the Sharia crisis, see Kendhammer, "Sharia Controversy in Northern Nigeria."

78. Dowd, "Understanding How Christians Respond," 33.

79. Suhr-Sytsma, "Forms of Interreligious Encounter," 677.

80. Deeper Life Church, officially known as Deeper Christian Life Ministry, is a well-known Pentecostal church that was very popular in the 1980s and 1990s and became "one of the largest Pentecostal enterprises in Nigeria" (Kalu, *African Pentecostalism*, 71).

81. Aihiokhai, "Alterity and Religious Violence," 588.

82. Iwuchukwu, *Muslim-Christian Dialogue*, 78.

83. See Exodus 14:5–29.

84. Suhr-Sytsma, "Forms of Interreligious Encounter," 681.

85. Dowd, "Understanding How Christians Respond," 35. I have been unable to find historical evidence to substantiate the claim of reprisal violence in the context narrated in the novel.

86. About the complexity of notions of forgiveness in relation to Christianity in Nigerian literature, see also chapter 1 of this book.

87. Suhr-Sytsma, "Forms of Interreligious Encounter," 680.

88. About the Bakassi Boys in southern Nigeria and their links to Christianity, see Harnischfeger, "Bakassi Boys."

89. See van Liere, "Image of Violence."
90. Suhr-Sytsma, "Forms of Interreligious Encounter," 676.
91. See, for instance, Ibrahim, *Sensational Piety*; Peel, *Christianity, Islam, and Orisa Religion*; Janson, *Crossing Religious Boundaries*; Williams, "Multiple Religious Belonging."
92. Iwuchukwu, *Muslim-Christian Dialogue*, x.
93. Okolocha, "War and Absurdity," 164.
94. Edwin, "Geopolitical and Global Topologies."
95. Aihiokhai, "Alterity and Religious Violence," 589.
96. Iwuchukwu, *Muslim-Christian Dialogue*, 176–77.
97. But see Iwuchukwu, *Muslim-Christian Dialogue*, 155–72, for a theological proposal toward Christian and Muslim religious pluralism.

Chapter 6

1. Soyinka, *Jero Plays*, 9, 20. *The Jero Plays* consists of two parts: *Trials of Brother Jero*, originally published in 1964, and its 1973 sequel, *Jero's Metamorphosis*.
2. Soyinka, *Jero Plays*, 10.
3. Omojola, *Yorùbá Music*, 146. See also Brennan, *Singing Yoruba Christianity*.
4. Ferrara, "Banality of Power," 259–60.
5. Casciano, "Popular Tales of Pastors."
6. Bergunder, "Cultural Turn."
7. The notion of Lagos, and Nigeria, as a "Pentecostal capital" comes from Ukah, "Prosperity, Prophecy."
8. Obadare, *Pastoral Power*, 4, 26–27.
9. See Cumpsty, "History, Humour and Spirituality."
10. See Osofisan, "Okey Ndibe."
11. Hallemeier, "Cosmopolitanism and Orality," 156.
12. Sackeyfio, "Okey Ndibe," 185; Hallemeier, "Cosmopolitanism and Orality"; Cumpsty, *Postsecular Poetics*.
13. Shankar, "For Love of God."
14. Kalu, *Embattled Gods*.
15. Kalu, *Embattled Gods*, 282.
16. I. Nkwocha, *Charismatic Renewal*, 176; Wariboko, "Pentecostalism in Africa." See also Rio, MacCarthy, and Blanes, "Introduction."
17. Lindhardt, "Presence and Impact," 14.
18. Wariboko, *Nigerian Pentecostalism*, 4, 40–53.
19. Achebe, *Things Fall Apart*, 109.
20. Wariboko, *Nigerian Pentecostalism*, 186.
21. This argument is developed by Brobbey, "Sacrilege as Commerce"; Hallemeier, "Cosmopolitanism and Orality."
22. Kalu, *Embattled Gods*, back cover.
23. Brobbey, "Sacrilege as Commerce," 81.
24. Hackett, "Revitalization"; Olupona, *City of 201 Gods*.
25. Osofisan, "Okey Ndibe."
26. See also pages 195–96 and 208 about Ngene "winking" at Ike.
27. Wariboko, *Nigerian Pentecostalism*, 55.
28. Obadare, *Pastoral Power*, xvii.
29. Wariboko, *Nigerian Pentecostalism*, 196.
30. See https://oxfordaasc.com/page/2771/ (accessed April 18, 2025).
31. Obadare, *Pastoral Power*, 87.
32. Obadare, "Charismatic Porn-Star."
33. Gaudio, "Modern Desires."
34. Mbembe, *On the Postcolony*, 212; Obadare, *Pastoral Power*, 91.
35. Adelakun, *Performing Power*, 112.
36. Obadare, "Charismatic Porn-Star," 605.
37. The notion of charismatic worship as orgasmic comes from Wariboko, "West African Pentecostalism," 6.
38. Crawley, *Blackpentecostal Breath*; Nadar and Jodamus, "'Sanctifying Sex,'" 2.
39. Obadare, *Pastoral Power*, 90.
40. About literary accounts of deliverance, see also chapter 2 of this book.
41. Cumpsty, "History, Humour and Spirituality," 30.
42. Kayode, *Gaslight*, 205.
43. Lauterbach, "Fakery and Wealth," 111.
44. Attanasi, "Plurality of Prosperity Theologies."
45. For the promise to Abraham, see Genesis 17:4–8.
46. Kalu, *African Pentecostalism*, 255.
47. Adichie, *Americanah*, 44; Akpan, *Fattening*, 50.
48. Adelakun, *Performing Power*, 117.
49. See, e.g., Leviticus 27:30.
50. Wariboko, *Nigerian Pentecostalism*, 234.
51. Casciano, "Popular Tales of Pastors," 62.
52. Lauterbach, *Christianity, Wealth, and Spiritual Power*, 63.

53. Akpan, *Fattening*, 65.
54. Adelakun, *Performing Power*, 110–12.
55. Gifford, "Prosperity"; Kalu, *African Pentecostalism*, 256.
56. Brouwer, Gifford, and Rose, *Exporting the American Gospel*; see also Ngoy, *Neo-Pentecostalism*, which also emphasizes North American influences.
57. Rimamsikwe, "Historical Study of Prosperity Gospel Preaching"; Ojo, *End-Time Army*, 206–9.
58. Kalu, *African Pentecostalism*, 260–63. Gifford also acknowledges this in *Ghana's New Christianity*, 47.
59. Umeogu et al., "Kolanut and Symbolismic Universe," 4.
60. Wariboko, *Nigerian Pentecostalism*, 235, 237.
61. Kalu, *African Pentecostalism*, 262.
62. Kirby, "Pentecostalism"; Nel, *Prosperity Gospel*.
63. For a discussion of the prosperity gospel and contextualization, see Ngoy, *Neo-Pentecostalism*.
64. Cumpsty, "History, Humour and Spirituality," 31.
65. Adabembe, "Commercialisation of Christianity."
66. Toivanen, "Cosmopolitanism's New Clothes."
67. Mbembe, *Out of the Dark Night*, 177.
68. Mbembe, "Afropolitanism," 60.
69. Wariboko, *Nigerian Pentecostalism*, 197. Emphasis mine.
70. Cumpsty, "History, Humour and Spirituality," 31.
71. See https://oxfordaasc.com/page/2771/ (accessed April 18, 2025).
72. See, e.g., Enang, *Nigerian Catholics*.

Conclusion

1. Wiles, "Three Branches," 281.
2. Fassin, "True Life," 52.
3. Ngũgĩ, *Globalectics*, 16.
4. Ukah, "African Christianities."
5. VanZanten, "World Christianity."
6. Gikandi, "Christianity and Christian Missions." See also Englund, "Introduction"; Marshall, *Political Spiritualities*.
7. Bediako, *Christianity in Africa*; Sanneh, *Whose Religion Is Christianity?*
8. About reverse mission, see Adogame, *African Christian Diaspora*, 169–90.
9. Adebanwi, "Writer as Social Thinker," 409.
10. Adogame, "Religion in African Literary Writings," 2, 3.
11. About Christianity as a public religion in Africa, see Englund, *Christianity* About world Christianity as a public religion, see Barreto, "World Christianity."
12. See Gikandi, "Christianity and Christian Missions"; Mugambi, *Critiques*.
13. I derive this term from Dube ("*Purple Hibiscus*," 223) who obviously refers to Ngũgĩ wa Thiong'o's book *Decolonising the the Mind*.
14. About alterity and the evasion of justice in world Christianity, see Womack and Barreto, "Introduction."
15. Maluleke, "Postcolonial Theology," 340, 338.
16. Womack and Barreto, "Introduction."
17. For instance, see Nwosu and Obiwu, *Critical Imagination*.
18. Wariboko, *Social Ethics*, 5.
19. Ndlovu-Gatsheni, "Decoloniality," 485.
20. See Adebanwi, "Writer as Social Thinker."
21. Ng'ang'a, "African Literature," 27.

Bibliography

Abani, Chris. *Song for Night*. London: Telegram, 2016.

———. *The Virgin of Flames*. New York: Penguin Books, 2007.

Abbey, Rose Teteki. "I Am the Woman." In *Other Ways of Reading: African Women and the Bible*, edited by Musa W. Dube, 23–26. Atlanta: Society of Biblical Literature, 2001.

Abraham, Tola Rotimi. *Black Sunday*. Edinburgh: Canongate, 2020.

Achebe, Chinua. *Arrow of God*. In *The African Trilogy*, 287–513. New York: Alfred A. Knopf, 2010.

———. *There Was a Country: A Personal History of Biafra*. London: Penguin, 2012.

———. *Things Fall Apart*. In *The African Trilogy*, 1–148. New York: Alfred A. Knopf, 2010.

Adabembe, Kehinde Oluwatoyin. "Commercialisation of Christianity in Nigeria: A Review." *Global Journal of Arts, Humanities and Social Sciences* 12, no. 2 (2024): 1–14.

Adamo, David T. *Explorations in African Biblical Studies*. Eugene, OR: Wipf and Stock, 2001.

———. *Reading and Interpreting the Bible in African Indigenous Churches*. Eugene, OR: Wipf and Stock, 2001.

———. "The Use of Psalms in African Indigenous Churches in Nigeria." In *The Bible in Africa: Transactions, Trajectories and Trends*, edited by Gerald O. West and Musa W. Dube, 336–49. Leiden: Brill, 2001.

Addei, Cecilia. "'Body of a Lion, Head of a Soldier': The Grotesque in Uzodinma Iweala's *Beasts of No Nation*." *Imbizo* 12, no. 1 (2021): 1–15.

Adebanwi, Wale. "The Writer as Social Thinker." *Journal of Contemporary African Studies* 32, no. 4 (2014): 405–20.

Adebanwi, Wale, and Ebenezer Obadare. "Introducing Nigeria at Fifty: The Nation in Narration." In *Nigeria at Fifty: The Nation in Narration*, edited by Wale Adebanwi and Ebenezer Obadare, 1–28. London: Routledge, 2013.

Adébáyọ̀, Ayọ̀bámi. *Stay With Me*. Edinburgh: Canongate, 2017.

Adeboye, Godwin O. *Can a Christian Be Cursed? An African Evangelical Response to the Problem of Curses*. Carlisle: Langham, 2023.

Adedeji, Femi. "Musical Revolution in Contemporary Christianity." In *Creativity and Change in Nigerian Christianity*, edited by David O. Ogungbile and Akintunde E. Akinade, 231–48. Lagos: Malthouse Press, 2010.

Adejunmobi, Moradewun, and Carli Coetzee, eds. *Routledge Handbook of African Literature*. London: Routledge, 2019.

Adelakun, Abimbola. "Pentecostal Panopticism and the Phantasm of 'The Ultimate Power.'" In *Pentecostalism and Politics in Africa*, edited by Adeshina Afolayan, Olajumoke Yacob-Haliso, and Toyin Falola, 101–18. New York: Palgrave Macmillan, 2018.

———. *Performing Power in Nigeria: Identity, Politics, and Pentecostalism*. Cambridge: Cambridge University Press, 2023.

———. *Powerful Devices: Prayer and the Political Praxis of Spiritual Warfare*. New Brunswick: Rutgers University Press, 2023.

Adeleke, Israel Oluwaseun, and Emmanuel Babatunde Omobowale. "Representations of Sectarian Extremism

in Selected Nigerian Novels." *Utuenikang: Ibom Journal of Language and Literary Review* 2, no. 1 (2023): 38–50.
Adeniji, Abiodun. "Nigerian Literature: Issues Then and Now." *Wenshan Review of Literature and Culture* 11, no. 2 (2018): 121–41.
Adepitan, Titi. "Ken Saro-Wiwa: Poetic Craft, Prophetic Calling." In *Before I Am Hanged: Ken Saro-Wiwa, Literature, Politics, and Dissent*, edited by Onookome Okome, 175–83. Trenton: Africa World Press, 2000.
Aderibigbe, Ibigbolade S., and Toyin Falola, eds. *The Palgrave Handbook of African Traditional Religion*. New York: Palgrave Macmillan, 2022.
Adichie, Chimamanda Ngozi. *Americanah*. London: Fourth Estate, 2013.
———. "Hiding from Our Past." *New Yorker*, May 1, 2014. https://www.newyorker.com/culture/culture-desk/hiding-from-our-past/.
———. "Miracle." *The Guardian*, November 7, 2011. https://www.theguardian.com/books/2011/nov/07/short-story-chimamanda-ngozi-adichie/.
———. "A Private Experience." In *The Thing Around Your Neck*, 43–56. London: Fourth Estate, 2009.
———. *Purple Hibiscus*. London: Fourth Estate, 2017.
———. *We Must All Be Feminists*. London: Fourth Estate, 2014.
———. "The Writing Life." *Washington Post*, June 17, 2007. http://www.washingtonpost.com/wp-dyn/content/article/2007/06/14/AR2007061401730.html.
Adogame, Afe. *The African Christian Diaspora: New Currents and Emerging Trends in World Christianity*. London: Bloomsbury, 2013.
———. "*Aiye loja, orun nile*: The Appropriation of Ritual Space-Time in the Cosmology of the Celestial Church of Christ." *Journal of Religion in Africa* 30, no. 1 (2000): 3–29.
———. *Celestial Church of Christ: The Politics of Cultural Identity in a West African Prophetic-Charismatic Movement*. Frankfurt: Peter Lang, 1999.
———. "Doing Things with Water: Water as a Symbol of 'Life' and 'Power' in the Celestial Church of Christ (CCC)." *Studies in World Christianity* 6, no. 1 (2000): 59–77.
———. "How God Became a Nigerian: Religious Impulse and the Unfolding of a Nation." In *Nigeria at Fifty: The Nation in Narration*, edited by Wale Adebanwi and Ebenezer Obadare, 101–20. London: Routledge, 2013.
———. "Ranks and Robes: Art Symbolism and Identity in the Celestial Church of Christ in the European Diaspora." *Material Religion* 5, no. 1 (2009): 10–32.
———. "Religion in African Literary Writings." *Studies in World Christianity* 16, no. 1 (2010): 1–5.
———. "Remembering to Forget, Forgetting to Remember: Memory, Trauma, and Religious Imagination in Africa." In *The Healing of Memories: African Christian Responses to Politically Induced Trauma*, edited by Mohammed Girma, 17–35. Lanham, MD: Lexington Books, 2018.
Adogame, Afe, and Akin Omoyajowo. "Anglicanism and the Aladura Churches in Nigeria." In *Anglicanism: A Global Communion*, edited by Andrew Wingate, 90–97. London: Church Publishing, 1998.
Afọláyan, Michael Ọládẹjọ. "Homage." In *Encyclopedia of the Yoruba*, edited by Toyin Falola and Akintunde Akinyemi, 154–56. Bloomington: Indiana University Press, 2016.
Agbaje-Williams, Ore, and Nancy Adimora, eds. *Of This Our Country: Acclaimed Nigerian Writers on the Home, Identity and Culture They Know*. London: Borough Press, 2020.
Aghahowa, Timendu. *The Bishop's Prodigal Daughter*. Lagos: Masobe, 2023.
Aihiokhai, SimonMary A. "Alterity and Religious Violence in Nigeria: Toward an Interfaith Theology of Recognition." *Journal of Ecumenical Studies* 57, no. 4 (2022): 569–94.

BIBLIOGRAPHY

———. "The Need for Prophetic Voices in the African Catholic Churches: The Nigerian Context." *International Journal of African Catholicism* 5, no. 1 (2014): 7–25.

Ajani, Ezekiel O. "Reinhard Bonnke's Crusades in Nigeria: An Analysis." In *Creativity and Change in Nigerian Christianity*, edited by David O. Ogungbile and Akintunde E. Akinade, 109–30. Lagos: Malthouse Press, 2010.

Ajayi-Lowo, Esther O. "The Same-Sex Marriage (Prohibition) Act in Nigeria: A Critique of Body Policing." In *The Politics of Gender*, vol. 9, *Teaching Gender*, edited by Adrienne Trier-Bieniek, 71–92. Leiden: Brill, 2018.

Ajibola, Opeyemi. "The Trauma Continuum: Narrating Deprivation, Dissent and Desecration in Elnathan John and Tricia Nwaubani's Fiction." *International Journal of Language and Literary Studies* 5, no. 3 (2023): 37–49.

Akinade, Akintunde E. *Christian Responses to Islam in Nigeria: A Contextual Study of Ambivalent Encounters*. New York: Palgrave Macmillan, 2014.

———, ed. *Fractured Spectrum: Perspectives on Christian-Muslim Encounters in Nigeria*. New York: Peter Lang, 2013.

———. "Sacred Rumblings: Reflections on Christian-Muslim Encounters in Nigeria." In *Fractured Spectrum: Perspectives on Christian-Muslim Encounters in Nigeria*, edited by Akintunde E. Akinade, 1–11. New York: Peter Lang, 2013.

Akinpelu, Oluwafunmilayo. "From Third-Generation Nigerian Literature in English to the Twenty-First Century." *Research in African Literatures* 54, no. 3 (2024): 147–65.

Akpan, Uwem. *Fattening for Gabon*. In *Say You're One of Them*, 31–139. London: Abacus, 2008.

———. *Luxurious Hearses*. In *Say You're One of Them*, 153–262. London: Abacus, 2008.

———. "My Parents' Bedroom." In *Say You're One of Them*, 263–89. London: Abacus, 2008.

———. "What Language Is That?" In *Say You're One of Them*, 141–52. London: Abacus, 2008.

Akpome, Aghogho. "An Overview of Modern Nigerian Literatures and Provisional Notes on 'Post-Dictatorship' Cultural Expression." *Imbizo* 12, no. 2 (2021): 1–17.

Alao, Abiodun. *Rage and Carnage in the Name of God: Religious Violence in Nigeria*. Durham, NC: Duke University Press, 2022.

Amadiume, Ifi. *Male Daughters, Female Husbands: Gender and Sex in an African Society*. London: Zed Books, 1987.

Amaefule, Adolphus Ekedimma. "'My God Tells Me' and 'My Bible Says': Nigerian Pentecostalism in Chimamanda Ngozi Adichie's *Americanah*." *Religion and Literature* 55, nos. 2–3 (2024): 233–55.

———. "The Roman Catholic Church in Nigeria and Liturgical Inculturation in Chimamanda Adichie's *Purple Hibiscus*." *Ecclesiology* 17, no. 1 (2021): 72–90.

Amoko, Apollo. "Autobiography and Bildungsroman in African Literature." In *The Cambridge Companion to the African Novel*, edited by F. Abiola Irele, 195–208. Cambridge: Cambridge University Press, 2009.

Anadị, Ugochukwu. "Fragments of Being on Earth and of the Earth." In *The Green We Left Behind: A Collection of Creative Nonfiction Stories from Nigeria on Climate Change*, edited by Unoma Azuah and Adaeze M. Nwadike, 58–64. Jackson, TN: CookingPot, 2022.

Anderson, Allan H. *African Reformation: African Initiated Christianity in the 20th Century*. Trenton: Africa World Press, 2001.

Anderson, Martha G. "Enchanted Rivers: True Stories about Water Spirits from the Niger Delta." In *Sacred Waters: Arts for Mami Wata and Other Divinities in Africa and the Diaspora*, edited by Henry John Drewal, 27–48.

Bloomington: Indiana University Press, 2008.

Anugwom, Edlyne Eze. *The Boko Haram Insurgence in Nigeria: Perspectives from Within*. New York: Palgrave Macmillan, 2019.

Anuonye, Darlington Chibueze. "Writing, the Gambler's Art: A Conversation with Chigozie Obioma." *World Literature Today* 97, no. 6 (2023): 44–46.

Anya, Ike. "In the Footsteps of Achebe: Enter Chimamanda Ngozi Adichie, Nigeria's Newest Literary Voice." iNigerian.com, October 10, 2003. https://www.inigerian.com/in-the-footsteps-of-achebe-enter-chimamanda-ngozi-adichie-nigerias-newest-literary-voice/.

Asad, Talal. *Formations of the Secular: Christianity, Islam, Modernity*. Stanford: Stanford University Press, 2003.

Asamoah-Gyadu, Kwabena J. *African Charismatics: Current Developments Within Independent Indigenous Pentecostalism in Ghana*. Leiden: Brill, 2005.

———. "'The Evil You Have Done Can Ruin the Whole Clan': African Cosmology, Community, and Christianity in Achebe's *Things Fall Apart*." *Studies in World Christianity* 16, no. 1 (2010): 46–62.

Asante, Molefi Kete. "Curse." In *Encyclopedia of African Religion*, edited by Molefi Kete Asante and Ama Mazama, 1:188–89. Thousand Oaks, CA: Sage, 2009.

Àsáwálé, Paul Olúwọlé. "Màmí-Wàtá." In *Encyclopedia of the Yoruba*, edited by Toyin Falola and Akintunde Akinyemi, 214. Bloomington: Indiana University Press, 2016.

Ashcroft, Bill, Gareth Griffiths, and Helen Tiffin. *The Empire Writes Back: Theory and Practice in Post-colonial Literatures*. 2nd ed. London: Routledge, 2002.

Ashplant, T. G., Graham Dawson, and Michael Roper. "The Politics of War Memory and Commemoration: Contexts, Structures and Dynamics." In *The Politics of War Memory and Commemoration*, edited by T. G. Ashplant, Graham Dawson, and Michael Roper, 3–86. London: Routledge, 2000.

Attanasi, Katherine. "The Plurality of Prosperity Theologies and Pentecostalisms." In *Pentecostalism and Prosperity: The Socio-economics of the Global Charismatic Movement*, edited by Katherine Attanasi and Amos Yong, 1–12. New York: Palgrave Macmillan, 2012.

Awondo, Patrick. "The Politicisation of Sexuality and Rise of Homosexual Movements in Post-colonial Cameroon." *Review of African Political Economy* 37, no. 125 (2010): 315–28.

Awoyemi-Arayela, Taye. "Nigerian Literature in English: The Journey so Far." *International Journal of Humanities and Social Science Invention* 2, no. 1 (2013): 29–36.

Aycock, Amanda. "An Interview with Chris Abani." *Safundi: The Journal of South African and American Studies* 10, no. 1 (2009): 1–10.

Azuah, Unoma, ed. *Blessed Body: The Secret Lives of Nigerian Lesbian, Gay, Bisexual and Transgender*. Jackson, TN: CookingPot, 2016.

Barreto, Raimundo C. "Introduction: World Christianity as Public Religion." In *World Christianity as Public Religion*, edited by Raimundo C. Barreto, Ronaldo Cavalcante, and Wanderley Pereira da Rosa, 1–15. Minneapolis: Fortress Press, 2017.

Barreto, Raimundo C., and Roberto Sirvent. "Introduction." In *Decolonial Christianities: Latinx and Latin American Perspectives*, edited by Raimundo C. Barreto and Roberto Sirvent, 1–22. New York: Palgrave Macmillan, 2019.

Bauer, Matthias, and Angelika Zirker. "Modern Debates: Christianity and Literature, Literature and Theology, and Religion and Literature." In *The Routledge Companion to Literature and Religion*, edited by Mark Knight, 58–68. London: Routledge, 2016.

BIBLIOGRAPHY

Baur, John. *2000 Years of Christianity in Africa: An African Church History*. Nairobi: Paulines, 2005.

Bediako, Kwame. *Christianity in Africa: The Renewal of a Non-Western Religion*. Edinburgh: Edinburgh University Press, 1995.

Bergunder, Michael. "The Cultural Turn." In *Studying Global Pentecostalism: Theories and Methods*, edited by Allan Anderson et al., 51–73. Berkeley: University of California Press, 2010.

Beti, Mongo. *The Poor Christ of Bomba*. London: Heinemann, 1971.

Bongmba, Elias K. "Interdisciplinary and Transdisciplinarity in African Studies: Theology and the Other Sciences." *Religion and Theology* 21, nos. 3–4 (2014): 218–50.

——. "On Love: Literary Images of a Phenomenology of Love in Ngũgĩ wa Thiong'o's *The River Between*." *Literature and Theology* 15, no. 4 (2001): 373–95.

Bongmba, Elias K., and Jill Olivier. "Introduction: The Challenge of Transdisciplinarity in Researching Religion and the Public." *Religion and Theology* 21, nos. 3–4 (2014): 211–17.

Brennan, Vicki L. *Singing Yoruba Christianity: Music, Media, and Morality*. Bloomington: Indiana University Press, 2018.

Brobbey, Gideon. "Sacrilege as Commerce: Materialism, Modernity and the Changing Igbo Metaphysics in Okey Ndibe's *Foreign Gods, Inc*." *Kairos: A Journal of Critical Symposium*, 7, no. 1 (2022): 71–84.

Brouwer, Steve, Paul Gifford, and Susan D. Rose. *Exporting the American Gospel: Global Christian Fundamentalism*. London: Routledge, 1996.

Bulawayo, NoViolet. *We Need New Names*. London: Chatto & Windus, 2013.

Burgess, Richard. *Nigeria's Christian Revolution: The Civil War Revival and Its Pentecostal Progeny (1967–2006)*. Oxford: Regnum Books, 2008.

Butu, A. W., et al. "The Impacts of Poor Solid Waste Management Practices on Ala River Water Quality in Akure, Nigeria." *Global Journal of Earth and Environmental Science* 5, no. 2 (2020): 37–50.

Canson, Patricia E. "Yemonja." *Encyclopedia Britannica*, August 15, 2014. https://www.britannica.com/topic/Yemonja/.

Casciano, Davide. "Popular Tales of Pastors, Luxury, Frauds and Corruption: Pentecostalism, Conspicuous Consumption, and the Moral Economy of Corruption in Nigeria." *Journal of Extreme Anthropology* 5, no. 2 (2021): 52–71.

Chennells, Anthony. "Inculturated Catholicisms in Chimamanda Adichie's *Purple Hibiscus*." *English Academy Review* 26, no. 1 (2009): 15–26.

Chigumira, Godfrey. "Mary as a Symbol of Inspiration for the Empowerment of Southern African Christian Women Disproportionately Infected/Affected by HIV and AIDS." *Black Theology* 12, no. 2 (2014).

Chitando, Ezra. "Fact and Fiction: Images of Missionaries in Zimbabwean Literature." *Studies in World Christianity* 7, no. 1 (2001): 80–94.

Chitando, Ezra, and Sophie Chirongoma. "Introduction: On the Title." In *Redemptive Masculinities: Men, HIV, and Religion*, edited by Ezra Chitando and Sophie Chirongoma, 1–28. Geneva: WCC Publications, 2012.

——, eds. *Redemptive Masculinities: Men, HIV, and Religion*. Geneva: WCC Publications, 2012.

Clarke, Michelle Louise. "New Waves: African Environmental Ethics and Ocean Ecosystems." In *African Environmental Ethics: A Critical Reader*, edited by Munamato Chemhuru, 153–72. Cham: Springer, 2019.

Comoro, Christopher, and John Sivalon. "The Marian Faith Healing Ministry: An African Expression of Popular Catholicism in Tanzania." In *East African Expressions of Christianity*, edited by Thomas T. Spear and Isaria N. Kimambo, 275–95. Oxford: James Currey, 1999.

Cooper, Brenda. "Resurgent Spirits, Catholic Echoes of Igbo and Petals of Purple: The Syncretised World of Chimamanda Ngozi Adichie's *Purple Hibiscus*." *African Literature Today* 27 (2010): 1–12.

Cordeiro-Rodrigues, Luís, and Ada Agada. "African Philosophy of Religion: Concepts of God, Ancestors, and the Problem of Evil." *Philosophy Compass* 17, no. 8 (2022): e12864.

Courtois, Cédric. "'Revolutionary Politics' and Poetics in the Nigerian Bildungsroman: The Coming-of-Age of the Individual and the Nation in Chigozie Obioma's *The Fishermen* (2015)." *Commonwealth Essays and Studies* 42, no. 1 (2019): 1–14.

———. "'Thou Shalt Not Lie with Mankind as with Womankind: It Is Abomination!': Lesbian (Body-)Bildung in Chinelo Okparanta's *Under the Udala Trees* (2015)." *Commonwealth Essays and Studies* 40, no. 2 (2018): 119–33.

Crawley, Ashon T. *Blackpentecostal Breath: The Aesthetics of Possibility*. New York: Fordham University Press, 2017.

Cumpsty, Rebekah. "History, Humour and Spirituality in Contemporary Nigeria: An Interview with Okey Ndibe." *Wasafiri* 36, no. 1 (2021): 25–31.

———. *Postsecular Poetics: Negotiating the Sacred and Secular in Contemporary African Fiction*. London: Routledge, 2023.

Curtin, Amanda. "2, 2 and 2: Chigozie Obioma talks about *The Fishermen*." February 23, 2015. https://amandacurtin.com/2015/02/23/2-2-and-2-chigozie-obioma-talks-about-the-fishermen/.

Daré, Abi. *The Girl with the Louding Voice*. London: Penguin, 2021.

Datta, Sreya Mallika. "Silence Is the Tool of the Unconcerned: An Interview with Chigozie Obioma." *Wasafiri* 35, no. 1 (2020): 57–62.

Deegan, Heather. "Religious Conflict in Kano: What Are the Fundamental Issues?" *Commonwealth and Comparative Politics* 49, no. 1 (2011): 80–97.

Dibia, Jude. *Walking with Shadows*. 2nd ed. Lagos: Jalaa Writers' Collective, 2011.

Dike, Onyinye. "Everyone Can Tell a Story: Adaobi Tricia Nwaubani's First Draft." *The Republic*, July 14, 2023. https://republic.com.ng/june-july-2023/first-draft-adaobi-tricia-nwaubani/.

Dike, Uzoma A. "Lament Psalms, the Christian Community and Governance in Contemporary Nigeria." *Wukari International Studies Journal* 7, no. 3 (2023): 217–30.

Douglas, Mary. *Purity and Danger: An Analysis of Concepts of Pollution and Taboo*. Routledge Classics. London: Routledge, 2002.

Dowd, Robert A. *Christianity, Islam, and Liberal Democracy: Lessons from Sub-Saharan Africa*. Oxford: Oxford University Press, 2015.

———. "Understanding How Christians Respond to Religious Persecution: Evidence from Kenya and Nigeria." *Review of Faith and International Affairs* 15, no. 1 (2017): 31–42.

Drewal, Henry John. "Introduction: Charting the Voyage." In *Sacred Waters: Arts for Mami Wata and Other Divinities in Africa and the Diaspora*, edited by Henry John Drewal, 1–18. Bloomington: Indiana University Press, 2008.

Dube, Musa W. *Postcolonial Feminist Interpretation of the Bible*. St. Louis: Chalice Press, 2000.

———. "*Purple Hibiscus*: A Postcolonial Feminist Reading." *Missionalia* 46, no. 2 (2018): 222–35.

———. "The Scramble for Africa as the Biblical Scramble for Africa: An Introduction." In *Postcolonial Perspectives in African Biblical Interpretations*, edited by Musa W. Dube, Andrew M. Mbuvi, and Dora Mbuwayesango, 1–28. Atlanta: Society of Biblical Literature, 2012.

———. "Service for/on Homosexuals." In *AfricaPraying: A Handbook on HIV/AIDS Sensitive Sermon Guidelines and Liturgy*, edited by Musa W. Dube, 209–14. Geneva: WCC Publications, 2003.

Dunn, Kate. "Four Questions for Adaobi Tricia Nwaubani." *Publishers Weekly*, September 6, 2018. https://www.publishersweekly.com/pw/by-topic/childrens/childrens-authors/article/77919-four-questions-for-adaobi-tricia-nwaubani.html.

Dunton, Chris. "Tuning into the Polyphony: The Emergence of LGBTQ+ Writing in Africa." *Research in African Literatures* 53, no. 4 (2023): 1–14.

Durrant, Sam. "Creaturely Mimesis: Life After Necropolitics in Chris Abani's *Song for Night*." *Research in African Literatures* 49, no. 3 (2018): 178–206.

Durrant, Sam, and Ryan Topper. "Cosmological Trauma and Postcolonial Modernity." In *The Routledge Companion to Literature and Trauma*, edited by Colin Davis and Hanna Meretoja, 187–200. London: Routledge, 2020.

Edwin, Shirin. "Geopolitical and Global Topologies in Fiction: Islam at the Fault Lines in Africa and the World." In *Routledge Handbook of African Literature*, edited by Moradewun Adejunmobi and Carli Coetzee, 261–75. London: Routledge, 2019.

———. *Privately Empowered: Expressing Feminism in Islam in Northern Nigerian Fiction*. Evanston: Northwestern University Press, 2016.

Effa, Allan L. "Releasing the Trigger: The Nigerian Factor in Global Christianity." *International Bulletin of Missionary Research* 37, no. 4 (2013): 214–18.

Egbedi, Hadassah. "Exclusive Interview with Uzodinma Iweala, Author, *Beasts of No Nation*." Ventures Africa, October 16, 2015. https://venturesafrica.com/exclusive-interview-with-uzodinma-iweala-author-beasts-of-no-nation/.

Egya, Sule E. *Nature, Environment, and Activism in Nigerian Literature*. London: Routledge, 2020.

———. "Not Yet Season of Blossom: Writing Northern Nigeria into the Global Space." In *Routledge Handbook of Minority Discourses in African Literature*, edited by Tanure Ojaide and Joyce Ashuntantang, 341–51. London: Routledge, 2020.

Ehirim, Nnamdi. *Prince of Monkeys*. Berkeley: Counterpoint, 2019.

Ekechi, F. K. "Colonialism and Christianity in West Africa: The Igbo Case, 1900–1915." *Journal of African History* 12, no. 1 (1971): 103–15.

Ekwuyasi, Francesca. *Butter Honey Pig Bread*. Lagos: Ouida, 2022.

Ellis, Stephen, and Gerrie ter Haar. *Worlds of Power: Religious Thought and Political Practice in Africa*. New York: Oxford University Press, 2004.

Emelone, Chioma. "Literature, History and Contemporary Development in Nigeria: A Study of Chigozie Obioma's *The Fishermen*." *Akwa Journal of English Language and Literary Studies* 7, no. 1 (2020): 21–37.

Emenyonu, Ernest N. *The Literary History of the Igbo Novel: African Literature in African Languages*. London: Routledge, 2020.

Emezi, Akwaeke. *The Death of Vivek Oji*. London: Faber & Faber, 2020.

———. "Who Is Like God." *Granta*, June 13, 2017. https://granta.com/who-is-like-god/.

Enang, Kenneth. *The Nigerian Catholics and the Independent Churches: A Call to Authentic Faith*. Nairobi: Paulines, 2012.

Englund, Harri, ed. *Christianity and Public Culture in Africa*. Athens: Ohio University Press, 2011.

———. "Introduction: Rethinking African Christianities beyond the Religion-Politics Conundrum." In *Christianity and Public Culture in Africa*, edited by Harri Englund, 1–24. Athens: Ohio University Press, 2011.

Erhijodo, Emmanuel E. "Traumatogenic Metaphors and Religious Motifs in Niger Delta Ecopoetry." *Journal of the British Academy* 12, nos. 1–2 (2024): a17.

Eze, Chielozona. "Afropolitan Aesthetics as an Ethics of Openness." In *Afropolitan*

Literature as World Literature, edited by James Hodapp, 131–50. London: Bloomsbury, 2020.

———. *Justice and Human Rights in the African Imagination: We, Too, Are Humans*. London: Routledge, 2021.

———. "'We, Afropolitans.'" *Journal of African Cultural Studies* 28, no. 1 (2015): 114–19.

Fagunwa, Omololu. *Nigerian Pentecostalism: A Brief History and the Untold Story of Assemblies of God in Nigeria*. Lagos: Cross Impact and Advancement Initiative, 2022.

Falola, Toyin. *Nigerian Literary Imagination and the Nationhood Project*. New York: Palgrave Macmillan, 2022.

———. *Understanding Modern Nigeria: Ethnicity, Democracy, and Development*. Cambridge: Cambridge University Press, 2021.

———. *Violence in Nigeria: The Crisis of Religious Politics and Secular Ideologies*. Rochester: University of Rochester Press, 1998.

Falola, Toyin, and Ogechukwu Ezekwem, eds. *Writing the Nigeria-Biafra War*. Woodbridge: James Currey, 2016.

Falola, Toyin, and Ann Genova. *Historical Dictionary of Nigeria*. Lanham, MD: Scarecrow Press, 2009.

Fassin, Didier. "True Life, Real Lives: Revisiting the Boundaries between Ethnography and Fiction." *American Ethnologist* 41, no. 1 (2014): 40–55.

Fastiggi, Robert. "Mary in the Work of Redemption." In *The Oxford Handbook of Mary*, edited by Chris Maunder, 303–19. Oxford: Oxford University Press, 2019.

Felch, Susan M. "Introduction." In *The Cambridge Companion to Literature and Religion*, edited by Susan M. Felch, 1–18. Cambridge: Cambridge University Press, 2016.

Feldner, Maximilian. *Narrating the New African Diaspora: 21st Century Nigerian Literature in Context*. New York: Palgrave Macmillan, 2019.

Ferrara, Mark S. "The Banality of Power in the Postcolony: Grifters, Tricksters, and Charlatans in Wole Soyinka's Jero Plays." *Partial Answers: Journal of Literature and the History of Ideas* 21, no. 2 (2023): 257–77.

Foster, Elizabeth A., and Udi Greenberg, eds. *Decolonization and the Remaking of Christianity*. Philadelphia: University of Pennsylvania Press, 2023.

Fourchard, Laurent. "Dealing with 'Strangers': Allocating Urban Space to Migrants in Nigeria and French West Africa, End of the Nineteenth Century to 1960." In *African Cities: Competing Claims on Urban Spaces*, edited by Francesca Locatelli and Paul Nugent, 187–217. Leiden: Brill, 2009.

Frederiks, Martha. "World Christianity: Contours of an Approach." In *World Christianity: Methodological Considerations*, edited by Martha Frederiks and Dorottya Nagy, 10–40. Leiden: Brill, 2021.

Fwangyil, Gloria Ada. "A Reformist-Feminist Approach to Chimamanda Ngozi Adichie's *Purple Hibiscus*." *African Research Review* 5, no. 3 (2011): 261–74.

Garner, Phillip Michael. *Theopoetics: Spiritual Poetry for Contemplative Theology and Daily Living*. Eugene, OR: Wipf and Stock, 2017.

Gaudio, Rudolf. "Modern Desires in Urban Nigeria." *Cultural Anthropology*, July 21, 2015. https://culanth.org/fieldsights/modern-desires-in-urban-nigeria/.

Gifford, Paul. "'Africa Shall Be Saved': An Appraisal of Reinhard Bonnke's Pan-African Crusade." *Journal of Religion in Africa* 17, no. 1 (1987): 63–92.

———. *Ghana's New Christianity: Pentecostalism in a Globalising African Economy*. London: Hurst, 2004.

———. "Healing in African Pentecostalism: The 'Victorious Living' of David Oyedepo." In *Global Pentecostal and Charismatic Healing*, edited by Candy Gunther Brown, 251–66. Oxford: Oxford University Press, 2011.

---. "Prosperity: A New and Foreign Element in African Christianity." *Religion* 20, no. 4 (1990): 373–88.

---. "Reinhard Bonnke's Mission to Africa, and His 1991 Nairobi Crusade." *Wajibu* 9, no. 1 (1994): 13–19.

Gikandi, Simon. "Christianity and Christian Missions." In *The Routledge Encyclopedia of African Literature*, edited by Simon Gikandi. London: Routledge, 2009.

---. "Diaspora and Pan-Africanism." In *The Routledge Encyclopedia of African Literature*, edited by Simon Gikandi. London: Routledge, 2009.

Gilette, Courtney. "Chinelo Okparanta on Her New Novel 'Under the Udala Trees' and Being a Champion of Love." Lamba Literary, October 7, 2017. https://www.lambdaliterary.org/2015/10/chinelo-okparanta-on-her-new-novel-under-the-udala-trees-and-being-a-champion-of-love/.

"Global Catholicism: Trends and Forecasts." Washington, DC: Center for Applied Research in the Apostolate, 2015.

Golo, Ben-Willie Kwaku. "The Groaning Earth and the Greening of Neo-Pentecostalism in Twenty-First-Century Ghana." *Penteco Studies: An Interdisciplinary Journal for Research on the Pentecostal and Charismatic Movements* 13, no. 2 (2014): 197–216.

Gray, Biko Mandela. "The Deliverance of Christian Queer." *Religious Studies Review* 46, no. 3 (2020): 321–24.

Green-Simms, Lindsey. "The Emergent Queer: Homosexuality and Nigerian Fiction in the 21st Century." *Research in African Literatures* 47, no. 2 (2016): 139–61.

Guignery, Vanessa. "Introduction: Contemporary Nigerian Literature in English: An Orchestra of Pluralities." *Études anglaises* 2 (2022): 131–46.

Habila, Helon. *The Chibok Girls: The Boko Haram Kidnappings and Islamic Militancy in Nigeria*. London: Penguin, 2017.

Hackett, Rosalind I. J. "Is Satan Local or Global? Reflections on a Nigerian Deliverance Movement." In *Who Is Afraid of the Holy Ghost? Pentecostalism and Globalization in Africa and Beyond*, edited by Afe Adogame, 111–32. Trenton: Africa World Press, 2011.

---. "Revitalization in African Traditional Religion." In *African Traditional Religions in Contemporary Society*, edited by Jacob K. Olupona, 135–48. St. Paul: Paragon House, 1991.

Hallemeier, Katherine. "Cosmopolitanism and Orality in Okey Ndibe's *Foreign Gods, Inc.*" In *The Limits of Cosmopolitanism: Globalization and Its Discontents in Contemporary Literature*, edited by Aleksandar Stevic and Philip Tsang, 141–58. London: Routledge, 2019.

Harlin, Kate. "'How Can a River Be Red?' Violent Petroculture in Chigozie Obioma's *The Fishermen*." *Journal of Postcolonial Writing* 55, no. 5 (2019): 685–97.

Harnischfeger, Johannes. "The Bakassi Boys: Fighting Crime in Nigeria." *Journal of Modern African Studies* 41, no. 1 (2003): 23–49.

Hartwiger, Alexander. "Orphans of the Nation: Transitional Justice Practices in Third Generation Nigerian Child Soldier Narratives." *Journal of the African Literature Association* 16, no. 2 (2022): 317–31.

Hawley, John C. "The God Who Speaks in Many Voices, and in None: African Novelists on Indigenous and Colonial Religion." In *Literary Expressions of African Spirituality*, edited by Carol P. Marsh-Lockett and Elizabeth J. West, 15–34. Lanham, MD: Lexington Books, 2013.

Heinz, Sarah. "Revision as Relation: Adapting Parable in Chigozie Obioma's *The Fishermen*." *Adaptation* 15, no. 1 (2022): 113–26.

Hellweg, Joseph. "Same-Gender Desire, Religion, and Homophobia: Challenges, Complexities, and Progress for LGBTIQ Liberation in Africa."

Journal of the American Academy of Religion 83, no. 4 (2015): 887–96.

Hoagland, Ericka A. "The Postcolonial Bildungsroman." In *A History of the Bildungsroman*, edited by Sarah Graham, 217–38. Cambridge: Cambridge University Press, 2019.

Hodapp, James. "Introduction: Africa and the Rest." In *Afropolitan Literature as World Literature*, edited by James Hodapp, 1–12. London: Bloomsbury, 2020.

Homewood, Nathanael J. *Seductive Spirits: Deliverance, Demons, and Sexual Worldmaking in Ghanaian Pentecostalism*. Stanford: Stanford University Press, 2024.

Ibeh, Chukwuebuka. *Blessings*. London: Viking, 2024.

Ibrahim, Murtala. *Sensational Piety: Practices of Mediation in Islamic and Pentecostal Movements in Abuja, Nigeria*. London: Bloomsbury, 2024.

Idowu, E. Bolaji. *Olodumare: God in Yoruba Belief*. London: Longmans, 1966.

Iduma, Emmanuel. *The Sound of Things to Come*. New York: Mantle, 2016.

Igboanusi, Herbert. "The Igbo Tradition in the Nigerian Novel." *African Study Monographs* 22, no. 2 (2001): 53–72.

Iheka, Cajetan. *Naturalizing Africa: Ecological Violence, Agency, and Postcolonial Resistance in African Literature*. Cambridge: Cambridge University Press, 2020.

Ihenacho, David Asonye. *A Critical Study of the Catholicism of the Igbo People of Nigeria*. Vol. 1 of *African Christianity Rises*. New York: iUniverse, 2004.

———. *Eucharistic Inculturation in Igbo Catholicism*. Vol. 2 of *African Christianity Rises*. New York: iUniverse, 2004.

Ijaola, Samson Oluwatope. "From Colonialism to Neo-colonialism: Christianity in Cultural Demythologization and Ecological Crises in the Niger Delta, Nigeria." *International Journal of Arts and Humanities* 5, no. 3 (2016): 161–78.

Ikechukwu, Eze. *Being a Christian in Igbo Land: Facts, Fictions and Challenges*. Berlin: Logos, 2013.

Ikeke, Mark Omorovie. "Christianity, Sacred Groves and Environmental Sustainability in Urhoboland: Eco-Theological Perspectives." *Abraka: Journal of Religion and Philosophy* 3, no. 1 (2023): 45–71.

Ilo, Stan Chu, ed. *Handbook of African Catholicism*. Maryknoll, NY: Orbis Books, 2022.

———. "Theology and Literature in African Christian Faith: Hearers of the Word in Africa." *Concilium* 5 (2017): 119–30.

"An Interview with Okey Ndibe." Oxford African American Studies Center. https://oxfordaasc.com/page/2771/. Accessed January 2, 2025.

Iweala, Uzodinma. *Beasts of No Nation*. London: John Murray, 2005.

———. *Speak No Evil*. London: John Murray, 2018.

Iwuchukwu, Marinus C. *Muslim-Christian Dialogue in Postcolonial Northern Nigeria: The Challenges of Inclusive Cultural and Religious Pluralism*. New York: Palgrave Macmillan, 2013.

Jackson, Jean-Marie, and Nathan Suhr-Sytsma. "Religion, Secularity, and African Writing." *Research in African Literatures* 48, no. 2 (2017): vii–xvi.

Jager, Colin. "Reconciliation in South Africa: World Literature, Global Christianity, Global Capital." In *The Routledge Companion to Literature and Religion*, edited by Mark Knight, 432–45. London: Routledge, 2020.

Janson, Marloes. *Crossing Religious Boundaries: Islam, Christianity, and "Yoruba Religion" in Lagos, Nigeria*. Cambridge: Cambridge University Press, 2021.

John, Elnathan. *Becoming Nigerian: A Guide*. Abuja: Cassava Republic, 2019.

John, Elnathan, and Àlàbá Ònájìn. *On Ajayi Crowther Street*. Abuja: Cassava Republic, 2020.

John Paul II. *Ecclesia in Africa: Post-Synodal Apostolic Exhortation*. Rome: Vatican, 1995. http://www.vatican.va/content

/john-paul-ii/en/apost_exhortations/documents/hf_jp-ii_exh_14091995_ecclesia-in-africa.html.

Johnson, Todd M., and Gina A. Zurlo. *World Christian Encyclopedia*. 3rd ed. Edinburgh: Edinburgh University Press, 2020.

Joseph, Celucien L. *Radical Humanism and Generous Tolerance: Soyinka on Religion and Human Solidarity*. Lanham, MD: Hamilton, 2017.

Jue, Melody. "Intimate Objectivity: On Nnedi Okorafor's Oceanic Afrofuturism." *Women's Studies Quarterly* 45, no. 1/2 (2017): 171–88.

Kalu, Ogbu, ed. *African Christianity: An African Story*. Trenton: Africa World Press, 2007.

———. *African Pentecostalism: An Introduction*. Oxford: Oxford University Press, 2008.

———. *The Embattled Gods: Christianization of Igboland, 1841–1991*. Trenton: Africa World Press, 2003.

———. "Sharia and Islam in Nigerian Pentecostal Rhetoric, 1970–2003." In *Religions in Africa: Conflict, Politics and Social Ethics; The Collected Essays of Ogbu Uke Kalu*, 3:87–106. Trenton: Africa World Press, 2010.

Kamalu, Ikenna, and Isaac Tamunobelema. "Linguistic Expression of Religious Identity and Ideology in Selected Postcolonial Nigerian Literature." *LWATI: A Journal of Contemporary Research* 10, no. 2 (2013): 100–112.

Kamau-Goro, Nicholas. "African Culture and the Language of Nationalist Imagination: The Reconfiguration of Christianity in Ngũgĩ wa Thiong'o's *The River Between* and *Weep Not Child*." *Studies in World Christianity* 16, no. 1 (2010): 6–26.

Kanu, Ikechukwu Anthony, ed. *African Eco-Theology: Meaning, Forms and Expressions*. Bloomington: AuthorHouse, 2022.

Kaoma, Kapya. *Christianity, Globalization, and Protective Homophobia: Democratic Contestation of Sexuality in Sub-Saharan Africa*. New York: Palgrave Macmillan, 2018.

Katongole, Emmanuel. *Born from Lament: The Theology and Politics of Hope in Africa*. Grand Rapids: William B. Eerdmans, 2017.

———. *The Sacrifice of Africa: A Political Theology for Africa*. Grand Rapids: William B. Eerdmans, 2011.

Kayode, Femi. *Gaslight*. London: Raven Books, 2023.

Kendhammer, Brandon. "The Sharia Controversy in Northern Nigeria and the Politics of Islamic Law in New and Uncertain Democracies." *Comparative Politics* 45, no. 3 (2013): 291–311.

Kendhammer, Brandon, and Carmen McCain. *Boko Haram*. Athens: Ohio University Press, 2018.

Kgalemang, Malebogo. "Novel Biblical Translation of Ngũgĩ wa Thiong'o." In *Postcoloniality, Translation, and the Bible in Africa*, edited by Musa W. Dube and R. S. Wafula, 176–91. Eugene, OR: Pickwick, 2017.

Kirby, Benjamin. "Pentecostalism, Economics, Capitalism: Putting the Protestant Ethic to Work." *Religion* 49, no. 4 (2019): 571–91.

Knight, Mark. "Introduction: Literature, Religion, and the Art of Conversation." In *The Routledge Companion to Literature and Religion*, edited by Mark Knight, 1–12. London: Routledge, 2016.

———. *An Introduction to Religion and Literature*. London: Continuum, 2009.

———, ed. *The Routledge Companion to Literature and Religion*. London: Routledge, 2016.

Kolapo, Femi J. *Christian Missionary Engagement in Central Nigeria, 1857–1891: The Church Missionary Society's All African Mission on the Upper Niger*. New York: Palgrave Macmillan, 2019.

Komolafe, Sunday Jide. *The Transformation of African Christianity: Development and Change in the Nigerian Church*. Carlisle: Langham, 2013.

Korieh, Chima J. "Introduction: History and the Politics of Memory." In *The

Nigeria-Biafra War: Genocide and the Politics of Memory, edited by Chima J. Korieh, 1–39. Amherst, NY: Cambria Press, 2012.

Kperogi, Farooq A. *Glocal English: The Changing Face and Forms of Nigerian English in a Global World*. New York: Peter Lang, 2015.

Krishnan, Madhu. *Contemporary African Literature in English: Global Locations, Postcolonial Identifications*. New York: Palgrave Macmillan, 2014.

Kuku, Damilare. "The Anointed Wife." In *Nearly All the Men in Lagos Are Mad*, 41–62. Lagos: Masobe, 2021.

Kwakye, Benjamin. *The Sun by Night*. Trenton: Africa World Press, 2006.

Lado, Ludovic. "Catholicism as a Lived Religion in Africa." *Religion Compass* 14, no. 12 (2020): 1–10.

———. *Catholic Pentecostalism and the Paradoxes of Africanization: Processes of Localization in a Catholic Charismatic Movement in Cameroon*. Brill: Leiden, 2009.

Lauterbach, Karen. *Christianity, Wealth, and Spiritual Power in Ghana*. New York: Palgrave Macmillan, 2017.

———. "Fakery and Wealth in African Charismatic Christianity: Moving Beyond the Prosperity Gospel as Script." In *Faith in African Lived Christianity: Bridging Anthropological and Theological Perspectives*, edited by Karen Lauterbach and Mika Vähäkangas, 111–32. Leiden: Brill, 2020.

Lauterbach, Karen, and Mika Vähäkangas, eds. *Faith in African Lived Christianity: Bridging Anthropological and Theological Perspectives*. Leiden: Brill, 2020.

Levey, David. "Tracing the Terrain: Religion and Writing in South Africa." *Literature and Theology* 13, no. 4 (1999): 275–83.

Lindfors, Bernth. *Comparative Approaches to African Literatures*. Amsterdam: Rodopi, 1994.

Lindhardt, Martin. "Presence and Impact of Pentecostal/Charismatic Christianity in Africa." In *Pentecostalism in Africa: Presence and Impact of Pneumatic Christianity in Postcolonial Societies*, edited by Martin Lindhardt, 1–52. Leiden: Brill, 2014.

Livingstone, Justin D. "Unfinished Forgiveness: Dynamics of Igbo Cosmology and Christian Theology in Chigozie Obioma's *An Orchestra of Minorities*." *Literature and Theology* 38, no. 1 (2024): 44–64.

Loimeier, Roman. *Islamic Reform and Political Change in Northern Nigeria*. Evanston: Northwestern University Press, 1997.

Lombardi, Bernie. "'Where Paradise Will Hopefully One Day Be': An Interview about Sexuality, Home, and Diaspora with Chinelo Okparanta." *Black Scholar* 48, no. 3 (2018): 17–26.

Ludwar-Ene, Gudrun. *New Religious Movements and Society in Nigeria*. Bayreuth: Bayreuth University, 1991.

Mabura, Lily G. N. "Breaking Gods: An African Postcolonial Gothic Reading of Chimamanda Ngozi Adichie's 'Purple Hibiscus' and 'Half of a Yellow Sun.'" *Research in African Literatures* 39, no. 1 (2008): 203–22.

Macaulay, Jide. "'Just as I Am, Without One Plea': A Journey to Reconcile Sexuality and Spirituality." *Ethnicity and Inequalities in Health and Social Care* 3, no. 3 (2010): 6–13.

———. "Spreading the News of God's Unconditional Love in Nigeria." In *Queer Ministers' Voices from the Global South*, edited by Lisa Isherwood and Hugo Córdova Quero, 126–31. London: Routledge, 2024.

Mackey, Allison. "Troubling Humanitarian Consumption: Reframing Relationality in African Child Soldier Narratives." *Research in African Literatures* 44, no. 4 (2013): 99–122.

Magesa, Laurenti. "Theology of Inculturation: History, Meaning, and Implications." In *The Routledge Handbook of African Theology*, edited by Elias K. Bongmba, 44–56. London: Routledge, 2020.

Makumbi, Jennifer Nansubuga. *Kintu*. Nairobi: Kwani Trust, 2014.

Maluleke, Tinyiko. "Postcolonial Theology in Africa: Looking Back and Looking Forward." In *The Routledge Handbook of African Theology*, edited by Elias K. Bongmba, 335–45. London: Routledge, 2020.

Marshall, Ruth. "Destroying Arguments and Captivating Thoughts: Spiritual Warfare Prayer as Global Praxis." *Journal of Religious and Political Practice* 2, no. 1 (2016): 92–113.

———. *Political Spiritualities: The Pentecostal Revolution in Nigeria*. Chicago: University of Chicago Press, 2009.

Mathuray, Mark. *On the Sacred in African Literature: Old Gods and New Worlds*. New York: Palgrave Macmillan, 2009.

Mbembe, Achille. "Afropolitanism." *Nka: Journal of Contemporary African Art* 20 (2020): 56–61.

———. *On the Postcolony*. Berkeley: University of California Press, 2001.

———. *Out of the Dark Night: Essays on Decolonization*. New York: Columbia University Press, 2021.

Mbiti, John S. *African Religions and Philosophy*. 2nd ed. Oxford: Heinemann, 1989.

Meyer, Birgit. "'Make a Complete Break with the Past': Memory and Post-colonial Modernity in Ghanaian Pentecostalist Discourse." *Journal of Religion in Africa* 28, no. 3 (1998): 316–49.

———. *Sensational Movies: Video, Vision, and Christianity in Ghana*. Berkeley: University of California Press, 2015.

Mignolo, Walter D., and Catherine E. Walsh. *On Decoloniality: Concepts, Analytics, Praxis*. Durham, NC: Duke University Press, 2018.

Mirmotahari, Emad. *Islam in the Eastern African Novel*. New York: Palgrave Macmillan, 2011.

Mu'azzam, Ibrahim, and Jibrin Ibrahim. "Religious Identity in the Context of Structural Adjustment in Nigeria." In *Identity Transformation and Identity Politics under Structural Adjustment in Nigeria*, edited by Attahiru Jega, 62–85. Uppsala: Nordiska Afrikainstitutet, 2000.

Mugambi, Jesse N. K. *Critiques of Christianity in African Literature*. Nairobi: East African Publishers, 1992.

Muo, Adaobi. "Recasting Traditional Adages in the Light of Christianity: An Examination of Selected Igbo Postproverbial Expressions." In *Postproverbials at Work: The Context of Radical Proverb-Making in Nigerian Languages*, edited by Aderemi Raji-Oyelade, 63–88. Osijek: Faculty of Humanities and Social Sciences, University of Osijek, 2024.

Murray, Stephen O., and Will Roscoe, eds. *Boy-Wives and Female Husbands: Studies in African Homosexualities*. New York: Palgrave, 1998.

Musila, Grace A. "Part-Time Africans, Europolitans and 'Africa Lite.'" *Journal of African Cultural Studies* 28, no. 1 (2015): 109–13.

Mustapha, Abdul Raufu. "Introduction: Religious Encounters in Northern Nigeria." In *Creed and Grievance: Muslim-Christian Relations and Conflict Resolution in Northern Nigeria*, edited by Abdul Raufu Mustapha and David Ehrhardt, 1–34. Woodbridge: James Currey, 2018.

Mustapha, Abdul Raufu, and David Ehrhardt, eds. *Creed and Grievance: Muslim-Christian Relations and Conflict Resolution in Northern Nigeria*. Woodbridge: James Currey, 2018.

Mutambara, Maaraidzoo. "African Women Theologies Critique Inculturation." In *Inculturation and Postcolonial Discourse in African Theology*, edited by Edward P. Antonio, 173–92. New York: Peter Lang, 2006.

Nadar, Sarojini, and Johnathan Jodamus. "'Sanctifying Sex': Exploring 'Indecent' Sexual Imagery in Pentecostal Liturgical Practices." *Journal for the Study of Religion* 32, no. 1 (2019): 1–20.

Nagy, Dorottya. "Recalling the Term 'World Christianity': Excursions into Worldings of Literature, Philosophy, and History." In *World Christianity:*

Methodological Considerations, edited by Martha Frederiks and Dorottya Nagy, 40–64. Leiden: Brill, 2021.
Ndibe, Okey. *Foreign Gods, Inc.* New York: Soho Press, 2014.
Ndlovu-Gatsheni, Sabelo J. "Decoloniality as the Future of Africa." *History Compass* 13, no. 10 (2015): 485–96.
———. *Epistemic Freedom in Africa: Deprovincialization and Decolonization.* London: Routledge, 2018.
Ndula, Janet N. "Deconstructing Binary Oppositions of Gender in *Purple Hibiscus*: A Review of Religious/Traditional Superiority and Silence." In *A Companion to Chimamanda Ngozi Adichie*, edited by Ernest N. Emenyonu, 31–43. Suffolk: James Currey, 2017.
Nel, Marinus. *The Prosperity Gospel in Africa: An African Pentecostal Hermeneutical Consideration.* Eugene, OR: Wipf and Stock, 2020.
Ng'ang'a, Abraham Waigi. "African Literature, Arts and Aesthetics in Christian Reflection: Engaging the Thought of Wole Soyinka." *Journal of African Christian Thought* 19, no. 1 (2016): 4–28.
———. "African Theology and African Literature: Rediscovering a Daring Intellectual Project." In *Religion and Social Reconstruction in Africa*, edited by Elias K. Bongmba, 269–82. London: Routledge, 2018.
Ngong, David Tonghou. *Senghor's Eucharist: Negritude and African Political Theology.* Waco: Baylor University Press, 2023.
Ngoy, Nelson Kalombo. *Neo-Pentecostalism: A Post-Colonial Critique of the Prosperity Gospel in the Democratic Republic of the Congo.* Eugene, OR: Wipf and Stock, 2019.
Ngũgĩ wa Thiong'o. *Decolonising the Mind: The Politics of Language in African Literature.* London: James Currey, 1992.
———. *Globalectics: Theory and the Politics of Knowing.* New York: Columbia University Press, 2012.
———. *The River Between.* London: Heinemann, 1965.
Nkwocha, Isidore Iwejuo. *Charismatic Renewal and Pentecostalism: The Renewal of the Nigerian Catholic Church.* Eugene, OR: Wipf and Stock, 2021.
Nkwocha, Levi U. C. *At the Feet of Abraham: A Day-to-Day Dialogic Praxis for Muslims and Christians.* Eugene, OR: Wipf and Stock, 2020.
Nkwoka, Anthony O. "The Role of the Bible in the Igbo Christianity of Nigeria." In *The Bible in Africa: Transactions, Trajectories and Trends*, edited by Gerald O. West and Musa W. Dube, 326–35. Leiden: Brill, 2001.
Nolte, Insa, Olukoya Ogen, and Rebecca Jones, eds. *Beyond Religious Tolerance: Muslim, Christian and Traditionalist Encounters in an African Town.* Woodbridge: James Currey, 2020.
Nwaubani, Adaobi Tricia. *Buried Beneath the Baobab Tree.* New York: Katherine Tegen, 2018.
———. "Killing for Airtime: How Boko Haram's Abubakar Shekau Manipulates Media." *World Policy Journal* 35, no. 2 (2018): 58–62.
———. "Media Turns Boko Haram into 'Superstar Monsters.'" CNN, May 19, 2014. https://edition.cnn.com/2014/05/19/opinion/boko-haram-media-opinion/index.html.
———. "Nigeria Community Divided over Boko Haram." *BBC News*, March 31, 2016. https://www.bbc.com/news/world-africa-35913016/.
———. "The Power of Religion" (Letter from Africa). *BBC News*, November 7, 2014. https://www.bbc.com/news/world-africa-29692580/.
Nweke, Paulinus Chukwudi. "Religious Peacebuilding in Nigeria." In *Religion in War and Peace in Africa*, edited by Margee Ensign and Jean-Pierre Karegeye, 16–23. London: Routledge, 2020.
Nwosu, Maik. "The Muse of History and the Literature of the Nigeria-Biafra War." In *Routledge Handbook of*

Minority Discourses in African Literature, edited by Tanure Ojaide and Joyce Ashuntantang, 276–92. London: Routledge, 2020.

Nwosu, Maik, and Obiwu, eds. *The Critical Imagination in African Literature: Essays in Honor of Michael J. C. Echeruo*. Syracuse: Syracuse University Press, 2015.

Obadare, Ebenezer. "The Charismatic Porn-Star: Social Citizenship and the West-African Pentecostal Erotic." *Citizenship Studies* 22, no. 6 (2018): 603–17.

———. *Pastoral Power, Clerical State: Pentecostalism, Gender and Sexuality in Nigeria*. Notre Dame, IN: University of Notre Dame Press, 2022.

———. *Pentecostal Republic: Religion and the Struggle for State Power in Nigeria*. London: Zed Books, 2018.

Obioma, Chigozie. *The Fishermen*. London: One, 2015.

———. "Pistols and Repentance: Street Evangelism in the City of Makurdi, Nigeria." *Esquire*, January 12, 2021. https://www.esquire.com/uk/life/a35178267/repentance-chigozie-obioma/.

Odeyemi, John Segun. *Pentecostalism and Catholic Ecumenism in Developing Nations: West Africa as a Case Study for a Global Phenomenon*. Eugene, OR: Wipf and Stock, 2019.

Oduyoye, Mercy Amba. "Biblical Interpretation and the Social Location of the Interpreter: African Women's Reading of the Bible." In *Reading from This Place*, vol. 2, *Social Location and Biblical Interpretation in Global Perspective*, edited by Fernando F. Segovia and Mary Ann Tolbert, 33–51. Minneapolis: Fortress Press, 1995.

———. *Daughters of Anowa: African Women and Patriarchy*. Maryknoll, NY: Orbis Books, 1995.

———. *Introducing African Women's Theology*. Sheffield: Sheffield Academic Press, 2001.

Oduyoye, Modupe. "Potent Speech." In *Traditional Religion in West Africa*, edited by E. A. Ade Adegbola, 203–32. Nairobi: Uzima Press, 1983.

Ofei, Josephine D., and Daniel Oppong-Adjei. "Sexual Identities in Africa: A Queer Reading of Chinelo Okparanta's *Under the Udala Trees*." *Asɛmka: A Bilingual Literary Journal of University of Cape Coast* 11, no. 1 (2021): 64–78.

Ogoti, Vincent R. "Soundscape and Narrative Dynamics in Chinelo Okparanta's *Under the Udala Trees*." *Journal of the African Literature Association* 13, no. 3 (2019): 291–305.

Ogungbile, David O., and Akintunde E. Akinade, eds. *Creativity and Change in Nigerian Christianity*. Lagos: Malthouse Press, 2010.

Oguntola-Laguda, Danoye, and Adriaan van Klinken. "Uniting a Divided Nation? Nigerian Muslim and Christian Responses to the Same-Sex Marriage (Prohibition) Act." In *Public Religion and the Politics of Homosexuality in Africa*, edited by Adriaan van Klinken and Ezra Chitando, 35–48. London: Routledge, 2016.

Ògúnyẹmí, Ernest O. "A Shifting Portrait." *Hopkins Review* 16, no. 3 (2023): 125–31.

Ojaide, Tanure. "Toward a Bioregional, Politico-Historical, and Sociocultural Identity of the Niger Delta." In *The Literature and Arts of the Niger Delta*, edited by Tanure Ojaide, 13–22. London: Routledge, 2021.

———. "Under New Pastoral Management." In *The Debt Collector and Other Stories*, 105–24. Trenton: Africa World Press, 2009.

Ojo, Matthews A. *The End-Time Army: Charismatic Movements in Modern Nigeria*. Trenton: Africa World Press, 2006.

———. "Pentecostal Movements, Islam and the Contest for Public Space in Northern Nigeria." *Islam–Christian Muslim Relations* 18, no. 2 (2007): 175–88.

———. "Reverse Mission." In *Encyclopedia of Mission and Missionaries*, edited by Jonathan J. Bonk, 380–82. London: Routledge, 2007.

Ojo-Ade, Femi. "The Black Man's Burden: Christianity in Black African Fiction." In *Essays in Comparative African Literature*, edited by Willfried Feuser and I. N. C. Aniebo, 125–56. Lagos: Centre for Black and African Arts and Civilization, 2001.

Okafor, Clement A. "Sacrifice and the Contestation of Identity in Chukwuemeka Ike's *Sunset at Dawn*." *African Literature Today*, no. 26 (2008): 33–48.

Okafor, Ikenna Ugochukwu. *Toward an African Theology of Fraternal Solidarity: Ube Nwanne*. Eugene, OR: Pickwick, 2014.

Okeke, Ifeanyi J. "The Human Person, Trees and Spirituality in Igbo Cosmology." In *African Ecological Spirituality: Perspectives in Anthroposophy and Environmentalism*, edited by Ikechukwu Anthony Kanu, 87–109. Bloomington: AuthorHouse, 2022.

Okolocha, H. Oby. "War and Absurdity: Viewing the Manifestations of Trauma in Uwem Akpan's 'Luxurious Hearses.'" *Matatu* 40, no. 1 (2012): 159–72.

Okorafor, Nnedi. *Lagoon*. London: Hodder & Stoughton, 2014.

Okparanta, Chinelo. "America." In *Happiness, Like Water*, 85–108. Boston: Mariner Books, 2013.

———. "Eko Hotel." In *The Gonjon Pin and Other Stories: The Cain Prize for African Writing 2014*, 216–38. Oxford: New Internationalist, 2018.

———. "Grace." In *Happiness, Like Water*, 123–52. Boston: Mariner Books, 2013.

———. "Runs Girl." In *Happiness, Like Water*, 67–84. Boston: Mariner Books, 2013.

———. "A Tribute to Chinua Achebe." *Agni Online*, July 1, 2013. https://agnionlin.bu.edu/essay/a-tribute-to-chinua-achebe/.

———. *Under the Udala Trees*. London: Granta, 2015.

Okwu, Augustine S. O. *Igbo Culture and the Christian Missions, 1857–1957: Conversion in Theory and Practice*. Lanham, MD: University Press of America, 2010.

Okyerefo, Michael Perry Kweku. "Christianising Africa: A Portrait by Two African Novelists." *Studies in World Christianity* 16, no. 1 (2010): 63–81.

Olajubu, Oyeronke. *Women in the Yoruba Religious Sphere*. New York: State University of New York Press, 2003.

Olali, David. "African Traditional Religion, Sexual Orientation, Transgender, and Homosexuality." In *The Palgrave Handbook of African Traditional Religion*, edited by Toyin Falola, 317–28. New York: Palgrave Macmillan, 2022.

Olayiwola, Elizabeth. "Nigerian Evangelical Film Genres: The Spectacle of the Spiritual." *Journal of African Cultural Studies* 32, no. 2 (2020): 115–30.

Olojo, Akinola. *Nigeria's Troubled North: Interrogating the Drivers of Public Support for Boko Haram*. ICCT Research Paper, no. 7. The Hague: The International Centre for Counter-Terrorism, 2013.

Olupona, Jacob K. *City of 201 Gods: Ile-Ife in Time, Space, and the Imagination*. Berkeley: University of California Press, 2011.

———. "Religion and Ecology in African Cultures and Society." In *Oxford Handbook of Religion and Ecology*, edited by Roger S. Gottlieb, 259–82. New York: Oxford University Press, 2006.

Oluwafemi, Babalola Emmanuel. "A Comparative Analysis of Christianity and Islam Concepts of Angels: The Panacea to Religious Harmony." *International Journal of Research and Innovation in Social Science* 4, no. 6 (2020): 451–57.

Omenka, Nicholas Ibeawuchi. "The Catholic Church and the Postwar Rehabilitation and Reconstruction in Nigeria, 1970–1975." In *New Perspectives on the Nigeria-Biafra War: No Victor, No Vanquished*, edited by Chima J. Korieh, 19–44. Lanham, MD: Lexington Books, 2021.

Omenyo, Cephas N. "Man of God Prophesy unto Me: The Prophetic Phenomenon in African Christianity." *Studies in World Christianity* 17, no. 1 (2011): 30–49.

Omobowale, Ayokunle Olumuyiwa, Helen Olubunmi Jaiyeola Akinade, and Mofeyisara Oluwatoyin Omobowale. "Ember-Months and Disaster Beliefs in Nigeria." *International Journal of Social Sciences and Humanities Review* 2, no. 2 (2011): 32–40.

Omojola, Bode. *Yorùbá Music in the Twentieth Century: Identity, Agency, and Performance Practice*. Rochester: University of Rochester Press, 2012.

Onah, Chijioke. "Decolonizing Trauma Studies: The Recognition-Solidarity Nexus in Uwem Akpan's *Say You're One of Them*." *African Literature Today* 41 (2023): 132–44.

Onapajo, Hakeem, and Abubakar A. Usman. "Fuelling the Flames: Boko Haram and Deteriorating Christian–Muslim Relations in Nigeria." *Journal of Muslim Minority Affairs* 35, no. 1 (2015): 106–22.

Onyinah, Opoku. *Pentecostal Exorcism: Witchcraft and Demonology in Ghana*. Dorset: Deo Publishing, 2011.

Oriogun, Romeo. *Sacrament of Bodies*. Lincoln: University of Nebraska Press, 2020.

Orobator, Agbonkhianmeghe E. "Ken Saro-Wiwa: Homage to a Prophet." *Hekima Review*, no. 15 (1996): 77–79.

———. *Religion and Faith in Africa: Confessions of an Animist*. Maryknoll, NY: Orbis Books, 2018.

———. *Theology Brewed in an African Pot*. Maryknoll, NY: Orbis Books, 2008.

Orogun, Daniel Oghenekevhwe. "Agencies of Capitalism: Evaluating Nigerian Pentecostalism Using African Moral Philosophies." PhD diss., University of Pretoria, 2020.

Osinubi, Taiwo Adetunji. "The Promise of Lesbians in African Literary History." *College Literature* 45, no. 4 (2018): 675–86.

Osofisan, Sola. "E. E. Sule: A Burden to Get It Right." *Africa Writer Magazine*, September 19, 2013. https://www.africanwriter.com/e-e-sule-a-burden-to-get-it-right/.

———. "Okey Ndibe: A Book Reading Should Be a Celebration." *African Writer Magazine*, April 1, 2014. https://www.africanwriter.com/okey-ndibe-a-book-reading-should-be-a-celebration/.

Otu, Kwame E. "When the Lagoons Remember: An Afroqueer Futurist Reading of 'Blue Ecologies of Agitation.'" *Feminist Africa* 2, no. 2 (2021): 29–46.

Ozumba, Aghaegbuna O. U., and Chineme O. I. Ozumba. *Dance of the Iroko*. N.p.: CreateSpace, 2014.

Papillon, Buki. *An Ordinary Wonder*. London: Dialogue Books, 2021.

Peel, John D. Y. *Christianity, Islam, and Orişa Religion: Three Traditions in Comparison and Interaction*. Berkeley: University of California Press, 2016.

———. *Religious Encounter and the Making of the Yoruba*. Bloomington: University of Indiana Press, 2000.

Potts, Matthew Ichihashi. *Forgiveness: An Alternative Account*. New Haven: Yale University Press, 2022.

Pucherova, Dobrota. "What Is African Woman? Transgressive Sexuality in 21st-Century African Anglophone Lesbian Fiction as a Redefinition of African Feminism." *Research in African Literatures* 50, no. 2 (2019): 105–22.

Quayson, Ato. *Calibrations: Reading for the Social*. Minneapolis: University of Minnesota Press, 2003.

Quinn, Molly Rose. "Chinelo Okparanta on Faith, War and Being Gay in Nigeria." *Literary Hub*, September 21, 2015. https://lithub.com/chinelo-okparanta-on-faith-war-and-being-gay-in-nigeria/.

Ramakrishnan, J. R. "Queerness, Womanity and Hope: A Conversation with Chinelo Okparanta, Author of *Under the Udala Trees*." *Electric Literature*, September 22, 2015. https://electricliterature.com/queerness-womanity-and-hope-a-conversation-with-chinelo

-okparanta-author-of-under-the-udala-trees/.

Ray, Benjamin C. "Aladura Christianity: A Yoruba Religion." *Journal of Religion in Africa* 23, no. 3 (1993): 266–91.

Richman, Naomi. "Homosexuality, the Created Body and Queer Fantasies in the African Deliverance Imaginary." *Journal of Religion in Africa* 50, nos. 3–4 (2021): 249–77.

———. "Machine Gun Prayer: The Politics of Embodied Desire in Pentecostal Worship." *Journal of Contemporary Religion* 35, no. 3 (2020): 469–83.

Rimamsikwe, Habila K. "A Historical Study of Prosperity Gospel Preaching in Nigeria, 1970–2014." PhD diss., University of Nigeria, Nsukka, 2017.

Rio, Knut, Michelle MacCarthy, and Ruy Blanes. "Introduction to Pentecostal Witchcraft and Spiritual Politics in Africa and Melanesia." In *Pentecostalism and Witchcraft: Spiritual Warfare in Africa and Melanesia*, edited by Knut Rio, Michelle MacCarthy, and Ruy Blanes, 1–36. Cham: Palgrave MacMillan, 2017.

Robbins, Joel. "Anthropology of Religion." In *Studying Global Pentecostalism: Theories and Methods*, edited by Allan Anderson et al., 156–78. Berkeley: University of California Press, 2010.

Sackeyfio, Rose. "Okey Ndibe, *Foreign Gods Inc.*" *African Literature Today* 33 (2015): 185–87.

Sakupapa, Teddy Chalwe. "The Decolonising Content of African Theology and the Decolonisation of African Theology: Reflections on a Decolonial Future for African Theology." *Missionalia* 46, no. 3 (2018): 406–24.

———. "Spirit and Ecology in the Context of African Theology: Christian Faith and the Earth." *Scriptura: Journal for Contextual Hermeneutics in Southern Africa* 111, no. 1 (2012): 422–30.

Sanneh, Lamin. *Whose Religion Is Christianity? The Gospel Beyond the West*. Grand Rapids: William B. Eerdmans, 2003.

Searle, Alison. "The Role of Missions in *Things Fall Apart* and *Nervous Conditions*." *Literature and Theology* 21, no. 1 (2007): 49–65.

Shankar, Shobana. "For Love of God." Africa Is a Country, September 7, 2015. https://africasacountry.com/2015/07/for-love-of-god-love-of-laughing-an-interview-with-okey-ndibe/.

———. *Who Shall Enter Paradise? Christian Origins in Muslim Northern Nigeria, c. 1890–1975*. Athens: Ohio University Press, 2014.

"A Short Biography of Papa Samuel Bilehou Joseph Oshoffa in Relation to the Celestial Church of Christ." Celestial Weekly, 2017. https://celestialweekly.com/wp-content/uploads/2017/11/A-short-biography-of-Papa-Samuel-Bilehou-Joseph-Oshoffa-in-relation-to-the-Celestial-Church-of-Christ-1.pdf.

Smith, Christopher C. "The Two Worlds of a Nigerian Christian Novelist: How Chigozie Obioma's Writing Draws on Western and African Expressions of Faith." *Christianity Today*, January 12, 2017. https://www.christianitytoday.com/ct/2017/january-web-only/chigozie-obioma-nigerian-christian-novelist.html.

Smith, Daniel Jordan. *To Be a Man Is Not a One-Day Job: Masculinity, Money, and Intimacy in Nigeria*. Chicago: University of Chicago Press, 2017.

Somtochukwu, Ani Kayode. *And Then He Sang a Lullaby*. London: Grove Press, 2023.

Soyinka, Wole. *The Burden of Memory, the Muse of Forgiveness*. Oxford: Oxford University Press, 1999.

———. *The Jero Plays*. London: Eyre Methuen, 1973.

———. *Of Africa*. New Haven: Yale University Press, 2012.

Stiebert, Johanna. "Lesbians, Lesphobia and the Bible: *Under the Udala Trees* as Data." In *Going the Extra Mile: Reflections on Biblical Studies in Africa and the Contributions of Joachim Kügler*, edited by Masiiwa R. Gunda et al.,

389–410. Bamberg: Bamberg University Press, 2024.
Stinton, Diane B. *Jesus of Africa: Voices of Contemporary African Christology.* Maryknoll, NY: Orbis Books, 2004.
Stobie, Cheryl. "Dethroning the Infallible Father: Religion, Patriarchy and Politics in Chimamanda Ngozi Adichie's *Purple Hibiscus.*" *Literature and Theology* 24, no. 4 (2010): 421–35.
Stone, Ken. "The Garden of Eden and the Heterosexual Contract." In *Bodily Citations: Religion and Judith Butler*, edited by Ellen T. Armour and Susan M. St. Ville, 48–70. New York: Columbia University Press, 2006.
Suhr-Sytsma, Nathan. "Forms of Interreligious Encounter in Contemporary Nigerian Fiction." *African Studies Review* 65, no. 3 (2022): 669–91.
Sule, E. E. *Sterile Sky.* Harlow: Pearson Education, 2012.
Sullivan-Blum, Constance R. "'It's Adam and Eve, Not Adam and Steve': What's at Stake in the Construction of Contemporary American Christian Homophobia." In *Lust and Loathing Across Time and Space*, edited by David A. B. Murray, 48–63. Durham, NC: Duke University Press, 2009.
Szolosi, Stephen M. "Uwem Akpan's *Say You're One of Them*: Invitations to Solidarity." *Christianity and Literature* 61, no. 3 (2012): 443–64.
Tadjo, Veronique. *In the Company of Men: The Ebola Tales.* London: HopeRoad, 2021.
Ter Haar, Gerrie. *How God Became African: African Spirituality and Western Secular Thought.* Philadelphia: University of Pennsylvania Press, 2009.
———. "A Wondrous God: Miracles in Contemporary Africa." *African Affairs* 102, no. 408 (2003): 409–28.
Thompson, Chantal P. "The Myth of the Garden of Eden and the Symbolism of the Baobab Tree in West African Literature." In *Francophone Post-colonial Cultures: Critical Essays*, edited by Kamal Salhi, 90–101. Lanham, MD: Lexington Books, 2003.

Thurston, Alexander. *Boko Haram: The History of an African Jihadist Movement.* Princeton: Princeton University Press, 2018.
Toivanen, Anna-Leena. "Cosmopolitanism's New Clothes? The Limits of the Concept of Afropolitanism." *European Journal of English Studies* 21, no. 2 (2017): 189–205.
Tunca, Daria. *Stylistic Approaches to Nigerian Fiction.* New York: Palgrave Macmillan, 2014.
Uchechukwu, Paul. "The Will of God." *Concilium* 5 (2019): 39–42.
Uchem, Rose N. *Overcoming Women's Subordination in the Igbo African Culture and in the Catholic Church: Envisioning an Inclusive Theology with Reference to Women.* Parkland, FL: Dissertation.com, 2001.
Uchendu, Egodi. "Being Igbo and Muslim: The Igbo of South-Eastern Nigeria and Conversions to Islam, 1930s to Recent Times." *Journal of African History* 51, no. 1 (2010): 63–87.
Udeagha, Nduka. "African Belief Systems, Ember Months, and Demonic Forces in Nigeria: The Pentecostal Influence." *Journal of Religion in Africa*, April 7, 2025. https://doi.org/10.1163/15700666-12340329/.
Udenwe, Obinna. *Satans and Shaitans.* London: Jacaranda, 2014.
Ugba, Abel. *Shades of Belonging: African Pentecostals in Twenty-First Century Ireland.* Trenton: Africa World Press, 2009.
Ukah, Asonzeh. "African Christianities: Features, Promises and Problems." Arbeitspapiere / Working Papers, no. 79. Mainz: Institute for Ethnology and African Studies, Johannes Gutenberg University, 2007.
———. "Contesting God: Nigerian Pentecostals and Their Relations with Islam and Muslims." In *Global Pentecostalism: Encounters with Other Religious Traditions*, edited by David Westerlund, 93–114. London: Bloomsbury, 2009.

———. *A New Paradigm of Pentecostal Power: A Study of the Redeemed Christian Church of God in Nigeria*. Trenton: Africa World Press, 2008.

———. "Prosperity, Prophecy and the COVID-19 Pandemic: The Healing Economy of African Pentecostalism." *Pneuma* 42, nos. 3–4 (2020): 430–59.

Ukpokolo, Chinyere. "Visible and Invisible Forces." In *Encyclopedia of the Yoruba*, edited by Toyin Falola and Akintunde Akinyemi, 337–38. Bloomington: Indiana University Press, 2016.

Umaru, Thaddeus Byimui. *Christian-Muslim Dialogue in Northern Nigeria: A Socio-Political and Theological Consideration*. Bloomington, IN: Xlibris, 2013.

Umeogu, Bona Christus, et al. "Kolanut and Symbolismic Universe: Towards the Creation and Constitution of Igbo Science and Arts." *Canadian Social Science* 15, no. 4 (2019): 1–6.

Unigwe, Chika. *The Middle Daughter*. Edinburgh: Canongate, 2023.

Unuabonah, Foluke Olayinka, and Oluwateniola Oluwabukola Kupolati. "The Pragmatics of 'It Is Well' in Nigerian English." *Poznan Studies in Contemporary Linguistics* 59, no. 1 (2023): 193–215.

Uwaegbute, Kingsley Ikechukwu. "Christianity and Masquerade Practices Among the Youth in Nsukka, Nigeria." *African Studies* 80, no. 1 (2021): 40–59.

Uwazuruike, Confidence. "Reporting Terrorism: Boko Haram in the Nigerian Press." PhD diss., Bournemouth University, 2018.

Uzoigwe, G. N. "Background to the Nigerian Civil War." In *Writing the Nigeria-Biafra War*, ed. Toyin Falola and Ogechukwu Ezekwem, 17–39. Suffolk: James Currey, 2016.

Vaaseh, Godwin A. "Political Uncertainty and Violence in Nigeria: Politicising the Boko Haram Insurgency in Northeastern Nigeria." *International Journal of Arts and Sciences* 8, no. 8 (2015): 403–16.

van Klinken, Adriaan. *Kenyan, Christian, Queer: Religion, LGBT Activism, and Arts of Resistance in Africa*. University Park: Penn State University Press, 2019.

———. "Pentecostal Plurality and Sexual Politics in Africana Worlds." In *The Pentecostal World*, edited by Jorg Haustein and Michael Wilkinson, 288–98. London: Routledge, 2023.

———. "Religion in African Literature: Representation, Critique and Imagination." *Religion Compass* 14, no. 12 (2020): 1–12.

van Klinken, Adriaan, and Ezra Chitando, eds. *Public Religion and the Politics of Homosexuality in Africa*. London: Routledge, 2016.

———. *Reimagining Christianity and Sexual Diversity in Africa*. London: Hurst, 2021.

van Klinken, Adriaan, and Johanna Stiebert, with Sebyala Brian and Fredrick Hudson. *Sacred Queer Stories: Ugandan LGBTQ+ Refugee Lives and the Bible*. Suffolk: James Currey, 2021.

van Liere, Lucien. "The Image of Violence and the Study of Material Religion, an Introduction." *Religions* 11, no. 7 (2020): 370.

VanZanten, Susan. "African Narrative and the Christian Tradition: Storytelling and Identity." *Christianity and Literature* 61, no. 3 (2012): 368–76.

———. "World Christianity." In *The Cambridge Companion to Literature and Religion*, edited by Susan M. Felch, 262–76. Cambridge: Cambridge University Press, 2016.

Vaughan, Olufemi. *Religion and the Making of Nigeria*. Durham, NC: Duke University Press, 2016.

Venbrux, Eric. "The Miraculous Medal: Linking People Together Like the Beads of the Rosary." In *Gender, Nation and Religion in European Pilgrimage*, edited by Catrien Notermans, 89–105. London: Routledge, 2012.

Wallace, Cynthia R. "Chimamanda Ngozi Adichie's *Purple Hibiscus* and the Paradoxes of Postcolonial

Redemption." *Christianity and Literature* 61, no. 3 (2012): 465–83.

Walls, Andrew F. *The Cross-Cultural Process in Christian History*. Maryknoll, NY: Orbis, 2002.

Walsh, Michelle A. "Taking Matter Seriously: Material Theopoetics in the Aftermath of Communal Violence." In *Post-traumatic Public Theology*, edited by Stephanie N. Arel and Shelly Rambo, 241–65. New York: Palgrave Macmillan, 2016.

Wariboko, Nimi. *Nigerian Pentecostalism*. Rochester: University of Rochester Press, 2014.

———. "Pentecostalism in Africa." In *Oxford Research Encyclopedia: African History*, October 26, 2017. https://doi.org/10.1093/acrefore/9780190277734.013.120/.

———. *Social Ethics and Governance in Contemporary African Writing*. London: Bloomsbury, 2023.

———. "West African Pentecostalism: A Survey of Everyday Theology." In *Global Renewal Christianity: Spirit-Empowered Movements*, vol. 3, *Africa*, edited by Vinson Synan, Amos Yong, and J. Kwabena Asamoah-Gyadu, 1–18. Lake Mary, FL: Charisma House, 2016.

Werner, Dietrich. "The Challenge of Environment and Climate Justice: Imperatives of an Eco-theological Reformation of Christianity in African Contexts." In *African Initiated Christianity and the Decolonisation of Development: Sustainable Development in Pentecostal and Independent Churches*, edited by Philipp Öhlmann, Wilhelm Gräb, and Marie-Luise Frost, 51–72. London: New York, 2020.

West, Gerald O. *The Stolen Bible: From Tool of Imperialism to African Icon*. Leiden: Brill, 2016.

Wiles, Ellen. "Three Branches of Literary Anthropology: Sources, Styles, Subject Matter." *Ethnography* 21, no. 2 (2020): 280–95.

Wilkens, Katharina. "Mary and the Demons: Marian Devotion and Ritual Healing in Tanzania." *Journal of Religion in Africa* 39, no. 3 (2009): 295–318.

Williams, Corey L. "Multiple Religious Belonging and Identity in Contemporary Nigeria: Methodological Reflections for World Christianity." In *World Christianity: Methodological Considerations*, edited by Martha Frederiks and Dorottya Nagy, 225–50. Leiden: Brill, 2020.

Wilson-Tagoe, N. "West African Literature in English." In *The Routledge Encyclopedia of African Literature*, edited by Simon Gikandi. London: Routledge, 2009.

Womack, Deanna Ferree, and Raimundo C. Barreto. "Introduction: Alterity and the Evasion of Justice in World Christianity." In *Alterity and the Evasion of Justice: Explorations of the "Other" in World Christianity*, edited by Deanna Ferree Womack and Raimundo C. Barreto, 3–26. Minneapolis: Fortress Press, 2023.

Yiğit, Ali. *Christianity and the African Counter-Discourse in Achebe and Beti: Cultures in Dialogue, Contest and Conflict*. London: Routledge, 2024.

Yishau, Olukorede. *In the Name of Our Father*. Lagos: Origami, 2018.

Zabus, Chantal. *Out in Africa: Same-Sex Desire in Sub-Saharan Literatures and Cultures*. Suffolk: James Currey, 2013.

Zeleza, Paul Tiyambe. "The Disciplinary, Interdisciplinary and Global Dimensions of African Studies." *International Journal of African Renaissance Studies* 1, no. 2 (2006): 195–220.

Zink, Jesse. "'Anglocostalism' in Nigeria: Neo-Pentecostalism and Obstacles to Anglican Unity." *Journal of Anglican Studies* 10, no. 2 (2012): 231–50.

Index

Abani, Chris, 3, 25, 37, 51, 79
Abel and Cain. *See* Cain and Abel
Achebe, Chinua, 1–4, 10, 17, 25, 69, 74, 83, 157, 159
   See also *Things Fall Apart*
Adam and Eve (biblical figures), 65, 68–71, 74–75, 118
Adamo, David, 39, 142, 186n27
Adebanwi, Wale, 21, 177, 181
Adelakun, Abimbola, 126, 131, 133, 163
Adichie, Chimamanda Ngozi, 3–4, 14, 19, 26, 30, 49, 79–84, 87, 94, 97, 101, 150, 180
   See also *Purple Hibiscus*
Adogame, Afe, 10, 20, 31, 111, 177
affirmation (of sexual diversity), 26, 53, 58–59, 64, 70, 76–77, 180–81
African indigenous religions. *See* indigenous religions
African-initiated (or independent/indigenous) churches, 16, 18, 27, 39, 73–74, 103, 110–11, 114, 123, 175, 179
African literature, 19, 29
   and Christianity, 2–5, 7–16, 79–80, 109, 155, 157, 177–79
   and ecology, 102–3
   and Islam, 11, 151
   and religion, 7, 9–10, 134, 174, 177, 180
Afropolitanism, 19, 171
   See also cosmopolitanism
agency
   female, 95–96, 99, 101
   religious, 3, 12, 95, 169, 178
Aihiokhai, Simon, 78, 127–28, 151
Akpan, Uwem, 3, 8, 24, 27, 42, 113, 144–45, 150–51, 166, 180
Aladura churches, 16, 18, 55, 110–11, 153–54
Alao, Abiodun, 133, 136–37, 139
altar, 42, 54–55, 84, 90, 150
alterity/othering, 27, 127–28, 133, 151, 179, 181
ancestors, 32–33, 47, 49, 74, 87, 113–14, 143, 158
   See also spirits
angel(s), 43, 55, 131
   Gabriel, 42–43, 92
   Holy Jimata, 111, 114
Anglicanism, 18, 20, 34, 62, 69, 157
apparition, 26, 30, 48, 79, 89–95, 100, 189n49

appropriation (of Christianity), 16, 22, 24, 68, 72–73, 108, 111, 177
Assemblies of God, 18, 110, 116–17, 119

baptism, 109, 114, 146–48
Beasts of No Nations, 25–26, 29–51, 176, 180–81
Biafra war. *See* civil war (Nigerian)
Biafra, Republic of, 25–26, 29–30, 36, 59–60, 79, 84
Bible, 33–36, 54, 60, 67–77, 108–9, 142
   queer interpretation of, 61–62, 70, 72, 74–75, 77
   as talisman, 38–39, 186n27
   See also Gospel
big Man culture, 80, 85, 96, 160, 179
bildungsroman, 24, 31–32, 66, 70, 82, 95, 99, 106
body. *See* embodiment
Boko Haram, 27, 128–36, 192n28, 192n35
Bonnke, Reinhard, 27, 109, 136–38, 176
Buried Beneath a Baobab Tree, 27, 127–35, 139, 176

Cain and Abel (biblical figures), 35–36, 108, 138, 185n22
capitalism, 104–5, 114, 155, 160, 170
Catholicism, 4, 14, 20, 26, 33, 36–37, 39, 42–43, 78–101, 146, 165, 172–73
   and relationship to indigenous religion, 80, 82, 87–88
   and relationship to Pentecostalism, 84, 89, 100, 148, 172–73
Celestial Church of Christ, 27, 110–12, 114–15, 118, 123, 153, 181, 191n40, 191n44
charismatic leadership, 28, 105, 153–55, 161–66, 172
charismatic movements, 18, 62, 103, 111, 127, 153
   See also Pentecostalism
child soldiers, 26, 29–32, 35–36, 45–46, 48–51
child(hood), 31, 33, 35–36, 41, 54–55, 65, 84–85, 106, 143, 156
Christian–Muslim relations, 11, 16, 27, 35, 125–52, 181, 192n28
civil war (Nigerian), 21, 24–26, 29–30, 35–36, 49, 59–61, 63, 65, 68, 78–79, 83–84, 139

INDEX

coexistence (interreligious), 125, 127–29, 136, 138, 149, 151–52, 159
colonialism/coloniality, 1–4, 6, 11–13, 15–16, 24, 68–69, 72, 81–82, 87–88, 113–14, 138, 177–79, 181
competition, religious, 2, 18, 100, 125–27, 138, 144, 149, 153–54
  See also market(place)
conversion, 1, 4, 12, 16, 36–37, 91, 134
cosmopolitanism, 157, 172
  See also Afropolitanism
critique, of religion/Christianity, 6, 10–14, 21, 27–28, 61, 66, 101, 103–5, 108, 123, 144, 155, 161, 170–72, 177–80
crucifix, 39, 41–42, 50, 84, 141, 173, 180
crusade, 27, 105, 109, 114, 136–38, 169
curse, 27, 44, 63, 70, 116, 118–21, 138, 142, 148

decolonization/decoloniality, 6, 12–13
  of Christianity/the Bible, 4, 6, 13, 72–73, 88–89, 178, 180–81
Deeper Christian Life Ministry (aka Deeper Life Church), 109, 146, 193n80
deity/ies, 85, 87, 112–14, 122, 156–58, 160–61, 169, 178, 191n46
  See also God; Goddess; Mami Wata
deliverance, 18, 26, 116, 176, 186n7
  from Boko Haram, 131
  from curses, 116, 119
  ministries, 5, 54–56, 154, 161
  of queer bodies, 52–59, 65–66, 76, 192n32
  reading for, 59, 76
demon(s), 110, 116, 131, 133
  of homosexuality, 55–58, 64–66, 192n32
  See also devil; spirits
demonization
  of homo/queer sexuality, 57–58, 76
  of indigenous religion, 87, 117, 158–59, 178
  of Islam, 127–28, 132–33, 151
  of poverty, 168
desacralization, 104, 108, 112–14, 117, 121, 123, 178
devil, 44, 46, 54–56, 58, 65, 116–18, 126, 132–33, 168
  See also Satan
devotion, 42
  family, 34, 84–86, 89–91, 116, 141
  Marian, 26, 43, 48, 80, 89–96, 100, 189n43
dialogue (interreligious), 127–28, 135, 140, 152
diaspora, 19–20, 111, 113, 171
Dube, Musa W., 61, 69–70, 72–73, 76–77, 81, 88–89, 97, 99

ecology, 22, 27, 102–24, 178, 181
  of religion, 108, 112

economy (religious), 64, 159–60, 162–64, 168
  See also market(place)
embodiment, 26, 53, 56–59, 76, 163
enlightenment, 22, 58–59, 95, 142
environment (natural), 27, 94, 102–24
  degradation/pollution of, 21–22, 102–4, 107, 113–14, 117–18, 121
  as sacred, 94, 104, 108, 112–13, 115, 117–18, 121–24, 178
eroticism/erotic economy, 53–54, 162–64
ethnicity, 24, 26, 59–60, 139–40, 121, 139–40, 150
Evangelicalism, 20, 35, 109, 136–37
evangelism, 16, 20, 27–28, 109, 126, 136–37, 146, 169, 176

family, 30–31, 33–34, 36–37, 69, 86, 91, 106, 109, 136–38
feminism, 59, 64, 72, 77, 81, 88–89, 92–93, 97, 99
Fishermen, The, 22, 27, 102–4, 106–24, 175, 177–78, 180–81
folktales, 37, 71–72, 74, 77
  See also mythology
Foreign Gods, Inc., 4, 21, 23, 27–28, 155–73, 171–72, 175–79, 191n46
forgiveness, 25–26, 31–32, 34–37, 45–51, 149
  divine, 45–48, 50–51, 66, 75
  interpersonal, 45, 50
fratricide, 35–36, 108, 116, 121

gender, 22, 55, 62, 64, 68–70, 79, 85, 92–97, 101, 178, 181
  diversity, 52–53, 55, 58,74, 79, 178, 181
  See also feminism; patriarchy
Genesis, Book of, 68–70, 74, 108, 118–19, 134
Gikandi, Simon, 1, 3, 16, 109, 176
God, 3, 57–58, 63, 71–72, 87, 91, 95, 122, 129, 147, 162–63, 166–67, 186n37
  as creator, 45, 70
  forgiveness from, 46–48, 51, 75
  presence, 40–44, 50, 53–54, 66, 141–43
Goddess, 33, 48, 104, 112–13, 116, 143, 191n46
  See also Mami Wata
Gospel, the, 108, 148
  of John, 43, 64, 120
  of Luke, 92
  of Matthew, 148, 184n54
  See also prosperity (gospel)

Hausa, 15, 30, 36–37, 60, 129, 139–40, 146, 149
healing, 30, 32, 39, 47, 49–50, 57, 66, 90–91, 111, 114, 135, 180–91, 189n43
  See also deliverance
heaven, 33, 44–45, 49, 158

INDEX

hermeneutics, 71–74, 77, 81, 142
heteronormativity, 53–54, 69, 76–77
Holy Spirit, 56, 73, 98, 114–15, 148, 159, 161
homophobia, 52–53, 66, 72, 74, 77
   in Christianity/church, 54, 57–58, 63, 72, 76, 154, 178, 181
homosexuality, 20–22, 26, 52–77, 178–81
   as an abomination, 54, 60, 64, 68–69, 72, 75–76, 178
humanism, 28, 42, 138–39, 144, 150, 172, 180–82
   dehumanization, 31–32, 41, 44–45, 50, 93, 95
   rehumanization, 30, 32, 49, 93 (*see also* rehabilitation)
hymn(s), 27, 84, 86, 108, 122–23, 153, 180 (*see also* music)

identity/ies,
   African, 10, 19–20, 95–96
   ethnic, 26, 82, 84, 96, 146–46
   gender/sexual, 52–53, 55–58, 65, 76, 96
   religious, 26, 82, 127, 132, 140, 146–46, 149–51
Igbo, 24–26, 30, 35–37, 59–60, 74, 80, 113, 139, 156
   Christianity among the, 16, 24, 34, 42, 51, 62, 67–69, 71, 78–79, 83, 88, 116–17, 157–58, 160
   identity, 26, 68, 82, 84, 88, 96
   indigenous religion, 33, 80, 87–88, 113, 116–17, 120, 160–61, 169
   mythology/folktales, 37, 47, 71–72, 74–75
imagination
   national/political, 21, 23, 105
   religious, 10, 13, 21–22, 26, 31, 35, 41, 49, 61, 76, 92, 94, 106, 124, 127–28, 180–82
   See also reimagination
Imitation of Christ, The, 148, 152, 181
inculturation, 3, 79, 81, 83, 86–89, 96, 100, 158, 175, 181
indigenous religions, 2–3, 33, 52, 58, 78, 80, 105, 112–14, 119, 143–44.
   and relationship to Christianity, 39, 78, 80–82, 87, 100, 111, 117, 127, 157–61, 169–70, 177–78
   See also mythology
interreligious relations. *See* Christian–Muslim relations; coexistence; dialogue; neighborliness; recognition
intertextuality, 14, 35, 43, 108, 122, 152, 180–81
Islam, 2, 27, 36–37, 125–28, 130–35, 144–45
   in African literature, 11, 151
   reform movements in, 125–26
   as a religion of peace, 130, 147, 149, 151
Iweala, Uzodinma, 25–26, 30–31, 36, 51, 54
Iwuchukwu, Marinus, 128, 135, 140

Jehovah Witnesses, 61, 67, 187n53
Jesus Christ, 39, 43, 51, 54, 89, 97–98, 101, 120, 134, 138, 186n41
   blood of, 148, 150, 159
   as a friend, 63–64
   statue of, 40–43, 46, 50 (*see also* crucifix)
   teachings of, 35, 57, 64, 108, 135, 148–49
justice, 11, 21, 77, 144, 179
   environmental/ecological, 27, 102–3, 105–6
   transitional, 29–30, 49

Kalu, Ogbu, 3, 62, 158, 160, 170
Katongole, Emmanuel, 43, 45, 186n37

Lagoon, 27, 104–6, 123
lived religion, 37, 39, 42, 80, 89, 100, 112
Luxurious Hearses, 27, 113–14, 144–51, 181

Mami Wata, 47–48, 55, 104, 106, 113, 191n46
market(place), religion as a, 19, 64, 100, 154, 171
   See also competition; economy
masculinity, 96–99, 190n66
   See also gender; patriarchy
Mass (Holy), 78, 84, 86, 90, 97, 99
material religion, 26, 37–42, 50, 84, 111, 150
   See also crucifix; medal; statue
medal(lion), 39, 50, 84, 90–91, 147–48, 150, 180, 189n42
memory, 12, 46–48, 142, 178
   Christianity as, 31, 33–37
   of the civil war, 25–26, 29–31, 36, 49, 51, 63
miracle, 57, 91, 93–95, 137, 186n37
mission, 15–16, 18, 84, 126, 88, 188n1
   and colonialism, 1–2, 13, 16, 69, 72, 78, 181
   See also reverse mission
missionaries, 20, 33, 68–69, 78
   Anglican/Protestant, 16, 34, 69, 116, 157, 178
   Catholic, 16, 83–84, 86, 88, 95, 113
   European, 1, 15–16, 38, 68–69, 74, 83–84, 86–88, 95, 113, 157–58, 178, 188n1
missionary Christianity, 18, 20, 22, 73, 100, 110, 113, 123, 157, 186n37
   and indigenous religion, 33, 38, 78–80, 83–84, 86–88, 126–27, 157–58, 175
Muhammed (Mohammad), the Prophet, 127, 130, 140

219

INDEX

mother(hood), 33–34, 36–37, 46–48, 50, 54, 65–66, 92–93, 96, 116
    and devotion/prayer, 44, 65, 134, 141–42
music (gospel), 34, 44–45, 116, 153–54
    See also hymns
myth(ology), 33, 37, 47, 74–75, 104, 108–9, 114, 134
    See also folktales

Ndibe, Okey, 4, 19, 21, 23, 27–28, 155–57, 160–62, 164–65, 170–73, 180
neighborliness (interreligious), 128–29, 135, 140–41, 144, 149–52
Ngũgĩ wa Thiong'o, 2–3, 10, 81, 109, 175, 177
Niger Delta, 102–3, 107, 112–14, 190n6
Nigerian literature, 5–6, 9, 13, 15–24, 29, 127, 153–55, 166, 181–82
    and ecology, 102–3, 123
    queer, 26, 52–59, 65, 76–77
Nwaubani, Adaobi Tricia, 27, 128–29, 135, 152

Obadare, Ebenezer, 22, 155, 161–64
Obioma, Chigozie, 19, 22–23, 27, 103–4, 106–10, 123–24, 180
Oduyoye, Mercy Amba, 38, 81, 85, 93, 95
Okorafor, Nnedi, 27, 104–5, 127
Okparanta, Chinelo, 21–22, 26, 59–62, 67, 74–75, 77, 112, 187n38
On Ajayi Crowther Street, 23, 54, 56–57, 154
Oriogun, Romeo, 53–54, 56
Orobator, Agbonkhianmeghe, 43, 82–83, 86–87, 89, 92–93, 95–96, 102, 118, 189n31,n51

patriarchy, 64, 69, 73–74, 77, 80, 85, 88, 95–96, 98–99, 101, 178, 181
peace
    Christianity and Islam as religions of, 130, 132, 135, 147, 149, 151
    divine, 122–23, 147
    interethnic and interreligious, 36, 45, 125, 128–29, 135, 140, 152
Pentecostalism, 4–5, 18, 53–56, 100, 103–6, 116–17, 125–27, 148–49, 153–73, 176
    emergence of, 4, 18, 62, 73, 84, 116
    representation in African literature, 4–5, 13–14, 21, 23, 28, 76, 155, 171
    as a public religion, 22, 110, 155, 171, 179
    and relationship to Catholicism, 84, 89, 100, 148, 172–73
    and relationship to indigenous religion, 55–56, 110, 157–61, 177–78 (*see also* demonization)
pentecostalization, 18, 28, 53, 56, 76, 100, 110, 171–72, 176

pilgrimage, 90–91, 93, 95
Pilgrim's Progress, The, 35, 185n21
pope, 85
    John Paul II, 79, 86
    Paul VI, 86
postcolonialism, and the transformation of Christianity, 3, 8, 12–13, 17–19, 22–23, 81, 100
power
    divine, 38, 43, 56, 65, 156–58, 163
    spiritual, 38–39, 56, 90–91, 109, 111–12, 116–17, 119–20, 127, 131, 159, 168
prayer, 36, 41, 60, 62–67, 80, 90–91, 111, 114, 142–43, 146–49, 164, 176
    Angelus, 42–43, 176
    of deliverance, 54–56, 58, 65–67, 116, 119–20, 131
    family, 34, 85–86, 89, 109
    for forgiveness, 34–35, 46, 66
    for healing, 91, 189n44
    indigenous, 85, 87, 161, 169
    mother's, 44, 134, 137, 141–43
    for protection, 65, 134, 137, 142, 148–49, 165
    of spiritual warfare, 66, 132, 158
    in tongues, 54, 148–49
    See also Rosary
priest, 23, 41, 46, 50, 54, 62–63, 162
    Anglican, 127
    Catholic, 14, 20, 37, 79, 83–86, 92, 95–97, 113, 144, 159, 165, 177
    Celestial, 111, 115, 118
    Indigenous, 33, 156, 159, 161, 169–70
prophecy/prophet, 27, 54–55, 57, 102–3, 105–8, 116–23, 143, 148, 153–54, 158
prosperity (gospel), 21, 27–28, 105, 154, 161–63, 175–72, 177
Protestantism, 16, 18, 33–35, 39, 62, 67, 89, 132
Psalms, Book of, 40, 43, 50, 142
public religion (Christianity as a), 7, 21–23, 110, 155, 171, 176–77, 180, 195n11
Purple Hibiscus, 4, 8, 14, 22–23, 26, 79–101, 166, 175–76, 178–81

Quayson, Ato, 21–22, 58
queer(ness), 26, 52–77, 178, 181

radicalization (religious), 127–28, 135, 138, 150–51
recognition (interreligious), 8, 128, 144, 150–52
Redeemed Christian Church of God, 18, 20, 127
redemption, 38–40, 43, 50, 57–58, 97–99, 173
    See also salvation

INDEX

rehabilitation, 32, 46, 48, 51, 186n49
reimagination, 10, 127
    of Christianity, 13, 59, 61–62, 75–77, 170–71, 180–82
    of the Virgin Mary, 92, 100
    See also imagination
religion and literature (study of), 7–10, 81
representation, of religion in literature, 1–3, 10–14, 37, 58, 61, 76, 79–80, 101, 108–12, 140, 151, 154, 165–66, 174–77
Revelations (Book of), 44–45, 122
reverse mission, 14, 20, 95, 177
revival, 24, 51, 60–61, 67–68, 79, 136
    (post-)civil war, 24, 51, 60–61, 67–68, 79
riots (interreligious), 127, 136–43, 145–46, 149, 151
    See also violence
river, 32, 47–48, 106–8, 112, 115, 117–23
    of peace, 122–23
    polluted, 114–15, 117–18, 122
    as sacred, 112–14, 121–22, 177
Rosary, 84, 86–87, 89–91, 94, 153

sacred, 11, 48
    environment as, 94, 104, 108, 112–15, 117–18, 121–24, 177
    objects, 37–43, 46, 50, 150, 160, 180
    queer body as, 53, 58
    scripture, 68, 73, 77 (*see also* Bible)
    trees as, 47, 74–76, 114, 134, 152, 186n41
saint(s), 39, 50, 148
    Christopher, 39
    Peter, 33
salvation, 40, 43, 50, 157, 169–70, 180
    See also redemption
same-Sex Marriage (Prohibition) Act, 52, 59, 61
Saro-Wiwa, Ken, 21, 31, 102–3, 124
Satan, 56, 132, 158–59, 168
    See also devil
satire, 23, 28, 147–48, 153–54, 157, 171
sexuality. *See* homosexuality; queer(ness)
Song for Night, 25–26, 29–51, 79, 180–81
Soyinka, Wole, 10, 17, 21, 23, 28, 50, 144, 153–54, 185n101
spirit(s), 30–33, 38–39, 47, 55, 74, 104, 110–17, 120, 135, 143, 156, 158, 160, 167
    of homosexuality, 54–56, 64–65
    See also ancestors; demon(s); Holy Spirit
spirituality, 11, 33, 54, 79, 100, 142–43, 172
    eco-, 47, 103, 112
    of resistance, 73, 93, 95
statues
    of Jesus, 40–43, 46, 50 (*see also*, crucifix)

    of Mary, 40–43, 50, 79, 90, 94–95, 110
    of Ngene, 156, 158, 160
Sterile Sky, 27, 128, 136–44, 150–52, 179
stigma/stigmatization, 42, 54, 56, 64, 76
Stobie, Cheryl, 81, 94, 96, 99, 101
suffering, 35, 38, 40–41, 43, 50, 93, 142, 144, 173
Suhr-Sytsma, Nathan, 11, 140, 149–50
suicide, 55–56, 107, 116, 134
Sule, E.E., 24, 27, 136, 143–44, 150, 152
Sunday school, 34–35, 45–46, 63, 110, 176
superstition, 95, 109, 116–17, 135, 159
syncretism, 111–12, 179, 191n40

taboo, 74–75, 115, 118, 120, 159
talisman, 148, 150
    Bible as, 38–39, 186n27
theology, 31, 38, 40–45, 49–51, 86, 102, 182
    African, 9–10, 12, 40, 43, 82–83, 93, 179, 182
    African feminist, 64, 72–73, 77, 79, 81, 88–89, 92–93, 95, 101
    Catholic, 83, 86, 173
    eco-, 27, 102–3
    interfaith, 128, 152
    and literature, 9–10, 12, 25, 83, 182
    queer, 70, 77
theopoetics, 26, 31, 37–45
Things Fall Apart, 1–2, 10, 14, 22, 83, 157, 159–60, 189n31
transnationalism, 27, 116, 155
trauma, 31–33, 38
    civil war, 25–26, 29–33, 35, 40, 49, 63, 180
    (post)colonial, 24, 26, 31, 51, 181
    queer, 53–56
tree(s)
    baobab, 134–35, 152
    iroko, 47, 186n41
    of knowledge (biblical), 74–76, 118, 177
    of life (biblical), 134–35
    as sacred, 47, 74, 114, 134
    udala, 74–76, 177

Ukah, Asonzeh, 17–18, 127, 175
Under the Udala Trees, 21–22, 26, 58–77, 176–78, 180–81

VanZanten, Susan, 8, 14, 81, 94, 175–76
violence, 29, 31, 35–43, 45, 49, 55–56
    colonial, 2, 6, 12, 87, 179–81
    gender-based, 22, 85, 96
    interethnic, 59–60, 121, 139–40
    (inter)religious, 27, 37, 128–29, 131–33, 136–46, 148–52, 179, 181 (*see also* riots)
    sexual, 41, 44–45, 48, 69, 131

Virgin Mary, 14, 26, 40–43, 48, 50, 79–80,
83–84, 89–96, 100, 110, 141, 180
    intercession by, 43, 48, 80, 91, 189n51
vulnerability, 102, 159, 162, 164, 167
    divine, 41–43, 186n37

warfare, spiritual, 27, 38, 66, 125–52, 158, 176
Wariboko, Nimi, 6, 56, 110, 126, 159, 161, 167,
170, 172, 180
water
    healing, 66, 114, 148
    inhabited by spirits, 104, 111–15
    polluted, 117–18, 121–22
witchcraft, 39, 85, 105, 127, 142, 159, 167–68
women, 34, 64, 68, 73, 77, 79, 92–93, 95–96,
99, 180
    See also gender; mother(hood)
World Christianity (study of), 5–6, 8, 12, 14,
18, 20, 81, 174–75, 177, 182

Yoruba(land), 106, 150
    Christianity among the, 16, 111, 114–15, 153
    indigenous religion, 55, 111–12, 114–15,
143–44, 191n46

www.ingramcontent.com/pod-product-compliance
Lightning Source LLC
Chambersburg PA
CBHW022051290426
44109CB00014B/1054